Reflections on the Pandemic

Reflections on the Pandemic

~

COVID and Social Crises in the Year Everything Changed

EDITED BY TERESA POLITANO

Rutgers University Press

New Brunswick, Camden, and Newark, New Jersey
London and Oxford

Rutgers University Press is a department of Rutgers, The State University of
New Jersey, one of the leading public research universities in the nation.
By publishing worldwide, it furthers the University's mission of dedication
to excellence in teaching, scholarship, research, and clinical care.

Library of Congress Cataloging-in-Publication Data

Names: Politano, Teresa, 1961– editor.
Title: Reflections on the pandemic : COVID and social crises in the year
everything changed / edited by Teresa Politano.
Description: New Brunswick : Rutgers University Press, [2024] | Includes
bibliographical references and index.
Identifiers: LCCN 2023018652 | ISBN 9781978831100 (hardback) | ISBN
9781978831094 (paperback) | ISBN 9781978831117 (epub) | ISBN
9781978831124 (pdf)
Subjects: LCSH: COVID-19 Pandemic, 2020—Literary collections. | COVID-19
Pandemic, 2020—New Jersey–New Brunswick–Anecdotes. | American
literature–21st century. | COVID-19 Pandemic, 2020—Social
aspects–New Jersey–New Brunswick. | Rutgers University. | Universities
and colleges–New Jersey–New Brunswick. | BISAC: LITERARY COLLECTIONS /
Essays | SOCIAL SCIENCE / Disease & Health Issues
Classification: LCC PS509.C63 R44 2024 | DDC 810.8/03561—dc23/eng/20230905
LC record available at https://lccn.loc.gov/2023018652

A British Cataloging-in-Publication record for this book is available
from the British Library.

References to internet websites (URLs) were accurate at the time of writing.
Neither the author nor Rutgers University Press is responsible for URLs
that may have expired or changed since the manuscript was prepared.

♾ The paper used in this publication meets the requirements of the American
National Standard for Information Sciences—Permanence of Paper for Printed
Library Materials, ANSI Z39.48-1992.

rutgersuniversitypress.org

Contents

Preface

On March 4, 2020, officials announced the first presumptive case of COVID-19 in the Garden State. Thirteen days later, Robert L. Barchi, president of Rutgers, the State University of New Jersey, announced that all in-person instruction at the university would be suspended for the semester and that all activities, including the spring commencement ceremony, would be canceled.

In hindsight, this swift action was to be applauded. The world had already entered an unprecedented era.

In reality, most of us had yet to grasp the severity of the situation. And amid the confusion and chaos surrounding the early news of the virus—and the giddy hope that this novel coronavirus would somehow peter out in a few short weeks—I found President Barchi's announcement particularly sobering. Barchi is a physician, uniquely qualified to make decisions about the public health of the university, home to more than 71,000 students and 23,600 faculty and staff.

Rutgers, as the state's premier research university—with more than three hundred research centers and institutes—was uniquely poised to respond to the crisis. Later in March 2020, the university established the Center for COVID-19 Response and Pandemic Preparedness, incorporating, among others, the university's strength as a global leader in the study of infectious diseases. Soon after, Antonio Calcado, leader of the university's COVID-19 task force, caught the virus and spent days isolated in a hospital on a ventilator.

The experience, he said, was humbling, making it easier, as an administrator, to err on the side of caution.

As the year progressed, researchers at the university developed a saliva test, conducted vaccine trials, developed strategies for contact tracing, and mapped data. One group of university researchers earned a $5 million grant from that National Institutes of Health to improve access to testing for underserved and vulnerable communities. University researchers also focused on other topics—the digital divide, mental health, education, the economy, the climate crisis, and health equity. Rutgers was one of the first institutions in the nation to allow students to graduate early from New Jersey Medical School, the School of Nursing, and the Ernest Mario School of Pharmacy, boosting the ranks of healthcare workers on the front lines.

In July 2020, as experts nationwide debated the survival of higher education, Jonathan Holloway, a historian and the university's first Black president, took office. During that summer of racial unrest following the murder of George Floyd, the university secured a $15 million grant for the study of global racial justice. In March 2021, Rutgers became the nation's first major university to require students to be vaccinated against COVID-19.

The intellectual complexity of the university is driven in part by its location. New Jersey is the nation's most diverse state, with the highest number of foreign-born residents and Rutgers consistently ranks as one of the nation's most ethnically diverse universities. New Jersey is also the nation's most densely populated state and, for much of the pandemic, was considered part of the epicenter.

In the transition from in-person to online learning, from an open, vital university to a largely empty campus, many students disappeared. They lost parents. They lost jobs. Their parents lost jobs. They lost Wi-Fi and thus access to learning. They lost hope. One student of mine witnessed the fierce strength of her mother, who had learned austerity growing up in Venezuela and could make arepas from whatever ingredients were in the pantry. Another student, who had returned home and was following a mandatory quarantine in a hotel room in China, emailed a polite request for an extension on her assignment because she had been in a coma.

In many ways, the years of the pandemic seemed like a hard stop to our lives. We were isolated in our bubbles, sheltering in place, limiting our contacts. We have now emerged to a world profoundly changed. We are still in recovery.

The contributors to this volume set out to document the COVID-19 pandemic moment, recognizing that this period was a particular time, with a particular feeling, affecting all of us. We have learned that history cannot be told from a singular point of view, so the pieces in this book were solicited from the various communities that make up Rutgers. Each contributor has a connection to Rutgers University, from president to poet, from surgeon to scholar, from artist to alumna, from student to staffer. Many of our scholars are moms. Mothers do not often write history, but they are not underrepresented here.

Rutgers was founded in 1766 as one of the nine original colonial colleges. Rutgers was home to the nation's first collegiate football game in 1869. As we like to say, the history of Rutgers is the history of the nation. As a university, we strive to be humane, innovative, resilient. We are a sprawling, diverse, public university—messy, questioning, and complex. This is a community project. Readers should feel free to skip around in the book—the structure of the book follows a general timeline from the beginning of the deep shutdown period through the full experience of the pandemic. The pieces are personal, creative, and scholarly in turn.

At the beginning of the pandemic, I was heartened by a poem shared by my friend and fellow New Jerseyan, Maricel Presilla. Maricel has won a James Beard award for *Gran Cocina Latina: The Food of Latin America*, an opus that represents thirty years of research and honors and preserves the recipes of everyday culinary experts. Maricel fled Cuba as a teenager and was the first Latin American woman invited as guest chef for the White House. She is founder of the International Chocolate Awards, has a PhD in medieval Spanish history, and has taught at Rutgers. After Super-storm Sandy, she rebuilt her award-wining Hoboken restaurants. When the pandemic hit, she closed them for good.

Maricel found solace in this poem by Antonio Machado (the translation is hers).

Caminante, no hay Camino

Caminante, son tus huellas
el camino y nada más;
Caminante, no hay camino,
se hace camino al andar.[1]

Path-walker, there is no Path
Path-walker, your footprints
and nothing else are the path;
Path-walker, there is no path,
the path is formed as you move.

Reflections on the Pandemic

Reflections in a COVID Photograph

JONATHAN HOLLOWAY

The first piece of advice new university presidents receive from their more experienced peers: "Find ways to extend your honeymoon period."

My presidency began on July 1, 2020. My first day in my actual office was July 6. It was a moment of high excitement, the first day of school for the new kid, as it were. It was also the occasion of my first presidential press conference. And it was during that press conference that my honeymoon period began to recede. The message that marked its ebbing? The opening sentences tell you what you need to know:

Dear Rutgers Students, Faculty, and Staff,

I am writing today to inform you that after careful consideration of all possible models for safely and effectively delivering instruction during the ongoing coronavirus pandemic, Rutgers is planning for a Fall 2020 semester that will combine a majority of remotely delivered courses with a limited number of in-person classes. Each of the chancellors will be communicating later today with more detail about what this means for the students they serve.

For me, making the decision to go remote was not difficult. All the public health indices and the science behind them made it clear that the best way to protect Rutgers' one hundred thousand–person community would be to move to a largely remote mode of education. Being remote would also give our healthcare providers and emergency responders—those who never got a day off during the pandemic and who regularly risked their lives to protect others— the best chance at managing the deployment of their resources. If the university had not gone remote, we would have facilitated the spread of the virus throughout New Jersey and could have overwhelmed the state's healthcare facilities. Going remote was obviously the right thing to do.

And in our socially mediated world where everyone enjoys a freedom to assert without evidence and to opine without facts, the immediate consequence of the decision was also obvious. Although the decision came as little surprise to most people, there was a vocal minority that had been holding on to the hope that the university would be fully open in the fall, that classes would be in-person, and that the university's new president would grow a spine and stand up to weak-kneed liberals who were overreacting to a flu-like virus that would have little effect on a college-aged population.

It is an understatement to say that this is not the presidency that I envisioned when I accepted the invitation to serve as Rutgers' twenty-first president. It was thrilling to walk into the board room in Winants Hall on January 21, 2020, warmly welcomed by the university's governing boards and other members of the Rutgers community. Yes, we were hearing about a coronavirus that was rattling health officials and political leaders overseas, but aside from a case or two in Seattle, this virus did not seem to pose a threat to the United States. That day, my focus was on the lovely embrace I received from Rutgers, the congratulatory phone calls from sitting members of Congress, and enthusiastic text messages on my phone and in my e-mail. The "foreign virus" was nowhere to be found in that day of celebration.

Over the next few weeks, however, it was obvious to everyone that the terms of everyday life had changed.

Back in Evanston, Illinois, where I was concluding my tenure as Northwestern University's provost, we watched the virus spread rapidly in Seattle and quickly begin to overwhelm New York City and New Jersey. By February, it was clear that the virus was coming to Chicago (we know in retrospect that it was already there) and that our world had changed. In my most selfish moment I felt sorry for myself, as the presidency I had accepted no longer existed. I did not know yet how much the virus would affect Rutgers, but it was clear that for the foreseeable future, I would be leading a response-and-recovery effort of some type.

Then, on March 10, 2020, three and a half months before I would begin my tenure as president, then-president Robert Barchi canceled classes leading up to spring break, told the community to prepare to not return after the break, and announced that the university would move to fully remote education. In acknowledging the "difficult and extraordinary situation" and the "imperative" of slowing the spread of the virus, Barchi, a physician, joined other university leaders across the nation in a lightning-quick move to a remote environment. Still in Evanston, I could tell that the recovery effort was going to be longer and more arduous than I had anticipated.

When a new president is announced, he or she starts to make regular visits to the university to get acquainted with the faculty, staff, and students; to understand the campus layout; to assess the leadership team, and to develop a nuanced understanding of campus climate and culture. This sort of transition work is critical so that the new president can start the job with confidence, ready from day one to make informed decisions about the next era of the university's history. I did not have the benefit of any of those opportunities but instead relied on three months of Zoom meetings to get acquainted and briefed. I felt deeply unprepared for the challenges that would come my direction.

With six years of senior administrative positions behind me, I had become accustomed to carrying the responsibility of difficult decisions. However, up to this point, there had always been a person or two above me in the org chart with final authority on major or controversial decisions. Now, the weight of the most challenging circumstances was mine to bear. This is right, and this is normal. The president is tasked with making decisions that could not otherwise be resolved, and inevitably, those decisions lead to someone being disappointed at best, often deeply angry. This, too, is normal.

But remember the realities of summer 2020: a relentless global pandemic, no vaccines in hand to mitigate the virus's effects, a presidential campaign that seemed designed to foment rage to sow social instability, and a racial reckoning that brought millions to the streets to protest what activists claimed were long histories of state-sponsored and extrajudicial violence against minorities. With each month, the levels of anxiety, frustration, and anger only seemed to grow. As far as I could tell, there was no university playbook or even presidential transition reports that could guide me through this thicket.

Given the circumstances, when it came to navigating the virus, planning our future recovery, and attending to all the social and political complexities and demands of the moment, the only viable path forward in my presidency required that I rely on science and data and that I be as direct and transparent as possible in my decision-making. This may sound simple to many, but there are few obvious moves one can make when it comes to leading a one-hundred-thousand-person community stretched across a state. As if I needed any confirmation of the situation's delicacy, I quickly came to learn that some viewed my decision to follow the science and data and to be direct and transparent—all critical to my plans to move the community forward safely—as deeply political and dishonest acts.

March 21, 2021:

We are committed to health and safety for all members of our community and adding COVID-19 vaccination to our student immunization requirements will help provide a safer and more robust college experience for our students.

In the weeks leading up to this announcement, my cabinet engaged in a series of prolonged and robust conversations about how we could ultimately return to in-person instruction, keep our community safe, and navigate the inevitable legal challenges to mandatory vaccinations. It may be hard to believe, but when we announced that Rutgers would require students be immunized against the coronavirus, we were not aware that we were the first major university to do so. What it meant to be in the vanguard became clear immediately: other university general counsels reached out to our attorneys seeking guidance, local and national media took notice and interviewed anyone at Rutgers they could find, and other public university presidents lamented to me that they wanted to do the same thing but that their state political leaders made it impossible to move forward in the same way. Despite the obstacles that many public university leaders faced, very quickly colleges and universities around the country took notice and followed Rutgers' lead.

Other factions took notice, too.

Exactly two months after we announced our immunization plan, roughly five hundred people gathered on our New Brunswick campus to raise their voices. Anti-vaccination activists led the way in organizing a protest against Rutgers' new policy. A motley crew joined them: Tea Party loyalists, Confederate flag defenders, MAGA enthusiasts, Libertarians, and even three Republican Party gubernatorial primary election candidates, at least one of whom looked increasingly uncomfortable as the audience's constituency took shape. It was a cauldron of anger, fueled by fear and stirred by politics.

I was sitting in my office about a half mile from the rally, beyond hearing distance of the crowd and its speakers. I knew the protest was happening, but I did not yet know the scale, nor did I know the diversity of the attendees. Then someone sent me a photograph

Brower Commons at Rutgers University in New Brunswick on May 21, 2021, during a noontime rally to protest the university's first-in-the-nation requirement that students be vaccinated against the COVID-19 virus. (Photo by Peter J. McDonough Jr.)

of the gathering, and I immediately realized that my twin commitments to follow science and data and to be direct and transparent in my decisions were not going to be received in the way that I had hoped.

Although I was unsurprised to see someone proudly wearing a red MAGA hat carrying the Gadsden ("Tea Party") flag, I was unprepared for the poster that equated Rutgers' vaccination policy with Nazi science schemes. And even though I was disappointed to see the "FU RU" poster (a "clever" declaration that embodied the creative banality of our era), I could not divert my eyes from the woman wearing a T-shirt that said "Masks = Slavery"—a cynical graphic mash-up of Black Lives Matter and Silence = Death T-shirts. This was the tripwire. It was there that I discovered the boundaries of our reasoned policy approach and our communications plan.

Universities are supposed to be places of preservation and discovery. There are precious few other institutions in the country that are charged with the dual missions of preserving the very best ideas expressed across time while also inviting new generations of curious people to challenge the veracity and value of those ideas. When the institutional culture is healthy and vibrant, a university is a place of tension and cognitive dissonance. But there are limits.

If the work of preservation and discovery is to proceed, there must be an understanding that everyone is chasing the truth and that we all have an interest in attaining it. Without the faith that there is something of value—this thing we call "the truth"—that can guide us to a better place because we understand our world in new and enlightened ways, we are left with a void. And it is this void into which I found myself staring when I looked at the picture. I am no stranger to campus protests of many different types. Taken as a whole, I believe them to be a critical part of a university's ecosystem, as they are as often an articulation of unmet local needs as they are the proving ground for ideas that might transform society. But when I looked at this picture, I encountered a space that was new to me, a space where emotionalism, ahistoricism, and provocative brinksmanship were the things that were most highly valued. This photograph proved the error of my earlier presumption. The protesters' desire to know, to debate, and to inform were being expressed in a symbolic language I did not understand. And if I could not understand their language, how could they understand mine?

I concede that the protest itself was an affirmation of the democratic principles that are at the core of this country's ideals. Further, as much as I found this protest to be antithetical to the university's values, I affirm the right for the individuals there to gather and to speak their piece. But this concession and affirmation do not mean that I am obliged to sit by idly while ethical scientific discovery was equated with Nazi barbarism and while violence was done to the past. Wearing a mask does not equate to slavery by any stretch of the imagination. But where to go? What to do?

This is the crossroads where we all find ourselves as we reflect on the myriad challenges of this pandemic. Social, political, economic, and epidemiological pressures have pushed people beyond a place of reason. We now find ourselves in an era where petty trolling and outrage are outpacing our capacity for grace, patient inquiry, and a search for a better world. Because of science and its abiding pursuit of the truth, we will physically survive this pandemic. But what have we lost in the process, and how will we get it back?

Yes, I imagined a very different presidency when I stepped to the podium to introduce myself to Rutgers and to talk about my commitment to academic excellence and my aspiration for a beloved community. And as the virus began its relentless spread in this country, I could see that my presidency would take on a different shape and contour than I had envisioned. Now, as we enter the third year of the pandemic, I find myself asking questions that travel beyond the boundaries of this university.

I am concerned about the durability of our democracy in an atmosphere damaged so deeply by rhetoric and polemics divorced from reality, from integrity, and from a shared faith that there is something redeemable in those we would otherwise consider strangers. As president, I will do what I can to protect the Rutgers community and to preserve its ability to be of service to the state. This is a big task.

As a citizen, I look at this photograph and realize that the work is so much bigger than that. And it is work that we must do together.

pantoum: 2020

EVIE SHOCKLEY

who could have predicted this?
      year of unyielding busyness giving way
to days of utter stillness & bewilderment,
         streets so quiet they invite coyotes' return.

      year of unyielding busyness giving way
to dread & longing for another's touch.
         streets so quiet they invite coyotes' return,
vehicles parked beneath clearing skies.

dread of & longing for another's touch,
      friendship become a vector for disease.
vehicles parked beneath clearing skies ::
      signs of another contagion we carry.

      friendship becomes a vector for disease,
necessity the mother of transmission.
      signs of another contagion we carry
passed around warehouses, factories, plants.

necessity is the mother of transmission.
      some, stuck at home, need soap, puzzles, steaks
   passed through warehouses, factories, plants
        by others who, essentially, need the work.

      some, stuck home, need toilet paper & tablets.
year of laboring & learning ever more remotely
        from others who, essentially, need the work
   that puts them in the virus's line of fire.

year of laboring & learning :: ever more remote
      from the distracting comforts of the old normal.
  what puts some right in the virus's line of fire?
      the viral load like other loads long shouldered.

      without the distracting comforts of the old normal,
it's harder not to see power, raw & rich, shift
        the viral load, like other loads long shouldered,
  onto the bodies of black & brown people, the poor.

it's harder not to see power, raw & rich, sifting
      through & into all our media feeds, feeding on us,
  on the lives of black & brown people, the poor.
      a march in isolation becomes a summer of marches.

      throughout our news feeds—feeding them & us—
images of injustice emptying or filling our lungs.
      a march of isolation becomes a summer of protests.
  whether from cops or covid, *i can't breathe* ::

evidence of injustice emptying or filling our lungs.
      coronavirus burns through the navajo nation.
  under knees or on ventilators: *i can't breathe.*
      chinatowns excised with breathtaking violence.

coronavirus burns through new parts of the nation
where mask-wearing's made ideologically toxic.
          anti-immigrant violence :: cutting, breathtakingly
     illogical, another symptom of diseased body politic.

with mask-wearing made ideologically toxic
          & medical expertise under increasing attack,
     illogic—one symptom of a diseased body politic—
          struggles with grief for primacy in our days.

          medical expertise warns of variants' attack,
as the numbers of the dead balloon, explode.
          struggles with grief take primacy, our days
     spent coping with curtailed rituals of mourning.

again, the numbers of the dead balloon, explode.
          we go through the motions, familiar & strange,
     try to cope with curtailed rituals of mourning,
               to extend our living through masks & screens.

          we go through the motions, familiar & strange.
year of too many shifts or too little travel,
               of laughing & crying through masks & screens,
     of dystopian fiction & quotidian disaster.

year of unemployment or too stressful travel,
          too much or too little time to contemplate
     dystopian depictions of quotidian disaster ::
          what sci-fi & science have been trying to tell us.

          too much to ask that we take time to contemplate
what led us to this paralysis & bewilderment.
          science & sci-fi have been trying to tell us ::
     we could have predicted this.   we did.

Mercy (As If)

MARK DOTY

Lucky she can do this, make her mercy system,
    knows people without work

or solace in the wan spring lockdown sun,
    hears their hunger tremble in waves

through apartment walls, into the dead streets.
    When did you ever walk three blocks

in the city and see no one? Lucky her method
    of enumeration, chalking on pavement

her coded grid, hopscotch mirror:
    open-mouthed grocery sacks, rowed,

standing at attention, numbered,
    though the tags aren't written

but remembered, a scramble of signs:
    who needs, when to deliver,

in what order, so much to be held
    that street and silence already tarnish

her memory. She has trouble enough.
　　So when my foolish old dog goes

padding over to sniff at the groceries
　　in their ranked sacks

she comes screaming out of nowhere
　　as if she wanted to tear us both apart,

and I can't help myself, I'm shouting back
　　at her, as if her threat were real,

because I protect my hapless dog as if
　　he were a physical extension of myself,

and it's only then I understand the dozens
　　of sacks standing open between us

are empty, nothing in them at all.

Writing My Last Book

RIGOBERTO GONZÁLEZ

I hadn't seen my friend Charles since 2019, just months before the beginning of the pandemic. Then, out of the blue, he sent me a text letting me know he was planning to come all the way from Upper Manhattan to visit me in Newark. I had moved to New Jersey only weeks before everything shut down. I didn't even have time to find a new dentist or a barber. For a year and a half, the only places I walked into were the market and the pharmacy. I didn't have any close friends in the area, so this was going to be a welcomed reunion.

The first thing we realized when we sat across from each other was that we had aged. He was now fifty-seven and I was fifty-one. And since we were both writers, we caught each other up on our current projects. That's when he made this arresting statement: "I feel a sense of urgency to complete these books because now I understand that I'm going to die."

That was a sentiment I had encountered before. But the writers who expressed such grim reality were much older. I was about to tell Charles that he was much too young to be doting on his mortality. Sure, we were middle-aged men and we had reached the stage when our daily meals were accompanied by an arsenal of pills to counter everything from high blood pressure to vitamin deficiencies, but we were doing these things because we wanted to improve the quality of the many years we knew we had left to live.

Instead, I held my tongue because up until that moment, I didn't recognize that I felt the same way—because of the pandemic.

Each year, I celebrated my birthday with my two college friends, Sandra and Janet, who were also born in 1970 and who also have summer birthdays. All three of us were single and childless, so we traveled to some glamorous place—Madrid, Old San Juan, Oaxaca—to have a good time spending our disposable income. The summer of 2020, we had to cancel our plans—a cruise journeying from Rome to Turkey—and instead celebrated our special day over Zoom. We sang a feeble rendition of "Las mañanitas" and blew out the candles to the cakes we had purchased for the occasion. Instead of cheering at the conclusion of the song, I started to cry. With all three of us immunocompromised, I was certain that none of us were going to make it to our next birthday.

How could I not think that? The numbers of deaths were rising each day. The city of Newark, with its airport and mass transit systems central to the tri-state area—features that had convinced me to relocate in the first place—was experimenting with complete shutdowns. On Mondays, no one was even allowed in the streets without specific purpose. When I went on my leisure walks (and thus breaking the rule), I disguised that fact by carrying my canvas shopping bag in case I got stopped by the police, who patrolled the area. "I'm going to buy groceries, officer," I'd say, holding up my proof. The act of sitting on my balcony, with its view of Broad Street, became sullied by the fact that I mostly saw ambulances careening back and forth. When winter came and the streets were thick with snow, I saw small cars get stuck on the road and I thought, *What a perfect metaphor for where we are in the world—stranded among the stranded.*

Knowing that I was not lucky, I prepared for my demise. I stopped spending money in order to leave something for my brother and his family, who depended on my remittances to Mexico each month. I worried that my brother would die before me and I wouldn't be able to pick up where he left off when I was all the way up here and his family way down there. I started calling my longtime friends weekly to have hour-long check-ins. Yes, I was lonely, but I wanted more time with their voices and to give them more time with mine. We didn't let the long silences spoil the call and we'd hear each other multitask the way it was when we were in the same room: chatting while cooking, while doing household chores, sometimes half-listening, sometimes at full attention. And finally, I wrote and wrote and wrote in order to finish what I believed was going to be my last book.

Although I had three projects anxious to get out of my head and onto paper, I decided rather quickly which one I wanted to work on: the book about my Purépecha grandmother, an Indigenous woman who took me in after I lost my parents. She was kind in some ways but cold in others. Abuela died in 2011, and the last time I lived with her, I was seventeen. Thirty-three years had gone by. And although I had written about her in my previous memoirs, she was not central to those stories. She would be in this one.

I chose it to be my last creative act because it was a book about uncertainty and incomplete narratives. I fled that home we shared with a man who treated us so poorly, and didn't look back until I started writing, when there was no one left alive to provide me with answers. I was going to write a book about a woman who was an important part of my life but who was still mostly a mystery to me. "I don't know" became my mantra each time I sat down at the computer. Yet I was living that phrase. When I dared to step out of my apartment, I didn't know if that was going to be the last time. When I hung up after a call, I didn't know if that was going to be the last time I would speak to that person. I had a renewed appreciation for that biblical platitude about living every day as if it could be the last because one day, it would be.

On the last day of my life, I wanted to be doing the one activity I loved best: writing. I set my alarm for 5:00 A.M. and forced myself out of bed and to the desk. Procrastination was not an option when the days were numbered. The COVID-19 death toll rose and rose around the world, and I thought what a cruel fate awaited those who took the next day for granted. Like many people, I was now walking a path of low visibility, unable to see past the next step. I couldn't remember the last time I had made plans for the near future, and it seemed foolish to do so, even careless. My poor isolated heart had nowhere to go and no one to visit.

Then I lost two writer friends to the pandemic. And my dance teacher from college. And a young woman with Down syndrome whom I used to look after on occasion. I poured that grief onto the page, mourning all the missed opportunities for connection with Abuela, whom I stopped visiting or even calling when my own life became complicated in my thirties. I was overcome by an intense survivor's guilt. My self-imposed punishment was sitting on a chair for long hours each day, shortening the distance between me and Abuela, one word at a time.

When November came around, I set up my altar for the Day of the Dead and placed photographs of my parents and Abuela at the center. These altars were beacons for the spirit world and guided our ancestors home on that sacred day. I always thought of my writing as a bridge between the living and the dead. But before the pandemic, I imagined that this bridge allowed memories and stories to travel toward me. During the writing of my last book, I felt myself traveling toward them. The pages of text were the vestiges I was leaving behind.

Whether I finished the book—meaning, whether I lived long enough to do so—I wanted some evidence that I had died doing something meaningful. I had nothing else within reach that was as important. The tongue-in-cheek response I used to give when I was asked how I was so productive ("I have no p's: no parents, no progeny, no partner, no pets, no plants") now made me feel unmoored rather than free.

The urgency to complete the book intensified as soon as I understood I was writing the final chapters. But so did my sense of impending doom. I decided to stay inside my apartment until I finished, even if the food was running out. I didn't want to take any risks. COVID-19 was everywhere, we were told. On mail, on door handles, on shopping carts, on fruit, on bags of chips. The only indulgence I allowed myself was to exercise by walking up and down the stairwell—what my friend Enrique once recommended after the gyms closed. But even that became too risky when I stumbled and refused to grab for the railing—there was coronavirus on it!—and I fell on my face.

Eventually, I did finish the book. I was so relieved I slept for days, but not before I sent the file to my friend Eduardo, my designated literary executor. "Just in case," I wrote in the email. I didn't have to explain further. That book was going to be a posthumous publication, I was sure of it. I didn't even dream about directing my attention to the next project because I didn't want to give myself false hopes that I could survive long enough for the next book.

Yet indeed I did. By then, the vaccines had become a reality, though perishing because of the virus had not.

I wish I could say that the second book I completed during the pandemic was written patiently, without the dark cloud of my mortality hovering above me. I wish I could say that I stopped dreading contracting the virus, even after the booster shot. I wish I could say that I felt safe again to imagine that I was going to have a long writing career that would accompany me into old age. But I can't say any of those things just yet. I am now working on the third book in the era of COVID-19, and I'm as anxious as ever about getting to see its completion. Before, my discipline was informed by my creative urges. Now it's fueled by the fear of leaving something unfinished. It's an unsettling motivation that I hope will dissipate as the pandemic shifts to endemic status. I want my creative life back and the luxury to say to myself, *I'll get to it when I get to it*. But until then, I'll be writing my last book until it finally is.

Taking the Court

STEVE PIKIELL

I will never forget the day: March 12, 2020. We were in Indianapolis for the Big Ten Tournament. The Rutgers men's basketball team was getting ready for the tipoff against Michigan.

We had just finished our warm-ups on the court and were headed back to our locker room. I was ready for my pregame speech. I was ready to tell the team that we wanted to be the ones cutting down the nets. We felt we could win the tournament.

There were six minutes on the clock before the game.

Kevin Warren, commissioner of the Big Ten, walked into the locker room and pulled me aside. The game, he told me, had been canceled.

I remember having to tell my team. How could I break this news to my seniors? What could I tell them to soften the blow of losing the opportunity to play in this conference tournament? What could I possibly say to make it better? We had won twenty games that year. We were playing really good basketball. We were confident going into that tournament that we were about to do some exciting things. We wanted to be the first team to win the conference tournament in school history.

Our players were waiting, sitting on the benches at Gainbridge Fieldhouse. Rutgers athletic director Pat Hobbs and I got straight to the point. We would not have the opportunity to play in the Big Ten tournament.

At that time, I offered my team an upside—we'd still play in the NCAA tournament. How could they cancel the NCAA tournament, the greatest event in all of sports? Maybe we'd play without fans, but I believed we'd still play.

In that locker room in Indianapolis, I was able to soften the blow with the fact that we were soon going to find out, on Selection Sunday, where we were headed. It had been more than thirty years since a Rutgers basketball team had played in the NCAA tournament.

We packed up, left Indianapolis, and got on our return flight. Before the plane had landed, the guys were attacking their phones.

One of the seniors, Akwasi Yeboah, came up to me on the plane right when we landed. He told me they had canceled the NCAA tournament.

I didn't believe him. "What? Is that true?"

Our sports information director confirmed the news; official notice had already been posted on the NCAA website. The 2020 NCAA tournament had been canceled. All the players knew before I knew.

In just seven hours, what could have been the best year in Rutgers men's basketball history was over. In just seven hours, the Big Ten tournament was canceled and the NCAA tournament was canceled. Our year was over, just like that. There were tears on the team plane.

I wasn't even able to tell our guys. The guys told me. They learned first from their phones. It seemed wrong that the guys had to get the news on their phones. I was the one still saying it couldn't be possible. I was the one who believed they'd figure out a way to play the NCAA tournament. After all the work we'd done, I just couldn't believe it.

We had just beaten Purdue in double overtime at their place on Senior Night. That was the road win we needed to prove we were good enough to get in the dance. We needed to win that game and we did.

That was the saddest day. That group of guys was so great. Yeboah's college career was over. Shaq Carter, another senior, got off the bus and headed to his dorm. Just like that, his career, too, was over.

I've had a few sad days in my life: the day my mother died, the day my father died. That day, the day our season abruptly ended, was as sad a day as I have had. All the hard work and all the sweat—we had no control over how our special season ended.

The guys on that team had taken Rutgers to the NCAA tournament for the first time in thirty years. Every article, every news show talked about the fact that Rutgers hasn't been to the tournament since Abraham Lincoln was president.

College basketball is a sport like no other. We try to do everything that we can to control our fate, to make it to the tournament on Selection Sunday. In 2020, I learned that you can't control everything. The following year, we made it to the NCAA tournament for the first time since 1991; we won our first game in the tournament since 1983. But the players from that 2020 team taught me to value every opportunity we have to take the court.

The New Normal

REVATHI V. MACHAN

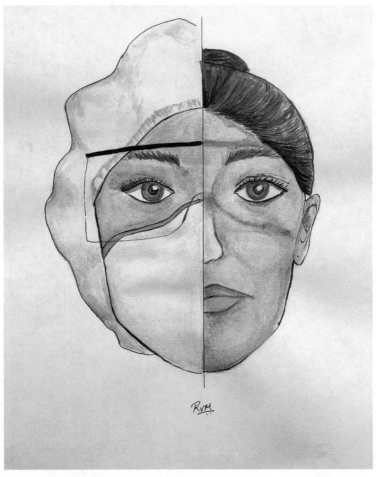

Revathi V. Machan, *The New Normal*. Mixed media piece made with watercolors, color pencils, markers, and gel pen, 12 × 12 inches. © Revathi V. Machan. Used with permission.

Emerging Not Stronger
or Weaker but Different

STEPHANIE BONNE

In the broad fabric of Rutgers University lies a wealth of minds, rich in diversity of thought. In one particular corner of the bio-medical sciences, a unique group of individuals exists. In my world, we are thinkers, teachers, and contributors to science, but we are also doctors who practice medicine in our daily lives. As such, we are tasked not only with the teaching of the next generation of caregivers. We must also model the principles of care for others in the medical sciences. Physicians represent a resource, and we are taught that we have unlimited capacity to handle whatever comes our way. This is my COVID-19 story.

> *In February of 2020, I sit in a kitchen with a few moms from my street.*
>
> *"Steph, what do you think is going to happen with this Wuhan virus?" I think for a minute.*
>
> *"I think it's going to be like SARS, or MERS, or Ebola. It will be a big deal overseas but won't affect us here very much."*

I spend my time thinking about public health. As a trauma surgeon, I take a particular interest in public health as it relates to injury. I spend my time combing public data sets that collect information about injury, violence, and firearm injury to try to separate the signal from the noise. How can we identify those who are at risk of becoming a victim of gun violence, and how can we prevent them from realizing that outcome? Can we stop gun violence? I believe we can because I know that public health works.

As the virus that comes to be known as SARS-COV-19 rages abroad, I take stock. Viruses can be dangerous, but our public health system in the United States is equipped to manage it, to keep it off our shores. I take for granted that public health systems do not just *exist*—they come from the combined work, expertise, and dedication of a significant number of individuals. I do not realize that our public health services have been silently gutted. We soon fail to contain the virus.

Elective surgery is suspended, we are told. "We have to cover the ICUs, because they are overwhelmed," I hear my boss say. "Stephanie, you'll spend the day shift in the pediatric ICU." The pediatric ICU is now a COVID unit and is full of adults.

I strap on my N-95 mask, wrap my head in cloth, grab my face shield, and walk into the nurses' station. A Haitian woman's blood pressure is dropping in the far room. I gown up and run to her bedside, plunging needles deep into her chest and wrists to get IV access, bringing over the crash cart.

I hold my cell phone to her face so her son, in California, can say, "Je t'aime, mama. Je t'aime" over and over, and speak to her in Creole. I push powerful blood pressure medications into her veins, past fingers and toes that are purple and black from blood clots. I leave the hospital, and she is still alive, a small victory as I sign her out to the next shift. "Maybe she will turn the corner," I say.

She dies anyway.

The next day, a new patient is in her bed. I had seen him the day before, but I had been focused on my Haitian woman. This patient is an African American man, whose sons thank him for his sacrifices working so many years in a kitchen so they could go to college. I do the same thing as yesterday. He dies too.

Part of trauma surgery is learning what to do if there is a mass casualty. We know the resources and capacity of the hospital, so if too many patients arrive at once, we prioritize the ones who can survive. If we get more than four patients with gunshot wounds, the patient who is shot in the head is left to die because his injuries are likely fatal anyway, and I direct the team to focus on the person who can survive. I know how to delegate resources, like staff, supplies, even blood. But I have never learned how to delegate myself because physicians are raised in a culture of hubris: "There is nothing we cannot handle."

> *April 2020: Freshly showered with antiseptic soap, I walk out of the hospital. I see the helicopter beacon running across the cancer center tower. I snap a short video and, without thinking, post it to social media.*
>
> *"I love seeing the helicopter beacon," I say. "It reminds me that we are still here."*
>
> *I drive to work on empty highways, empty streets. I wonder if this is the apocalypse, as if I am in one of the blockbuster movies I had seen in college. Not yet. We are still here. I am still available to my patients and the hospital is still there for all of us.*

When the pandemic hit, I saw, for the first time, my expertise as a limited resource, and for the first time, I felt as though this crisis was something that we, collectively, could not handle. There is a limit to what I can do, and my team is exhausted, demoralized, and suffering. Sometimes still, two years later, I wake up at night and wonder if I should have let the Haitian woman die so I could have taken care of the dad who cooked to put his sons through school. Or, I wonder, would he have died anyway?

"Hi, all! How are we holding up?"

I am back to taking care of trauma patients today, a welcome respite from my colleagues who are still managing overfilled makeshift ICUs of COVID patients.

It is not long until the pager goes off.

"Forty-year-old male, GSW to legs, tourniquet in place."

I rush down to the trauma bay to a man who is wincing in pain. We work quickly to evaluate him and find all his injuries. He has a gunshot wound just below his knee; the exit wound a little farther down his leg. I release the tourniquet and am met with a geyser of blood squirting in my face from his leg wound. We rush to the operating room so I can get control of the bleeding and care for his wounds. While he is asleep, I receive news from the anesthesiologist. "He didn't complain of a cough or anything, but his COVID test is positive." I am grateful for a moment that I wore my N-95 mask the whole time I was with him.

I finish operating and tuck him safely into his hospital room. I learn that he goes by "Christopher." I learn that he was shot when he was walking to the store to buy milk for his four-year-old daughter. Someone drove by and sprayed bullets. Christopher watched two strangers die in the street.

Although I spend my academic life trying to better understand public health problems, none of these exist in a vacuum. My patient has two problems at once: a gunshot wound and COVID. He is a young black man, and he is subject to high risk for both problems. How could I, or how could public health, have protected this man from the dual public health problems of gun violence and COVID?

Now that I have learned that I have a limited capacity, I wonder if my time is better spent tending to the sick and wounded or trying to mitigate the upstream factors that lead patients to our hospital doors? Both of Christopher's diseases are preventable, and both prey on those who are most vulnerable. In a single patient,

I see the manifestation of the failure of investment in public health solutions. I wonder if we will ever be able to solve these problems.

Before I leave the hospital, I take a scalding shower, swab my nose with alcohol-soaked Q-tips, and rinse with the burning mint of some Listerine. I mask up again and head home. I enter through the basement door, strip down, take a second scalding shower, rub down my cell phone and glasses with antibacterial wipes and throw my clothes straight into the washer. After a few minutes of nice deep breaths in my own bathroom, I mask back up, put on some sweats, and go downstairs to ask my kids about their day of Zoom classes and remote learning.

I leave the hospital feeling pretty good. I have helped this delightful and funny young man navigate two tough issues. I know he will be okay because of my help. But my good feelings turn again to despair and worry. I was in the room when they put in the breathing tube. I was close to his face when we evaluated him in the trauma bay. Is it safe for me to go home to my husband and children? What if one of them becomes sick because of me, because I have chosen a career that offers the rewards of helping the sick and injured? I wonder if I am really needed at home or if my mothering skills are an expendable resource, at least for now.

"Dr. Bonne, Evan hasn't finished any of his work for three weeks. He is never on camera. I need him to participate more in class." I cringe reading this email from my son's fourth-grade teacher.

"Buddy, come over here," I say to him. "What's going on with school?"

"Nothing," he says, choking through tears. "It's fine."

Two months into the pandemic and it hits me. The kids are not okay. My usually bright, gifted, and funny young man is struggling.

A few conversations later, we figure out the problem. He hates being alone, despite the lovely workstation I set up with activities, pictures, snacks, and his own space in our guest room. None of it means anything if he cannot see his friends. He worries about me all the time. He is nine.

We are navigating a new world of health care, zipping ourselves in and out of sealed rooms, reviewing data about zinc and remdesivir and prone positioning. Like many parents, we still must navigate the world of remote preschool and Google classroom.

In addition to navigating remote hospital meetings, a disrupted schedule, and the sinking feeling in the pit of my stomach whenever I sneeze, I come home to the same challenges as the rest of my community. Some kids are lonely and unproductive. Others find new hobbies and flourish. As a family, we learn to hike as our burning desire to leave the house translates into a newfound love of state parks. My aging parents in Michigan need groceries delivered, and I am the only one who can navigate Amazon Prime. The sandwich generation becomes a reality, and I realize that although I need support, I also need to be present and available to the people who need me most.

I don my "Doctors Against Gun Violence" T-shirt because later today, I will post my picture to Facebook. A selfie with a Band-Aid on my shoulder, after my first COVID vaccine. It is December 24, 2020. A vaccine is all I really wanted for Christmas.

My kids are vaccinated a few days after my birthday, in November 2021. "This is it," I think. The fear and dread for me, my family, and my patients—maybe it is done. Life will never be the same, but maybe we can live life again like we did before, with delight in each other's presence, with hugs, and with companionship.

Only a month later, the omicron variant wreaks havoc in the New York area. We find ourselves with the same visiting restrictions that require families of dying patients to say goodbye on FaceTime and mothers to scream guttural screams over a small screen by the side of the bed. This time, the threat to our hospitals is not that they are overrun with patients, but our already gutted and shoestring staff is overtaken by the virus, and we are unable to staff our wards and operating rooms.

What I miss most are the smiles, the small touches. I still have my most important people—a vaccinated family that tests for COVID before we see each other, friends who socially distance outside, and colleagues who work together in a meaningful way. But we hesitate now. A sympathetic smile from a colleague who touches your hand when you have had a terrible death in the trauma bay is now replaced by a shrug and a wink from behind a mask. The hug from a girlfriend you have not seen in a few months is now replaced by a Zoom happy hour. A "come on in" invitation from a parent down the street is replaced by a wave from the porch. My work is grim. Seeing someone's face or feeling their touch can mean the difference between feeling understood and feeling alone.

COVID leaves us in our personal bubbles, a safe but lonely place for humans, who from the beginning of time were never meant to be alone. We must learn to be a resource to each other in a new way and find new meaning in our relationships in ways we never have before.

"Level 1 trauma, GSW to pelvis, unstable."

It is the seventh trauma in twenty-four hours, and our operating room, which had been flooded, was sealed off for construction. We put this man on an operating room table in the middle of the emergency room. Our anesthesia colleagues secure a breathing tube while we slam blood into his veins, desperate to work as quickly as possible. The large blood vessels in his pelvis were hit by the bullet. We operate on him right there in the trauma bay and fix all the bleeding.

He is still extremely sick and requires months of hospitalization, but six months later, he visits our ICU to thank the nurses for their care. He teaches poetry to youth in the high schools in Newark to try to help them understand their own trauma and prevent violence.

With economic stress comes increased violence, and 2020 and 2021 presented a significant economic stress to the world. People will resort to whatever they need to do to care for their children and to feed their families. As one pandemic waned, another pandemic—gun violence—takes its strongest hold on America in thirty years. We do not hold our cell phones for the families to say goodbye, but we go to the waiting room more often than we have in our careers to tell a mother that her son or daughter is dead. "There was nothing we could do. His heart stopped before he got to the hospital." Or worse, "The bleeding was too much. I couldn't stop all of it in time. I'm sorry."

Words that convey inherent guilt or feelings of inadequacy. If I had just worked faster, gave more blood, anticipated more injury, maybe I could have saved him. Feelings that then get quashed by incredible colleagues who remind you that some injuries are fatal no matter what you do or how fast you operate.

COVID deaths relent but are almost immediately replaced by the sharp uptick in violence in our communities, an equally raw emotional scar to bear by those who work in medicine and just want the best outcomes for our patients. One wave of the pandemic gives way to another.

Today too, as in April 2020, we are still here, downtrodden and demoralized, but still staffing the hospital for all who need us.

Public health works. When we embrace the principles of public health and invest in the systems needed to implement public health approaches, we can solve hard problems together. The social determinants of health that affect vulnerable populations matter, and we must strive to undo the inequity, racism, and historical trauma in our society. We must care for each other. We must look to our neighbor and friend and see the hurt and ask questions. Just like the kids are not okay, some of us are not okay either, and we must talk about this.

We will emerge from the pandemic not stronger or weaker but perhaps different. For the first time in my lifetime, we are recognizing how fragile our healthcare system is and how the crux of the public health and healthcare systems relies on people. People are our most important resource. The staff, the nurses, the doctors—they are finite and not to be taken for granted. When we take for granted our system, full of people doing their work, as I did when I first spoke to my neighbor in March 2020, we fail to recognize our weaknesses and work to correct them.

Focusing on our humanness gives me immense hope. If we reframe our problems as human ones, we can address other public health issues. Just as COVID has threatened our very existence, so will inequity, structural inequalities, climate change, and violence. If we treat these issues with the same fervor and focus, we may truly find ourselves on the way to an equitable, sustainable, and prosperous society.

Looking for a Better End Game

MARY E. O'DOWD

On Friday, March 13, 2020, I picked up my children from school and took them to the playground. This was to be our last day of in-person school for two weeks. That same day, the *Princeton Planet* reported the first local presumptive case of COVID-19. Watching my kids play, I felt a sense of eeriness, not because I was superstitious (although the date seems fitting in retrospect), but because only five children were on the playground—my three boys and another two, who all played together. The other mother asked what I thought about the situation, and I tried to explain what was bothering me.

"I am having a hard time seeing the end game," I began. "We are closing schools before we have one case in town, and we are likely to see an increase in cases. If we close with zero cases, how will we reopen when we do have them?"

On our walk home, I recall thinking that this day was likely our last day of school. I did not yet see the size of the storm headed for our children and our families.

In my previous job as New Jersey's commissioner of health, I led the state's response to the 2014 West African Ebola epidemic. I had been part of the state Department of Health's response for the 2009 H1N1 flu pandemic, Hurricane Irene, and Superstorm Sandy. Closing schools was never recommended during either of those infectious disease events. In fact, during H1N1, much of our effort was dedicated to explaining why schools should remain open. In January 2020, as Rutgers University wondered how a new health scare would affect international programs, I was asked to participate in the response team.

As part of my efforts to synthesize the evolving information, I listened to the weekly Centers for Disease Control and Prevention (CDC) telebriefings on the novel coronavirus. I came to appreciate and trust the comments from Nancy Messonnier, director of the CDC's National Center for Immunization and Respiratory Diseases. She was calm, transparent, and spoke in the public health language I knew and understood. I recognized the significance of the World Health Organization's declaration of a public health emergency and the import of the aggressive action the CDC took to issue quarantine orders affecting air travelers from Wuhan, China. The CDC had not exercised quarantine power in more than fifty years.

In her carefully worded January comments, Messonnier gave "evidence-based recommendations" for "this time." My experience as a public spokesperson meant that I heard her intended message loud and clear: This is a big problem that we do not yet understand, but we are acting aggressively because we are very concerned. I had been in similar situations when I needed to communicate with the public, but information was changing so quickly that we could not keep up. Now I was on the other side, and I could only assume that they had more information that needed to be confirmed because sharing it too soon, or being wrong, might cause a panic.

When Messonnier mentioned she was talking to her family about preparing for "community spread," I knew what she meant; I had practiced pandemic response plans. I started to bulk purchase shelf-stable food. When my husband, who works at a hospital, came home one day saying that we better buy supplies, I pointed to shelves full of mac and cheese and toilet paper and said, "That was done weeks ago."

This is all to say, I was reasonably well prepared from a professional standpoint. I could see the future in a way many could not; I anticipated that school closures would last longer than two weeks and have a significant societal impact. I was informed. Yet I never imagined how bad it was going to be from my perspective as a mother.

In March 2020, I was appointed as an inaugural member of the state Department of Health's COVID-19 Professional Advisory Committee, created to ensure that New Jersey's response was based on the latest scientific, medical, ethical, and public health evidence. I supported the commissioner by sharing tactical advice based on the previous multistate emergencies I had gone through. A formal national training program for health commissioners does not exist—you rely on those who have weathered previous storms.

As the lockdown lingered and federal and state guidance continued to change, my role within Rutgers evolved. I became a liaison between the operational response team at Rutgers and the state health department. I urged state leadership to verbally combat the negative stigma we saw our Asian students and faculty experiencing and pursued clarification when guidance did not address the dynamics of student housing. As a Rutgers graduate, I remembered the shared bathrooms in freshmen dorms, off-campus apartments crammed with students, and parties at fraternity houses that, well, let us just say the memory of walking on those sticky floors has not been forgotten. I helped interpret governmental public health actions, debating with the team when Rutgers should act in advance of public health guidance. Rutgers emerged as a national trendsetter, recalling students from abroad ahead of CDC direction and later as the first university to mandate vaccination.

In the early months of the pandemic, I was often home alone with my eight-year-old third grader, Patrick; my four-year-old preschooler, Jack; and my one-year-old, Kevin. My husband was working long days at the hospital. I was anxious, sleep deprived, my patience diminished.

With three boys at home, my work-life balance was overturned. As someone passionate about public health, I was eager to help the university and the health department with any expertise I could offer, but I also had a personal reason for wanting to do more. In April, my friend Colette, a mother of three children, died of COVID-19; her loss was publicly recognized by Governor Phil Murphy. She was an extraordinarily kind woman and an exceptional public health advocate. Colette's death reinforced my desire to help us find our way through this difficult period—quitting was not an option. At the same time, I felt guilty about not doing more for my children. While I attended virtual meetings, my kids watched TV. The stress and isolation began to take a toll on all of us.

Patrick, who loved school and is very social, became lonely and bored with schoolwork. I would find him snacking in the kitchen. He played games online and got lost in Harry Potter books, but he was struggling. Jack began to hide under the table during his Zoom preschool classes, and I would try to drag him back with fraying patience. One day, he escalated the battle by urinating on my desk. When he finally told me that it was just "too sad to see friends on the computer and not be able to be with them," we dropped out of Zoom classes. Jack only went back online so he could say goodbye to his friends whom he never saw again because he switched schools.

I knew my sons needed more attention and stimulation. At first, I was able to be creative. The easiest strategy before the pandemic, the neighborhood playground, was now roped off with yellow police tape. We are lucky to have a large backyard. I led an outdoor art class, served picnics for home school lunch, built a firepit, and devised a clothesline snack delivery system to the tree house. Between work meetings and school sessions, I would try to get us all outside for exercise, but getting three boys out of the house at the same time and on deadline almost never went well. Once outside, the "fun" physical activities seemed to morph into forced marches, with the boys complaining nonstop. My inventiveness and patience waned.

As the initial wave of cases began to subside and testing became more readily available, with federal approval of the first saliva test developed by Rutgers scientists, the university began to urgently pursue a strategy for reopening. As chair of the Testing and Contact Tracing Subcommittee, I authored our testing strategy. Balancing testing science against our operational capacity, we created a Testing Protocol Action Group comprised of the university's clinical, legal, ethical, and epidemiological experts. This was coupled with the contact tracing component crafted by my cochair Perry Halkitis, dean of the School of Public Health. This collective work, launched in the summer of 2020, allowed for a gradual repopulation of campus while maintaining what was often referred to as "an island of health in a sea of disease," referencing the low rates of COVID cases on campus relative to the rest of the state.

During the next phase of the pandemic, I tried to interweave my two parallel universes. I spent many working hours reading the latest public health reports, and I tried to insert the best mitigation tactics into my family life. Many of the policymakers I knew professionally did not have the benefit, or challenge, of seeing the world through the same divergent lenses. Many of the families in my community did not have access to the scientific experts I regularly questioned in my professional life. As the vaccine became closer to reality, my initial hesitancy was assuaged by talking with these experts. I recognized the potential benefits of sharing my perspective. I began hosting a Rutgers podcast, *On the Pandemic*, interviewing experts first on vaccines and then broader topics including mitigation strategies, education, mental health, athletics, and the impact of the pandemic on children and the healthcare workforce. I frequently tried to challenge my guests to provide relevant guidance to the public and to influence policymakers by highlighting some of the hidden actors and less acknowledged implications of the pandemic. I regularly shared examples from my three sons, so often that my mom started to joke about it. I continue to think that asking these questions makes a difference.

Putting families' perspectives on the table is the first step toward making their needs a priority.

In November 2021, *JAMA Pediatrics* published a meta-analysis of twenty-nine studies, estimating that depression and anxiety in children and adolescents globally had doubled since before the pandemic.[1] In June 2020, when it looked as if New Jersey had survived its first wave, I began to see evidence of deeper damage to my children. We finally felt safe enough to reunite with my brother's family for a weekend visit to the Jersey Shore. While our children are close in age and have a strong friendship, their behavior was striking. All seven of them wanted to be in constant physical contact. They would share seats and lie on top of each other on the couch. They seemed like a pack of lion cubs, constantly climbing all over each other, clearly obliterating the six-feet-apart edict. Over the summer, we prioritized keeping the cousins together as much as possible, and with this increasing companionship, I saw their spirits rise. In their newfound happiness, I began to appreciate how lonely and sad they had become. The CDC and Kaiser Family Foundation both indicate that the prevalence of anxiety, depression, and substance use in the general population and particularly in youth have increased significantly because of the traumatic impact of the pandemic.[2] This situation calls for the prioritization of increased investment in mental health, with an emphasis on vulnerable populations, as part of our recovery plan.

Meanwhile, my oldest son had gained weight, and his body mass index had spiked. As his doctor talked about the need to be more active, Patrick tried to hide his stomach. The sad, embarrassed look on his face brought tears to my eyes. I wanted to scream, "We aren't walking to school because school's not open. He can't play with his friends because that isn't consistent with the lockdown. The playgrounds are covered in police tape. And trying to motivate my nine-year-old to get real physical activity while dragging around his little brothers is nearly impossible!"

By the time the official reports were published saying that the pandemic had led to weight gain in children,[3] I was already deep into my recovery plan for Patrick. A new mother-son dynamic had begun: constant arguments over how much time he had been active versus in front of a screen. Appealing to his love of data and my desire to stop the debate, we bought Fitbits. (This became a pandemic "win." We now participate in a four-generation family Fitbit group where my great-aunt in her eighties is usually ahead of the rest of us, a motley crew aged five to seventy-two.) I signed Patrick and his brother Jack up for every organized sports program I could find. In June 2021, at his ten-year-old well visit, Patrick had made dramatic improvement. Equally satisfying was his sense of pride.

In September 2020, despite the insanity of virtual education for five-year-olds, Jack started kindergarten. Although virtual school certainly gave him access to teacher-guided reading and math instruction and the valuable skill of muting himself on Zoom, he would miss what might be the most critical aspect of kindergarten: social learning. I hired two middle school students to run a playgroup for Jack and a few other kids. These sessions were outside, and the girls were amazing—playing games that required lots of running in addition to arts and crafts. The unanticipated benefit was that the parents developed a spontaneous peer support group, a well-established tool in improving mental health.

I hired a tutor to sit with Jack during his online class sessions so that he had the support (and, let's face it, discipline) to get through each assignment. I felt incredibly privileged to have the resources to make these things happen, as I know many mothers do not. However, it was not surprising to discover that my son was behind in reading when he returned to in-person education. I dedicated a podcast to reports demonstrating that children, particularly those who spent their kindergarten year in virtual school, are behind socially, emotionally, and academically, and preexisting disparities have been exacerbated.

My youngest continued to thrive despite the pandemic. Kevin experienced a home full of the energy and stimulation that would have been lacking if his brothers were at school each day. He was one of the lucky younger children who had involved grandparents as well as older siblings. I also recognized that COVID remained a threat, and unlike the rest of his family, Kevin, being under five, had to wait the longest to have access to the protection of vaccination.

I have watched this pandemic from the lens of a public health leader and a mother. I have learned through reading the reports and my lived experience the negative impacts of this pandemic on mothers and children. I am extraordinarily privileged in terms of economics, education, race, family support, and community safety. During this pandemic, neither of my parents died and I never worried whether my family would have enough to eat. And even still, I, like mothers around the globe, have suffered. I have watched my children struggle despite being able to throw all my privileges at their problems.

As many reports reinforce, the brunt of the societal consequences of this pandemic have been borne by women and mothers. Women were forced out of the workforce due to unemployment or childcare obligations. Our society is dependent on its health care, social services, and education systems. These sectors are disproportionately staffed by women and have faced extraordinary disruptions and shortages. When schools and childcare programs closed, the fragility of the infrastructure that supports working families was exposed. Hospitals were confronted with an exodus of women. The adverse effects on women's careers, as well as their mental, physical, and economic health, continue to be documented. I was fortunate to be able to do my job remotely from home, which allowed me to keep working while supporting my family's needs. And still, like many women, I had many dark days where it was difficult to get out of bed. I felt like I was walking through water. I lost sleep over the next day's enormous task: I would have to get up and motivate my family through the day of activities, while handicapped by the constant worry that I could never do enough. When the alarm rang, I woke up exhausted and had to give myself a pep talk to force myself out of bed.

The National Women's Law Center published reports showing that whereas men were able to recoup their jobs lost from the pandemic by February 2022, women did not accomplish this until September 2022, with persisting inequities related to childcare, race, and wages.[4] In the essential workforces of education and health services, which are more than 75 percent female, the February 2022 data showed that men made up 100 percent of the jobs gained while women lost jobs.[5] These findings are consistent with earlier New Jersey data analysis conducted by the Rutgers Center for Women and Work.[6] Rutgers, like so many other organizations, has launched a task force focused on learning from the pandemic and how to create a caring, inclusive work environment. Put simply, we must support working families. The United Nations Children's Fund (UNICEF) recommends flexible work arrangements, paid parental and sick leave, breastfeeding and childcare support, child benefits, and fair wages. In return, UNICEF argues, these policies will increase gender equity, worker engagement, productivity, and retention.[7]

As we reimagine the end game to this pandemic and move into a new era, we must take on a new mission. We need to prioritize helping families, particularly mothers and children, fully recover—socially, physically, emotionally, professionally, and academically. We must mitigate additional damage to individuals and help women and families thrive. In rebuilding, we need to meaningfully engage a diversity of families to ensure a full appreciation for the scope of needs and to develop truly effective support systems. Rutgers has been recognized during the pandemic for its scientific contributions and public health leadership. We can continue this legacy in the recovery era by leading efforts in community engaged research in the development and implementation of effective and equitable workforce policies. If we want a more resilient society, we will need to address the profound and tragic inequities uncovered by the pandemic. Our future depends on it.

Pandemic Dispatches
(East Africa–North America)

ANGELIQUE HAUGERUD

2020–2022, NEW JERSEY—I travel by FaceTime three thousand miles westward to my mother's ninetieth birthday celebration, on the penultimate day of February 2020, as pandemic time commences.

I am grateful, a year later, for my first COVID-19 vaccine. Images of U.S. vaccine recipients' relief and joy snowball across social media and television news broadcasts. Novel virus, novel vaccine. Months later, after second doses and boosters, new COVID variants lurk and no one knows how long, or against what types of virus mutations, vaccines and boosters may be effective. Limbo. Meanwhile, I experience clichéd privilege—online grocery deliveries, Zoom meetings, at-home work, and walks in a beautiful park.

2020–2022, KENYA—An ocean and a continent away, Kenya, like other African countries, has a stunningly inadequate COVID vaccine supply during the pandemic's first two years. Wealthy nations hoard vaccines, and patent waivers for mRNA vaccines are absent. By mid-2021, just 11 percent of people in Kenya (which the World Bank classifies as a middle-income country) have been vaccinated through the COVID-19 Vaccines Global Access program directed by the World Health Organization and the Coalition for Vaccine Preparedness.

Vaccine seekers in Nairobi, a city I have been fortunate to visit many times, line up before dawn and wait for hours in 2021, only to be told the supply is exhausted. By early 2022, as people in wealthy countries get third doses, just 16 percent of people in Africa—versus about 60 percent of the world's population—have received at least one COVID vaccine dose.[1] Vaccine apartheid is real.

MARCH 14, 2021, NAIROBI—"That's the world order and we had better get used to it," Alex Muteti (a prosperous Kenyan business-man and research interlocutor I have known for more than a decade) writes to me via WhatsApp, after remarking, "I think we must wait for the First World to get done with [vaccinating] their populations first before they pass on the surplus [of COVID vac-cines]." An implicit moral hierarchy of humans. World order, world disorder?

JULY 22, 2021, NAIROBI—Vaccine sentiments: Mr. Muteti alerts me via WhatsApp text message about a poignant article published that day on CNN's website by Kenyan journalist Larry Madowo (formerly with the BBC). Madowo's headline: "My Uncle Died before He Could Get a COVID Vaccine, and I Got Mine in a U.S. Drugstore."[2] His uncle, writes Madowo, "was the third family member who had died in the pandemic that I didn't get a chance to mourn properly or see laid to rest." The journalist adds, "The oft-repeated mantra that 'we're in this together' rings hollow when a privileged few have more vaccines than they need and a great many have nothing. . . . Many people like my grandmother have died, or will die, because of the accident of where they live. Her heart is now failing, and mine is breaking."

As Mr. Muteti and I exchange text messages about journalist Madowo's story and about obstacles to wider global vaccine distribution, Mr. Muteti says, "COVID's Delta variant is causing havoc here in Nairobi. . . . The hospitals are overwhelmed and out of beds in Nairobi . . . [and people] are worried about their dwindling incomes." And then he writes, "I really don't know where and when this will end, Prof. Just hoping that it doesn't leave us too heartbroken to recover."

The heartbreak is global. Numbers are a crude proxy for its extent: nearly one million U.S. COVID-19 deaths reported to the Centers for Disease Control and Prevention by March 2022, with a higher COVID-19 death rate per capita in the United States than in other large high-income countries.[3] Reported deaths in India in early 2022 are more than a half million; in Brazil 656,000; in the United Kingdom 163,000; in Colombia 139,000; in Mexico 321,000; in Kenya 5,600; in Egypt more than 24,000; in Uganda 3,600; and in Indonesia nearly 153,000.[4] Although these numbers reflect widely varying data collection capacities, multiplying each figure by nine (for the likely minimum number of close friends and family members grieving each death) begins to hint at the extent of heartbreak.

The high COVID death rate in the United States arises in part from vaccine refusal but also from the failings of profit-driven medical care and many years of cuts to public health budgets. Unlike other wealthy countries, U.S. health care is a consumer good rather than a right. The country lacks universal public health insurance (for those of pre-Medicare age), a strong public health data system, or medicines affordable for all. During the pandemic's first wave, U.S. healthcare workers faced dire shortages of masks and other protective equipment, and they endured exhausting work hours. Some succumbed to COVID.

COVID caregivers worldwide became heroes during the pandemic's early months. In 2020, a ritual of tribute arose across the globe. In New York City, at 7:00 P.M. each day, people in the streets and in balconies and windows applauded and cheered for healthcare workers. Similar public displays—daily or weekly—occurred in India, Spain, Italy, England, the Philippines, and other countries.

Street artists also paid tribute and musicians performed in hospital courtyards. The Eiffel Tower displayed the word "Merci."

FEBRUARY 8, 2022, EAST BRUNSWICK, NEW JERSEY—Dr. Andrea Harangozo, a highly respected pulmonary and critical care physician who has worked long hours in the intensive care unit throughout the pandemic, shares her thoughts on the experience with me via email:

> Pulmonary and critical care physicians take on all comers, people from any socioeconomic status, around the world, from the 1980s HIV epidemic to the present phase of the COVID-19 pandemic that started in 2020. Physicians continue to fulfill their Hippocratic Oath despite being devalued to the level of "provider" before the pandemic. We and all "front-liners" risk our lives each day. We continue as physicians, fighting a fight against a pandemic that has become a political football despite the science we believe in. We again witness life and death. We and our (critically ill) patients and families learn the lesson of patience as we watch some live, some die, despite our science and our politics. We watch the inequitable results of the systems we are forced to deal with, and we still strive to win the battle.

The battle surges again as the ultra-transmissible omicron variant traverses the globe in late 2021 and early 2022. In November 2021, South Africa—which has excellent epidemiological capacities—detects the omicron variant in a foreign traveler, among others, and very responsibly reports the new variant to the world. The travel ban that other countries impose precipitously on parts of Africa angers many since the variant's global spread soon becomes scientifically evident. The international travel restrictions on eight southern African countries (lasting five weeks in the United States and a bit longer in Europe), depress African economic growth and are imposed just as South Africa's economically vital tourist season is about to start. The United States at the same time opens its borders again to other international tourists. How did this politicized start to the omicron wave look to my Nairobi correspondent?

November 28, 2021, Nairobi—"Probably the [omicron] variant is roasting the globe, but we are all focusing on southern Africa?" Mr. Muteti writes to me via WhatsApp. He appends a scathing critique of the travel ban by South African author Graeme Codrington from LinkedIn. I then share with Mr. Muteti a November 27, 2021 *New York Times* article titled, "As New Variant Circles the Globe, African Nations Are Blamed and Banned." He replies, "Thanks Prof. I hope that it [omicron] won't have a global impact but at the same time, shame on these guys!"

Stark global inequalities of power and wealth, already at record levels and set to increase even more, shape COVID death rates. Compared with rich countries, in lower- and middle-income countries, about twice as large a share of COVID-19 patients die from the virus.[5]

The world's billionaires, meanwhile, have seen the "biggest surge in [their] . . . wealth since records began," with the planet's ten richest people (all men) doubling their wealth—to $5 trillion.[6] The world's wealthiest person in mid-2021 (Jeff Bezos, with a net worth of more than $200 billion) increased his assets by more than $320 million *per day* during the pandemic's first year— acquiring about three times more in *one second* than many people in the United States make in a week.[7] "The increase in Bezos' fortune alone," reports Oxfam,[8] "could pay for everyone on earth to be safely vaccinated."

At the opposite end of the wealth spectrum, workers who deliver food by bicycle to customers in cities such as New York earn an average of barely $8 per hour, excluding tips, if they work at least forty hours per week.[9] They often face hazardous work conditions. In New York during the pandemic, these delivery workers formed watch groups to help protect one another from robbers who sometimes assaulted the workers as they tried to steal their electric bikes. After organizing, the New York City bicycle delivery workers won new protections such as the right to use customer restrooms in restaurants where they pack orders, greater employer transparency on workers' earnings and tips, and the right to limit their delivery work travel distances. But since they are still classified as independent contractors, they remain ineligible for unemployment benefits and workers' compensation.

As billionaires and large corporations with familiar brand names (and often anti-union stances) made mega-profits during the pandemic, low-wage workers in the United States sold their blood plasma to help pay for groceries and rent. Some slept in their cars because they could not afford rent. Many relied on government assistance such as food stamps and missed meals because they could not afford them. Thus, taxpayers subsidize the mega-profits of corporations that pay low wages and paltry taxes. The trick of trickle-down economics.

While more than 700 billionaires in the United States have vastly expanded their wealth during the pandemic, 3.7 million U.S. children fell back into poverty in early 2022 when Congress failed to extend the Child Tax Credit ($300 per month).

By early 2022, Africa—which has 17 percent of the world's population—has received about 6 percent of the vaccine doses produced globally.[10] By February 2022, Kenya is one of six African countries selected to receive, through the World Health Organization, the mRNA technology required to produce its own COVID-19 vaccines, and the pharmaceutical company Moderna pledges not to enforce its COVID vaccine patents.

By March 2022, Africa has experienced four waves of COVID. The fourth wave—omicron—passes through Nairobi fairly quickly, with many catching what they call Nairobi flu during the holiday season. By March 2022, COVID infections in Kenya have declined sharply and the government lifts mask mandates. For how long, no one knows.

MARCH 12, 2022, NAIROBI—Mr. Muteti sends photos of a family outing with foreign visitors on a sunny Saturday. "Get it done" (with "it" highlighted in coral) is emblazoned across the front of his T-shirt as he stands smiling, shoulder to shoulder with his two European visitors. I ask if it seems that COVID is mostly finished in Nairobi for now, and he replies, "Indeed it is, Prof. We've even dropped the mask mandates a few days ago." He then adds, "I'm however worried that we already have Deltacron in France." I reply, "Great that things are good now [in Kenya] on the COVID front! Yes, keeping an eye on Deltacron and hoping for the best!" Mr. Muteti's answer: "That's the only thing we can do for now. Be positive and enjoy the moments, Prof!"

MARCH 13, 2022, NAIROBI—Mr. Muteti writes, via WhatsApp, "Hey Prof! New variants or not, I'm certain that resilience will keep us here for many years to come."

May it be so. For many years to come. *Baraka tele* (Swahili for "bounteous blessings"). And may those in power understand that "resilience" need not be taught. Nor is it a substitute for food, water, health care, or shelter—or for a global order that is abundantly more just.

War of the World

How Humans Became a Destructive Force of Nature

PAUL G. FALKOWSKI

Ultimately, Rutgers recovered from the COVID pandemic. The period was surreal and severely influenced all our lives. During that time, I was reminded that, as a teenager, I loved to read science fiction. It was a literature that captured my imagination and immersed me in other worlds and times beyond New York City in the 1960s. Isaac Asimov, Robert A. Heinlein, Ray Bradbury, and Arthur C. Clarke were among my favorite authors. But when I was about fourteen, my father, who was born in 1901, suggested I might enjoy reading the "classics"—Jules Verne and H. G. Wells, the literature of his youth.

I read *The War of the Worlds* in a day. It is a short, gripping melodrama where superintelligent Martians invade England and begin to destroy the towns and later London. Their machines killed the best human military defenders, and the Martians themselves showed no mercy. In the end, the anonymous narrator, threatened with death and at wits' end, suddenly realizes that the Martians are dying. They were killed by some mysterious microbe. They were "slain, after all man's devices had failed, by the humblest thing that God, in his wisdom, has put upon this earth."[1]

The Martians had no immunity to the microbes, but humans did by virtue of evolution and selection; "to no germs do we succumb without a struggle," the narrator wrote. Wells allowed that there were no bacteria on Mars, and hence, when the Martians drank and ate, "our microscopic allies began their overthrow." In the epilogue, the narrator says, "In all the bodies of the Martians, no bacteria except those already known as terrestrial species were found." It was a glorious ending that saved humans from destruction and, for probably the first time in literature, gave microbes a heroic role.

At fourteen, I was not sophisticated enough to read any deep meaning into *The War of the Worlds*, which was first published in 1898. At the time, I just thought it was a short, engrossing, readable, somewhat stilted book with a satisfying ending. Only later did I realize, after reading Wells's *A Short History of the World*, that there was something more to the author and it piqued my curiosity.

Wells studied biology and was a proud champion of Charles Darwin's theory of evolution by natural selection. Retrospectively, it is rather remarkable that Wells allowed that humans acquired immunity from microbial-borne diseases while the Martians would succumb. That plot twist probably was credible to the readers at the time; a suspension of disbelief in a book that described a highly improbable set of events.

The concept was so believable because in 1898 England, microbes killed lots of people. The average life expectancy was about forty-six years.[2] Plagues had decimated Europe in previous centuries. Between 1889 and 1894, more than a million people around the world died from an influenza known as the Russian flu.[3] From 1851 to 1910, more than four million people in England and Wales died of tuberculosis alone,[4] not to mention cholera and all manner of food and water poisoning. Child mortality for those under the age of five was extraordinarily high in England, at 329 deaths per thousand births in 1800 and 228 deaths per thousand in 1990. That means that approximately 22 percent or one in every four children born in the late 1890s died before reaching five years of age.[5] The mortality rate from communicable, microbial diseases was a check on human population growth for centuries. That dramatically changed at the dawn of the twentieth century.

Fifty years before the publication of *The War of the Worlds*, John Snow, an English physician widely viewed as the father of contemporary epidemiology, revived the germ theory of contagious diseases, which had been postulated almost two centuries earlier by Nicolas Andry, a French physician. Snow was concerned about the water supply in London, which between 1849 and 1854 appeared to be responsible for two major outbreaks of cholera around Broad Street (now called Broadwick Street) in the Soho district of the city.[6] Snow reported that the 1854 outbreak of cholera killed approximately 1,263 people in seven weeks in that area of the city alone,[7] which was horribly crowded, and where sewage was disposed of in the street. In London, the 1853–1854 epidemic claimed more than ten thousand lives, and there were twenty-three thousand deaths for all of Great Britain.[8] Snow hypothesized that a microbe (a "germ") in the common well water, which was used by the residents of the area, was responsible for the cholera outbreak. This hypothesis was regarded very skeptically at the time; the competing "miasma" hypothesis was that diseases were communicated in the air from rotting organic matter. Indeed, the word "malaria" (bad air) is derived from the belief in miasma—and it was not altogether incorrect with respect to malaria, if we assume that the vector of the disease, female mosquitoes, are airborne. However, Snow was nothing if not pragmatic; the various private companies in London that delivered water from the polluted Thames River to wells in the city had different water treatment protocols. Companies that had higher filtration standards did not have outbreaks of cholera. Snow realized that something in the water from a single pump on Broad Street was responsible for the cholera epidemic. Snow also realized that men working in a brewery that used the water from the Broad Street source did not get cholera because they boiled the water in the making of beer.

Snow's discovery sparked an interest in cleaning up water supplies for drinking. Coincidentally, it was only a few years later, in the summer of 1858, when the Thames became so thick with sewage that it became unbearable to breathe the air near the river. The "Great Stink" led to the construction of underground sewage systems in London and the beginning of waste treatment. Simultaneously, flush toilets, which had been invented in England in 1596, became increasingly popular, leading to increasing demand for indoor plumbing. The separation between the potable water supply and waste removal, now so common throughout the developed world, was designed by engineers in England and then applied later throughout Europe and the United States. This phenomenon was one of the first transformations in the history of humans that would lead to a great decrease in infant mortality and, subsequently, an increase in life expectancy. It was the beginning of the real war of the world by humans against microbial disease.

In retrospect, it seems remarkable that it took so long for someone to discover that germs could transmit diseases to water that was contaminated by human waste. In the present world, it took only a few weeks to identify that COVID-19 was a viral disease, but it led to the death of millions of people around the world. It took almost two years to develop a vaccine, but that technology was based on the research of others more than a century ago.

In a milestone of science, during the mid- to late nineteenth century, Robert Koch and Louis Pasteur developed empirical vaccines against anthrax. These two giants of microbiology were standing on the shoulders of William Jenner who, in 1796, developed the first trial vaccination against smallpox, although he had no real understanding of the cause of the disease. Regardless, at the close of the nineteenth century, the basic concept of acquired immunity, although a scientific mystery, was starting to be understood. For most readers of *The War of the Worlds*, how microbes killed the Martians was largely irrelevant. What was relevant was that microbes could believably kill these alien creatures.

There was one hitch in *The War of the Worlds* that gave me pause: the narrator averred that the reason the Martians were so susceptible to death by terrestrial microbes was because there were none on Mars. Massive, highly intelligent organisms like the Martians described in *The War of the Worlds* could not have evolved without having some much simpler, unicellular ancestors. Of course, Wells (or the narrator of the book) could not have understood that at the time. Furthermore, although Darwin knew about microbes, he did not take them into account in his opus *On the Origin of Species*, which was first published in 1859. It was not until 1977 that Carl Woese and George Fox established that all organisms were related to each other by a molecular nanomachine, the ribosome, which is responsible for synthesizing the proteins in every cell on this planet.[9] One surprising result of Woese and Fox's research is that now we know that virtually all the organisms on Earth are fundamentally microbes! Indeed, the macroscopic world of animals and plants, which is so familiar to us, represents a tiny sliver of biological diversity.

Moreover, Darwin did not really know the age of the Earth. This issue was resolved almost a century after the publication of the first edition of *On the Origin of Species*. In 1956, Clare Patterson, then a young scientist at the California Institute of Technology, reported that the Earth was formed 4.55 billion years ago. This calculation was based on the radioactive decay of uranium isotopes into lead isotopes in meteorites, rocks that were formed early in the evolution of our solar system, some of which impacted our planet. That age was more than a million times older than Darwin dared estimate and sparked a tremendous interest in what the Earth was like before the evolution of animals, and later, plants, which were apparent much later in the fossil record. Indeed, the first fossil animals are "only" about 635 million years old.

In short, microbes rule the planet. Rutgers has a long history of understanding environmental microbiology. Indeed, Selman Waksman won a Nobel Prize for discovering antibiotics (a term he coined) in the soils around Cook Campus.

However, we are in a perpetual war with microbes. Because of overuse of antibiotics around the world, microbes have become increasingly resistant to our drugs. We are now faced with diseases that, in the past would have been simply treatable with antibiotics, are now virtually untreatable. Although we know how to treat water and sewage so it does not cause disease, increasingly these civil engineering efforts cost money that society is not willing to spend.

Humans have become a destructive force of nature. We have genetically bred and engineered plants that feed and serve us, while simultaneously decreasing the roles of microbes in making this planet habitable. We view the planet as our own but do not know how to manage it. Unless we learn from nature how to treat water, how to make food and fibers, and how to make this planet sustainable, we are a doomed species.

The COVID crisis was a peek into the war. It spurred great efforts to develop antiviral medications and to help develop vaccines. The effort is ongoing. Microbes do not stop working because we have vaccines or new drugs. The viruses that cause the disease will continuously mutate. New viruses will evolve. New microbes will evolve. Humans will need to continuously develop new vaccines and medications to protect our species from infection and to reduce the effects of the diseases in the infected. The war of the world against microbial diseases will never end.

Jordan Casteel, *Jared*, 2020. Oil on canvas, 90×78 inches / 222.6×198.12 cm, JC2020-002. © Jordan Casteel. (Courtesy of Casey Kaplan, New York.)

Jared (2020)

JORDAN CASTEEL

Jordan Casteel's (b. 1989, Denver, CO) practice is rooted in community engagement. Her own photographs of family, friends, and people whom she encounters are the source for her paintings. Casteel's nearly life-sized portraits and cropped compositions of subjects in their natural environments chronicle personal observations of the human experience.

Jared is a large-scale portrait depicting Casteel's friend—a former doorman of the Harlem building where the artist resides. From the frequency of the artist passing in and out over the years, Casteel developed a meaningful, family-like connection with Jared, whom she intimately painted during the coronavirus pandemic in 2020. Jared is seated at the reception desk, looking through slender framed glasses to engage with the viewer. He wears a dark suit with a blue necktie emblazoned with Superman's red-and-yellow *S* logo, evidence of a lifelong affinity for the DC Comics character. He is posed casually next to a plastic Superman action figure, brought to work from his personal collection. The muscular figurine is perched on the lid of a metal trash can, speckled with magnets from local businesses. Casteel draws our focus to the details in the cropped space of the canvas. The warm wood paneling that serves as a backdrop for the figure also allows the intricacies of the space to stand out—a multicolored bouquet of roses rests on the desk and a red wiry electrical cord falls from the surface, leading the viewer's eyes downward to Jared's shiny black motorcycle boots.

Reflections on Being Human
in the Twenty-First Century

YALIDY MATOS

The murder of young Black men, women, boys, and girls at the hands of police officers and others; the death and mistreatment of Guatemalan and Salvadoran children in the custody of Immigration and Customs Enforcement; the disproportionate punishment placed on Black boys and girls in K–12 schools; the negative psychological effects of immigration enforcement on immigrant school-aged children; refugee crises across the globe; the #MeToo movement; the #BlackLivesMatter movement.

This never-ending list of bad news was the motivation for a course I created and taught at Rutgers in the spring of 2020. I decided to sign up to teach this course because the question of how to exist in a world of constant bad news was bubbling inside of me, and I felt an urgent need to teach my way out of it. I titled the Honors College seminar, "How to Be Human in the Twenty-First Century: A Critical Race and Black Feminist Theory Contemplation." At the time, the degradation, denigration, and dehumanization of human life seemed endless. I wanted to offer a course that interrogated social justice issues using a critical race theory and Black feminist lens.

Critical race theory was born in legal studies in the 1970s after advances in civil rights stalled. People who develop critical race theory posit that racism is both ordinary and endemic and that the racialization of groups is bounded by time and space; thus, different groups can be racialized in different ways throughout time and space. Critical race theorists also recognize the role of intersectionality; some individuals are doubly and triply oppressed by forces and others have conflicting intersecting and overlapping identities. Finally, critical race theory is an analytical tool that does not follow legal claims of neutrality. Using a Black feminist lens augments critical race theory as an analytical tool. Black feminist theory has a few distinguishing features including the centering of the experiences of Black women as distinctive and as resulting in a particular consciousness and a focus on the essential contributions of Black women to U.S. society. Black feminist theorists also understand Black women's struggles within the wider struggle for human dignity, empowerment, and social justice.

Using these two lenses to contemplate what was happening in the United States and the world gave my class a common language to understand how race operates for us all, the ways our identities position us as both having privilege and as being disadvantaged, and how to center the voices of those in the margins. If we understand those who suffer the most, then we can start any conversation or debate or disagreement from a place of empathy, compassion, and understanding. A central expectation of the class was for students to become aware of their own positionality without attaching valence to it and to understand how positionality affects a person's worldview—both what we see and our limitations as well. At the end of the day, to understand another's humanity is to see your own first.

I also wanted to offer my students ways to think about humanity and being human people first. Guiding questions that framed our inquiry included: "How do we as a people, as a society come to comprehend what is happening all around us and maintain a level of hope? How do we focus on the equally significant acts of human kindness across the globe, in our own country, state, county, college campus?" I wanted, needed, to know how do we build bridges to connect across differences rather than being divided by railroads and walls that separate without any connection?[1] Moreover, can we move beyond even bridges and come together rather than building any infrastructure that keep us apart? I wanted to create and teach a course where students felt safe, seen, at home.

Midway through the spring semester, our lives were upended by COVID-19. The students and I were forced to shift our methods of teaching and learning over spring break as a lockdown and remote learning were instituted for the rest of the semester. The contemplation of being human could not have been timelier.

The questions I posed to my students became increasingly urgent during the lockdown. How do we think about being human when so much of what makes us human, connection and relationships, is stripped away?

As a midterm project, which was due during lockdown and after spring break, the students created art projects alongside personal reflections. I took inspiration for this assignment from the poetry and writings of Audre Lorde and Claudia Rankine. In her essay "Poetry Is Not a Luxury," Lorde says,

> For women, then, poetry is not a luxury. It is a vital necessity of our existence. It forms the quality of the light within which we predicate our hopes and dreams toward survival and change, first made into language, then into idea, then into more tangible action.
>
> Poetry is the way we help give name to the nameless so it can be thought. The farthest external horizons of our hopes and fears are cobbled by our poems, carved from the rock experiences of our daily lives. . . .
>
> In the forefront of our move toward change, there is only our poetry to hint at possibility made real. Our poems formulate the implications of ourselves, what we feel within and dare make real (or bring action into accordance with), our fears, our hopes, our most cherished terrors.[2]

I was intentional in asking the class to create art during a time that necessitated art to move us forward, to remind us of our existence—of our existence as full intersectional human beings. As Lorde makes clear in her essay, women's lives, as gendered beings, require poetry to survive, especially Black women and women of color who often fall through the cracks of existence. I wanted students to grapple with their multiple identities and to grapple with what it means to live and experience life as intersectional beings. I wanted students to use art to grapple with their dreams, hopes, terrors, and fears and to realize where those things could be nurtured.

The projects I received back from the students cracked me open. The artwork and corresponding reflections were deep, complex, and authentic. One student drew an American flag where the red stripes were visibly bleeding into the white stripes. Another student wrote the words "Get over it. Get over it" repeatedly with interspersed pictures of Mamie Till crying over Emmett Till's casket and of Trayvon Martin, among others. Allowing oneself and being allowed to show up as your authentic self, in ways that are engendered by art, is part of what it means to be human. The students spoke of empathy, of privilege, of oppression and discrimination, of blood, of bigotry, of identity, of shattered mirrors, of family, of generational trauma and hope, of bridges, of feminism, of culture, of dreams, of butterflies, of settler colonialism, of positionality, of difference, of diversity, of pain. These are all aspects of the human experience.

Teaching this course meant so much to me. I wanted to replicate my own undergraduate experience in one course, Feminist Theory, that created a space of belonging and empowerment for me. As an undergraduate student at Connecticut College, I constantly felt that I did not belong and was made to feel that way both consciously and unconsciously by peers and professors alike. Micro and macro aggressions abounded. The feeling and experience of being a woman of color on a predominately white campus often relegated me to the margins. On many occasions, I relegated *myself* to the margins by moving from the sidewalk for white students to walk and by remaining silent in classes when students were offensive or ill-informed. So when I finally made the decision to not be silent, I began to take control of my own learning. My experiences as a woman of color at a predominately white liberal arts institution inform my pedagogical values, the way I approach teaching and learning, and the courses I teach, including the course described in this essay. It was in a similar course, Feminist Theory, taught by Mab Segrest, that I had as an undergraduate, where I began to feel more at home, not at the college but inside of myself.

I came into myself and became a more fully human version of myself because I saw myself depicted in readings and learned to give language to my own experiences as a woman of color, first-generation college student, 1.5-generation immigrant, and native Spanish speaker. I wanted to provide that kind of classroom experience in this course, where students were able to bring their full selves to class, even through a Zoom screen, and where the midterm assignment created a space to merge the personal and the political, the knowledge of books, and well as the knowledge of our bodies. I wanted to empower my students not only with knowledge about critical race theory and Black feminist thought but empower them to be their authentic selves and to wrestle with difficult topics that may or may not implicate them personally.

At the end of the day, we are all different in many ways and some of us are more privileged than others, but these differences do not have to divide us. They can, in fact, bring us closer if we are open to listening. In many of the reflections of my students who carried privileges, the students named and wrestled with those realizations, with what they had learned thus far. And in many of their reflections, students spoke of the ways their intersectional identities (consisting of multiple, intersecting factors, including but not limited to gender identity, race, ethnicity, and class) were doubly harmful. As a junior in college, in my Feminist Theory course, I felt heard and seen not only because the professor heard me and saw me but because I learned *to hear and see myself* as a whole human being worthy of a whole human experience. In my own course, I wanted to provide my students with even just a sliver of this experience.

After teaching this course in the spring of 2020, I went on fellowship and sabbatical for a year, and I deepened my understanding of humanity, including my own. I spent a lot of time contemplating isolation. One of the things the pandemic has taught us—or at least those of us brave enough to learn something from it—is that in stillness, there is clarity. As bell hooks artfully states in her book *all about love*, "Knowing how to be solitary is central to the art of loving. When we can be alone, we can be with others." Amid the forced stillness, the lockdown, the forced boundaries, I was also able to gain clarity. The more I leaned into stillness, the more I accepted aspects of my life that were not going to change in the short term and maybe even the long term, I began to see the parts of me that needed healing, the parts of my humanity that needed love. What the pandemic forced me, and a lot of us, to do was ask questions of ourselves: Am I happy with my current life? At this job? What parts of myself have I moved to the back burner or that are not even on the stove? What parts of myself feel relieved? Which parts feel constricted? What parts of myself need love? If we are honest with ourselves, amid turmoil and death, the silver lining to these questions is that it can lead to better humans, neighbors, colleagues, friends, family members because there is a way that violence, death, and pain can plant the seeds of love and solidarity and a shared human experience that simultaneously considers difference, a tenet of Black feminist theory. It is in the consideration, and as Lorde argues, the recognition, acceptance, and celebration of difference that, I believe, we can learn how to be kinder and more loving human beings to one another.

Selected Reading List

Coates, Ta-Nehisi. *Between the World and Me*. New York: Spiegel & Grau, 2015.

Collins, Patricia Hill. *Black Feminist Thought: Knowledge, Consciousness, and the Politics of Empowerment*. New York: Routledge, 2000.

Delgado, Richard, and Jean Stefancic. *Critical Race Theory*. 3rd ed. New York: New York University Press, 2017.

Fung, Amy. *Before I Was a Critic I Was a Human Being*. Toronto: Book* Hug Press, 2019.

Lorde, Audre. *Sister Outsider: Essays and Speeches*. Berkeley: Crossing Press, 2007.

Ng, Celeste. *Little Fires Everywhere*. New York: Penguin, 2019.

Rankine, Claudia. *Citizen: An American Lyric*. Minneapolis: Graywolf, 2014.

The Building Bridges Issue, *Yes!* magazine.

Risking Delight in the Middle
of a Pandemic

YEHOSHUA NOVEMBER

At dusk, mid-March, one of those first evenings of the pandemic, I walked down my suburban New Jersey street to deliver two bags of flour—one whole wheat, one white—to a couple in their sixties. Because of the lighting at that hour, I could see straight into their living room. They must have been playing music on their record player. He must have spontaneously taken her hand and lifted her into a dance.

I left the bags inside the screen door and made the trip back home, a chilly breeze beginning to gust. How exhilarating and fresh, how beautiful to renew love in that way. And despite the many drawbacks and inconveniences of quarantine, how beautiful it was to have time to learn the teachings of the Jewish mystics and then pray alone, at my own pace, for a couple of months—the home filled with words of prayer, my children beside me (or escaping up the stairs as I called after them to remain beside me).

One night, in April, I took a walk with my eldest daughter and my son. Soon, we stood before a lake, moon and stars reflecting off the black waters. My son, who had finally emerged from the Zoom cave of our guest room and agreed to join us, imitated the loud squawking of a fleet of ducks. Away from his laptop screen, he appeared alive and free, his body housing a soul that now called out unimpeded, a mini resuscitation of the spirit that overreliance on technology had smothered.

I felt renewed when I finally returned to communal prayer at a makeshift outdoor synagogue under a neighbor's oak tree. Was I really seeing, in the flesh, the faces of those I had prayed beside for almost a decade?

Through his mask, a rabbi with a Bronx accent chanted the Torah portion on the burning of incense in the Holy of Holies, offering precise instruction on an ancient practice that produced a cloud of smoke symbolizing all that transcends reason. We, too, were attempting to resume our ordinary routines, uncertain of what would happen or the cosmic message that might be encoded in the pandemic. The sound of the Torah reading rose over the white garage and potted plants. I recalled the Hasidic teaching that the Divine voice that spoke at Sinai was called "great" and "unceasing" because—not confined to that moment or desert geography—it would continue to flow, for eternity, through any voice that would ever read words of Torah. A ladybug landed on my knee.

In the other universe of hospitals, friends' fathers and mothers were dying. Instead of traditional shiva visits, neighbors bearing trays of hot food and organizing prayers of comfort in the homes of the bereaved, we logged on to console mourners framed by squares on screens too narrow to hold their disorientation, their sorrow. Death was always surreal, but now, its aftermath seen second-hand, we could not be sure if we were dreaming.

Spiritual leaders, with shelves of holy books behind them, stared into webcams, citing dates and texts, trying to explain precisely what was happening. Emails came from the university outlining possible layoffs and pay cuts. My heart fluttered before I realized I had misread a few important words in an announcement from Human Resources.

Was it fair, not having lost a loved one, to draw theological conclusions about what all the changes wrought by the pandemic meant? Was it selfish and small-minded that I relished the freedom from my commute, teaching poetry from my basement as my students mourned another kind of death—that of their college social lives? People all around the world were dying or struggling to scrape by. Those more fortunate empathized, but the world's overarching sadness remained in the background for me, almost like the college logo shifting in and out of distortion whenever administrators moved their heads during a cyber meeting.

Many secretly, or not so secretly, felt untethered from the less important things, reborn, which reminded me of a Jack Gilbert poem about delight in the face of suffering:

> The poor women
> at the fountain are laughing together between
> the suffering they have known and the awfulness
> in their future, smiling and laughing while somebody
> in the village is very sick. There is laughter
> every day in the terrible streets of Calcutta,
> and the women laugh in the cages of Bombay.
> If we deny our happiness, resist our satisfaction,
> we lessen the importance of their deprivation.
> We must risk delight. We can do without pleasure,
> but not delight.[1]

Explanations for suffering—or joy in its wake—make me feel uneasy. It is true, however, that the majority of us remain quite blessed in obvious ways. Allowing ourselves to get caught in a thicket of despair, therefore, "lessen[s] the importance" of all those who have suffered or moved on to another place. "We can do without pleasure," Gilbert writes. Certainly, this is not a time to book exotic vacations and sport Hawaiian shirts. However, to honor those who have suffered, "we must," Gilbert warns, "risk delight."

Delight. A sense of wonderment and newness, especially when encountered in the ordinary or familiar, in that which we have overlooked in our habituation. In Hebrew, *Ta'anug*. A delight, the

Jewish mystics say, felt most profoundly not in a departure from daily life but a delight simply because. Joy in being oneself. Joy come what may. We may not understand the magnitude of this chapter of misfortune, like all the other chapters of misfortune, for many years. For now, we might pursue a form of delight, tuning into the wonderment behind the quotidian, revivifying our connection to our loved ones and—the old counterintuitive secret to experiencing the deepest delight—inconveniencing ourselves to assist others.

Days of 2020

Fear without Knowledge

MARK DOTY

I'm living in the molten center of a crisis, in a small apartment in what was once a five-story townhouse, on a block in the Chelsea neighborhood of New York City blessed by trees. There's a nineteenth-century church, a laundromat, and a school for disabled young people, but otherwise, the block is entirely residential, though you'd never know from the hurrying or idling traffic, as drivers weary of 14th Street choose this one as an alternative, and at some point, every day an irritable driver leans on his horn, inspiring a host of others until a big truck's air horn hostages everyone's attention till it's over.

But not now, not for weeks. It's startling to realize that I miss that aggressive clash, all bluster and swagger. Now the noise seems like a sign of life, a brash assertion that going somewhere, taking on a task, picking up and delivering *matters*, ensuring that life as we know it continues. Does it? In the lockdown, the way we live now, it's hard to know how things go on. The evidence—the empty sidewalks, the uncanny quiet—is partial. We define these times by everything that isn't happening.

It's odd to dwell in the shell-shocked center of an emergency and feel at a distance from it too. I'm healthy; no one I love is ill or has died. I try to maintain a faith that this will not change, though I lost a colleague at work, a brilliant older scholar I liked very much but knew only a little from exchanges at meetings and an occasional sly joke in the hallway. My city's been rocked by the coronavirus, but I've remained, for now, in a personal zone of relative safety. I know this may well be a useful illusion, a strategy for staying on an even keel while I can.

I've felt this way before. In 1983, my new partner and I left behind his apartment in a crumbling townhouse in Boston's Back Bay and my sublet loft in an old piano factory in the South End and moved into half a country house south of the city. AIDS was a presence on the horizon, stories of men sickening and dying miserable deaths while everyone stood helpless around them, terrified of contagion. We considered ourselves lucky, followed the news, paid attention to our health, tried to have faith in the same sort of zone of safety I'm occupying now. That imaginary territory vaporized when a friend grew ill and in a few months died on another friend's couch. We would know more about the virus, as years went by, but not enough to prevent the death of my partner, Wally, in 1994, of a viral brain infection that left him half-paralyzed and childlike, a sweet man capable of laughter till the very end.

Almost forty years after the appearance of HIV, the awful uncertainty of fear without knowledge is back. Will masks protect us? How much distance do we need to keep between ourselves and others? Can we have sex if we don't kiss? Is it even okay to pet someone's dog?

It's always been a joy for me to have a dog, but in these times, Ned feels crucial to me in new ways. A ten-year-old golden retriever, he likes unhurried, lengthy walks, with stops along the way, and though he's allegiant to routine, he also takes visible pleasure in new streets to explore. If it weren't for him, I'd likely limit my going out to trips to the surly, densely stocked market on 7th Avenue or the nearby deli beloved for the saintly guy nearly always behind the register, benevolence incarnate, who calls his loyal customers *honey* or *sweetness* and wraps and bags our purchases as if they were treasures.

But Ned needs a good long walk daily, along with a few shorter trips outside. The latter used to be mostly opportunities for him to lie on the sidewalk like a resting lion and receive the attention of neighbors. But now, it's usually just the two of us. Even when we walk the long blocks to Union Square, a favorite destination, we might pass two or three people on the way. *In New York City*, I say to Ned, *how can this be?* One early evening in the lockdown, we arrive at the dog run in the square and find the fenced area empty, a sign on the locked wire gate proclaiming indefinite closure. Ned sits down, looks into the unoccupied park, looks back at me, back into the park. He isn't ready to leave, waits to see if something might change. We'll repeat this scene a dozen times; before the dog run opens again, we'll both have stopped expecting it.

That evening, or soon after, on the walk back home, something embarrassing happened, although no one knew it but me. It was nearly twilight, and we were walking west on a block where large apartment buildings, perhaps ten or twelve stories, face one another across the street. There were no cars at all, so we walked right down the center of the street as if we owned it, a two-creature procession between two walls of windows and balconies. Suddenly, windows were raised and terrace doors opened, and little groups of people appeared and began to clap and cheer. Some were banging on pots and pans or blowing horns. The thought occurred to me that Ned and I were doing something remarkable: we were walking bravely, undefended except for the mask I wore across my mouth and nose—we were the world going on. Were they cheering for us?

The next day, around the same hour, there was a commotion outside my apartment, and when I opened a window and looked to one side, I saw people in the building beside me, on the same floor as mine, leaning out the window and applauding, while they played a recording of "The Star-Spangled Banner." Then I understood that, as I'd suspected a moment after I thought I'd been acclaimed by the citizens of 15th Street, the applause was not for me.

Another early, cooling evening we walk south, toward what used to be Saint Vincent's Hospital, which once cared for thousands of people with AIDS. As if there could be no more hospital there after that maelstrom, Saint Vincent's went into bankruptcy and was sold; where the hospital stood are now condos and townhouses, crisp and suburban in aspect. Across the street is a new park, a green triangle with park benches and adolescent trees. In one corner stands the New York City AIDS Memorial: white steel, open to the light and air, it resembles folded paper, origami architecture. I like it, but what's best are the words impressed into the concrete below. The artist Jenny Holzer arranged much of the text of Walt Whitman's signature poem, "Song of Myself" in a grand spiral beneath one's feet. It starts at the tight center with *I celebrate myself* and spirals on and on until it reaches the poem's remarkable final line, *I stop somewhere waiting for you.* When Whitman says *you* here, he means you and me and anyone; we are of his tribe, and he makes himself our prophet. It's the great American poem of fellow feeling, of democratic equality, of faith in each other and our possibilities, and perfect for this spot, a vision of the extraordinary society we might yet become.

But as if the city intends to point us toward a paradox, something else looms on the street that borders the memorial, something that summons my attention just as profoundly. West 12th separates the park from the only remaining medical building, a portholed white-tiled structure that seemed awkward until its Valley of the Dolls–era style suddenly looked glamorous again. It's Lenox Health Greenwich Village, a medical facility with a huge emergency room, the only one on this side of Manhattan, from the island's southern tip all the way to Midtown.

Parked on the street, set apart from any other vehicle, there's a trailer, a long rectangular box you might see pulled behind a truck barreling down the interstate. It's white and spotless. Where you'd usually see a pull-up door at the back, there is a long, sloping ramp concealed by a canopy of white vinyl so that no one can see as the gurneys are pushed up, bearing the bodies of those who have died of COVID-19. There's no more room for them in the hospital. How many might such a truck hold?

I know what the temporary morgue is the moment I see it and stand for a minute taking it in, listening to the hum of the cooling unit, looking back at the memorial where the poem unwinds on the pavement, a permanent encapsulation of hope, and back to the white box that holds the remains of my fellow citizens who will perhaps be buried, for now, in mass graves on islands in the East River. The dead ennobled by the monument, the dead in the cool truck, waiting, maybe unclaimed—I think of them while Ned and I walk the nearly empty blocks home.

A Litany for Survival

NAOMI JACKSON

When I was a girl, my Bajan grandmother insisted that my older sister and I recite Psalm 23 every night before bed. I didn't yet know what death was, but I knew that there was something sinister and brave about repeating the words "Yea, though I walk through the valley of the shadow of death, I will fear no evil." I learned that Christians were foot soldiers in an army helmed by an almighty God and that their faith would shield them from danger. Fearlessness wasn't a bad idea to instill in two Black girls growing up in 1980s Brooklyn, where the threat of violence was palpable, a lump you felt in your throat every time you passed the police or a group of guys who could quickly turn from admirers into assaulters.

My parents emigrated to the United States from Barbados and Antigua in the late 1970s. They were determined to cloak their children in an armor of education, etiquette, and religion—to protect us from a world that, in the words of Audre Lorde, "we were never meant to survive." I was ten when Gavin Cato, a seven-year-old Black boy born in Guyana, was hit and killed by a Hasidic Jewish driver in Crown Heights, two miles from our home. I was old enough to know that the rebellion that followed was connected to the suspicion that characterized relations between the Hasidic Jews and West Indians who lived alongside each other in that corner of Brooklyn. The riots interrupted the regular rhythms of my life. White reporters came to Sunday services at our all-Black

Episcopal church; adults' voices lowered to a whisper when we entered the room. For the first time, I understood that there was something hated and precarious about being a Black child in America.

Psalm 23 came back to me when I became pregnant last summer, at the age of thirty-eight. I'd long stopped repeating it before bed, but I hadn't forgotten it. Five years after my granny's passing, I'd realized what faith was for: it was meant to be a balm in times when certainty was out of reach. I'd been praying for a baby for years, though the intensity of my wish to be a mother waxed and waned. My desire was mostly a secret. I had friends who talked about basal body temperatures and dieted to prepare for pregnancy, but that approach felt uncomfortable to me—too ostentatious and too confident. I knew women who had struggled to conceive and others who had lost babies. Assuming that you could get pregnant at my age and that your child would survive seemed like laughing in the face of God.

I met the man who would become my husband in the winter of 2017. By that summer, we'd married, and within eighteen months, we had begun trying to conceive. We told almost no one what we were up to. Last June, I started texting a friend for weight-loss secrets, convinced that my jeans were tight because I had been eating too much cafeteria food at my new job. String by string, all my waist beads popped off, then my breasts ached, and I was often nauseous. My husband pointed out the obvious, but I was in denial until I took a pregnancy test that came back positive. Over the Fourth of July weekend, we told our families that we were expecting.

Having a Black child in America has always been an act of faith. In the antebellum South, one in every two children born to an enslaved woman was stillborn or died within a year. If they lived, the babies were often sold away from their mothers. Black women in the Jim Crow era feared that their children would be sexually assaulted or lynched and that the crimes would go unreported, unsolved, and unpunished. Still today, we worry that our children will not survive. The gap between infant mortality rates for Black and white babies is wider now than it was during slavery. And the lives that follow hold many dangers. Images of Black mothers mourning their murdered sons and daughters—from Mamie Till to Kadiatou Diallo to Samaria Rice and Tamika Palmer—are achingly familiar. George Floyd's pleas for his mother in his final moments drove home what we already knew: despite our best efforts and fiercest love, we may not be able to keep our children safe.

But our children are not the only ones in danger. As I began seriously considering having a child, I started to read more about the risks that pregnancy poses to Black women in the United States. American women are more likely to die in childbirth than women in the rest of the developed world, and Black women are three to four times more likely to die than white women, regardless of income or education. In New York City, Black women are nearly twelve times as likely as white women to die during childbirth or in the postpartum months. We have higher rates of infertility, fibroids, preeclampsia, and postpartum health problems. I read testimonies from Beyoncé, Serena Williams, Tatyana Ali, and Allyson Felix, all of whom had traumatic birth experiences, including preeclampsia, pulmonary embolisms, and emergency C-sections. If a doctor doubted Serena Williams when she recognized the symptoms of blood clots, which she had experienced before, how would a Black woman without the protection of celebrity fare?

And I was no one's ideal patient. My medical chart was littered with problems, including Graves disease, thyroid nodules, and an increased risk of thyroid cancer. I had been diagnosed with uterine fibroids in 2014, and an MRI in February 2019 showed multiple leiomyomas. The obstetrician-gynecologist I consulted warned me that I could experience pain and other complications if I got pregnant, if I was able to get pregnant at all. I had also been diagnosed with bipolar disorder. My recovery from a particularly bad episode in 2018 included a two-week stay on the psychiatric ward at Mount Sinai Hospital in Manhattan. I knew that the risk of relapse for people with bipolar disorder is considerable during pregnancy and the postpartum period; I had read the grim data about postpartum psychosis and suicidal ideation. My psychiatrist, a Black woman whom I credit with aiding my recovery, was alarmed when I told her that I was pregnant. She quickly cycled me off divalproex sodium, a medication proven to cause birth defects, and thankfully none of my symptoms returned.

On top of my very real risk factors, the statistics on Black maternal mortality amplified my anxiety and distress. Well-meaning friends shared anecdotes and offered unsolicited advice. One friend told me about the death of a mutual acquaintance's baby. Another told me about her friend's miscarriage. A third, concerned about how the stress I was under was affecting the baby, predicted that I would have a preterm birth. A fourth insisted that I ask my doctor for a steroid shot to strengthen the baby's lungs in case he came early. I tried my best to shield myself from their fears and projections, but I felt overwhelmed. I held my breath, waiting for the worst to happen.

During my pregnancy, I worked as a staff writer at a philanthropic foundation that provides grants to social science researchers, including several studying the benefits of paid family leave policies. I felt lucky to get the job just as a visiting professorship I'd had at Queens College was ending. But the human resources department said I was ineligible for the foundation's own three-month paid childcare leave because I hadn't been an employee long enough, despite having also worked there for more than a year in my twenties. Instead, I had to hope that the baby would wait to be born until I qualified, after twenty-six weeks of full-time employment, for New York State Paid Family Leave, which would pay 60 percent of my salary for ten weeks. I whispered *January 29* like a mantra. I told the baby to hold on and had a few friends pray on it, too.

Meanwhile, I planned for my delivery. I dreamed of a home birth with a midwife. My stepmother's great-grandmother, known as Cousin Lou, had been a midwife who rode on horseback through the Jamaican countryside at all hours of the night to deliver babies.

She accepted payment in whatever form families had—soap, fabric, food—and sometimes worked for free. But a home birth was out of the question because of my age and other risk factors. Even if it had been an option, I learned that these days, fewer than 2 percent of the nation's fifteen thousand licensed midwives are African American. Until the mid-twentieth century, most Black women gave birth at home with the aid of Black midwives, but that tradition was stigmatized and erased as Black people gained access to hospitals and midwives who lacked formal training were barred from the profession. The low number of Black midwives today makes it hard for Black women to receive culturally responsive care in their own communities, a privilege that many white women take for granted.

It took me a month after my positive pregnancy test to find an ob-gyn. I wanted to work with a Black woman. Research supports what I already knew from experience—that African Americans being cared for by Black doctors are more satisfied with their treatment; they have better health outcomes and longer life expectancies. My primary care physician, psychiatrist, dentist, and dermatologist are all Black women, but I couldn't find a Black female ob-gyn who would take me on as a patient. According to the Association of American Medical Colleges, about 5 percent of physicians in the United States are Black, including about 11 percent of the nation's ob-gyns.

I ended up back at Mount Sinai, the site of my acute psychiatric care the year before. I settled into a comfortable rapport with a white female doctor, a maternal-fetal medicine specialist. My husband came with me to my first appointment on August 1, 2019. We were stunned to find that I was already twelve weeks along and carrying not one but two fetuses. A blood test and ultrasound later confirmed that they were identical twin boys. I was overjoyed. I spent much of the next month on the phone with family members, trying to figure out where these twins had come from.

The trouble began two weeks later, when I went in for a follow-up appointment with another doctor in the same practice. One of the fetuses I was carrying was smaller than the other due to a rare disorder known as twin-twin transfusion syndrome in which twins unevenly share blood. I asked the doctor whether I should come back in a few days to check on the struggling fetus. She replied that it didn't matter—he would probably die anyway. I was stunned by her callousness. I went home and prayed for a sign to tell me what was happening, but I felt nothing. When I returned to the hospital the following week, the heart of the smaller fetus had stopped beating.

My grief was intense and complicated. This summer, I spoke with Dorothy Roberts, a legal scholar of race and reproduction and a mother of four, and she reminded me that "there is still a very prominent belief that there is something wrong with Black women's bodies, and every poor outcome is because of us." We shouldn't be having babies, the thinking goes, because our wombs are "harmful and defective." Even though I knew better, I found it hard not to blame myself for the loss of my second son.

Our doctor warned us that the surviving twin might also have suffered brain damage and could have developmental delays. She reminded us that terminating the pregnancy was an option. New York State requires doctors to inform patients with pregnancy complications of their right to an abortion, but I still bristled, thinking of the history of forced sterilization among Black women in the United States.

My husband and I knew that we would see the pregnancy through. But I was unsure how to process the strange fact of carrying one living and one dead fetus. My beloved niece kept referring to Auntie's twins long after the co-twin had passed; I found myself both wanting to tell her to stop and happy that the idea lived on with her.

I asked the doctor what it would be like to deliver the deceased co-twin. She described the fetus as a "pressed rose" that would come out along with the placenta. I thought of the white rosebush in my late-granny's garden in Barbados, and the rosebushes outside our house in the Bronx that always reminded me of her. I thought of Our Lady of Guadalupe, the patron saint of Mexico, who is revered as a protector of pregnant women, infants, and the unborn. In devotional images, she often stands with the sun behind her and the moon at her feet, encircled by a wreath of red and pink roses.

The doctor said that if I made it to the six-month mark without further problems, I'd likely carry the surviving fetus to term. Midway through my sixth month, I had a dream that a surgeon was removing my uterus. I woke up moaning and hyperventilating, convinced that all that was left of the baby was a bloody sheet. As my due date neared, I worried less about qualifying for paid family leave and more about making it out of the delivery room alive.

My doctor wanted to schedule an induction. I heard her concerns about avoiding a stillbirth, the risk of which increases significantly after thirty-nine weeks for women over forty. Still, I wanted to aim for an unmedicated childbirth. When I was twelve, I had a seizure that left me afraid of sleeping alone and inspired a lasting need to remain in control and aware of my surroundings. During a hospital stay after I was diagnosed with bipolar disorder, I was sedated with psychiatric meds and was unconscious for several hours. I woke up groggy and afraid in an unfamiliar hospital room. For weeks afterward, I was unable to write my name clearly and developed a stutter whenever I was nervous or overly tired. I vowed I would never again take medications that compromised my sense of autonomy.

At my thirty-eight-week appointment, my blood pressure tested above the acceptable range, meaning that I could have preeclampsia, a condition that can result in seizures that are life threatening for both mother and baby. Preeclampsia is 60 percent more prevalent in Black women and more likely to affect women above thirty-five. My doctor wanted me to go to the labor-and-delivery floor for monitoring. I knew that she was trying to ensure that I didn't become another statistic, but I resented what felt like her efforts to control me. I declined further monitoring that day, agreeing only to come back for my appointment the following week.

Over the weekend, my husband cleaned, painted, and organized the baby's bedroom and tried to keep me calm. I spoke with my doula, Nicole Jean Baptiste of Sésé Doula Services in the Bronx, about my birth plan. Nicole's services were a gift from an ob-gyn friend of mine who told me that continuous support from doulas during childbirth is associated with decreased C-section rates and less frequent use of epidural anesthesia. Years ago, in Boston, my friend helped deliver the baby of a Black woman who died from complications after she left the hospital. She wanted to ensure the same thing didn't happen to me.

When I returned to the hospital the following Monday for a blood pressure screening, my reading was high again. I agreed to the induction. I knew that I'd never forgive myself if my stubbornness led me to lose the baby or endanger my health. I was relieved to be introduced to a Black female doctor who would be part of my care team.

The day before the induction, the Black ob-gyn discussed possible plans with me. She suggested I take the drug misoprostol to induce contractions. I hesitated. I'd just read about Tatia Oden French, a thirty-two-year-old Black woman from Oakland, California, who developed an amniotic fluid embolism (AFE) after being given misoprostol; both she and her daughter died after she gave birth via C-section. French, a psychologist who had written her dissertation on traumatic brain injuries among Black women who had suffered domestic violence, questioned the use of misoprostol, but ultimately gave in after a nurse reportedly asked her, "You don't want to go home with a dead baby, do you?" There is no proven link between misoprostol and AFE, and the drug is widely used to induce labor, but my distrust of the medical establishment was so thorough that I refused to take it. One of racism's subtlest legacies is to make it harder for Black people to know when our fears are rational.

The induction was scheduled for early evening on February 4. I tried to stay calm, but inside, I prepared for a fight. I knew that my medical chart, which lists my bipolar diagnosis, was readily available to every nurse and doctor who interacted with me. So in addition to the routine threat of being labeled a stereotypical angry Black woman, I worried that I would be dismissed as a "crazy" person. But I told myself I would rather be seen as belligerent than be dead.

I wasn't wheeled down to the labor-and-delivery floor until around three o'clock the next morning. From the beginning, I was at odds with the hospital staff. After having to wait nearly twelve hours, now I was being rushed. A Foley balloon was inserted in my cervix to encourage dilation. When I told the resident who inserted it that she was hurting me, she said that if I couldn't handle that pain, I wouldn't be able to make it through my labor without medication. I had to repeat over and over again that I didn't want an epidural—I was terrified of being unable to move.

Three and a half hours into my labor, the resident offered to break my water, which I knew would intensify my contractions to such an extent that I might be in too much pain to refuse the epidural. When I asked why she was in such a hurry, she admitted that she wanted to complete the task before her shift ended. I was livid and asked her to leave my room. Later that morning, I sparred with the nurse, who pressured me to increase my intake of Pitocin—a synthetic hormone that causes contractions—every hour to keep my labor going at a healthy clip. My doula, Nicole, later noticed that despite my request that the nurse stop upping the Pitocin, she had increased the dose when we weren't looking.

My sister, Shari, arrived around nine o'clock that morning, and my husband went home to rest. Shari and I did squats, led by Nicole, to encourage the baby down the birth canal. We listened to Mahalia Jackson and Kendrick Lamar. As the day wore on, the doctors and nurses stopped coming to my room regularly. I couldn't help but wonder whether it was because they didn't want to hear my mouth. I lumbered around, dragging my IV behind me, because standing was more comfortable than sitting or lying down. At around 2:45 P.M., the Black ob-gyn came to check on me because she could see on the monitors outside my room that I was pushing; she warned me to stop before I tore myself. I insisted that the baby was coming soon and begged her not to leave. She assured me that the baby was still a ways away and promised she'd be back in twenty minutes.

Twenty minutes later, she was nowhere in sight. I swayed between Nicole and my sister and asked them if they were ready to catch a baby. Shari ran to the nurse's station to tell them that the baby was coming. The staff promised her they would page the doctor, but they seemed unconcerned and made no move to come check on me. When Shari returned to the room, Nicole told me to reach down and see if I could feel the baby's head. I could. Shari went to the doorway and started yelling for help, but the baby couldn't wait any longer. After one push, my son was born into Nicole's hands.

I wept as I held my son to my chest and fed him for the first time. I marveled at his full head of hair and impossibly bright brown eyes. He put one tiny finger to his chin like an infant philosopher. I was shocked to finally touch him, as I had never really allowed myself to believe that things would turn out okay. I was at Mount Sinai, one of the leading hospitals in the country, and I had just delivered a baby without a doctor or nurse present. I was both enraged and comforted that after the battles over admission and induction and medication, I'd had something akin to a home birth, with my healthy baby boy born into the loving arms of the family I'd created to receive him.

I remember asking Shari to search the placenta for the little pressed rose the doctor had promised me. I worried that if I saw it myself, I would never be able to forget it, and the happy occasion of my son's birth would be imprinted with sorrow. My sister held my hand and told me that the co-twin looked as if he were asleep. Nicole stroked my hair and reminded me that I would always be a mother of two.

These past few months, I've often wondered why I'm still here in the United States. I've always imagined what my life would have been like if my parents had never emigrated, or if I were to move back to the Caribbean, which I also consider home. Five years ago, I applied for and received Antiguan and Barbudan citizenship. But I haven't left. As much as I think about living elsewhere, for better or worse, I've thrown in my lot with Black people in America.

This spring, while I cared for my newborn, at least three more Black women in the United States died during or after giving birth. In April, Amber Rose Isaac, twenty-six years old, died at Montefiore Medical Center in the Bronx after delivering her son, Elias, via C-section. She had requested in-person doctor's visits for several weeks before she was finally admitted to the hospital and diagnosed with HELLP syndrome, a complication of preeclampsia in which the red blood cells that carry oxygen to the body start to break down. Wogene Debele, an Ethiopian mother of four in Takoma Park, Maryland, died on the same day, before she was able to hold her son, Levi. Unique Clay, a postal worker and mother of three in Chicago, died of COVID-19 just days after being released from the hospital where she had given birth.

I am grateful to have a healthy baby because I know it could have easily gone another way for him, or me, or both of us. I appreciate bedtime, diaper, and feeding routines, which help take the edge off the awful and infuriating news: the pandemic that has disproportionately affected Black communities, the police killings of Black people, and the brutal response to the attendant rebellions in cities across America. The night before New York City was put under curfew, my husband went out in the small hours of the morning to do laundry, a practice he'd started a few months before, to mitigate the risk of COVID-19 infection. I stayed awake, nursing the baby while sirens blared and helicopters flew low overhead, trying to will my husband back to us unharmed. I dreamed about another place we might live, where a mundane trip to the laundromat might not incite such anxiety and fear.

My faith lies in God and Black women, as it always has. I know that we have the answers to this seemingly intractable problem. Scholars such as Deirdre Cooper Owens, Dána-Ain Davis, and

Lynn Roberts are producing groundbreaking research on reproductive justice. National organizations like the Black Mamas Matter Alliance are pushing for legislative change that would transform maternal health care. And at the state and local levels, Black-led organizations are developing new models of culturally congruent care. Jamaa Birth Village in Ferguson, Missouri, and Ancient Song Doula Services in Brooklyn are providing childbirth education classes, parent support groups, and doula and midwifery care that centers on Black women and their communities. Bx (Re)Birth and Progress is advocating for the construction of the first freestanding birth center in the Bronx, which has some of the worst health, economic, and education indicators in the United States.

To be a Black mother in America is to know that your children never truly belong to you, that any number of forces or actors might take them from you at any moment. I pray that this will not always be the case. Since giving birth, I have been comforted by the image of the pregnant Virgin of Guadalupe—a woman with the sun at her back, the moon at her feet, surrounded by roses.

Sojourner Truth, Founding Mother, by Grace Lynne Haynes for the *New Yorker*, August 3 and 10, 2020. (Courtesy of the artist.)

Sojourner Truth, Founding Mother

GRACE LYNNE HAYNES

This piece was created to mark the hundredth anniversary of the ratification of the Nineteenth Amendment. Sojourner Truth, an advocate for abolition and women's rights, was born enslaved. Her enslaver was Johannes Hardenbergh Jr., the brother of Rutgers University's first president, Jacob R. Hardenbergh.

A Letter to Juneteenth on the Embodied History of Life in 2020

GREGORY PARDLO

July 30, 2020

Dear Juneteenth,

You're a celebrity all of sudden? Don't get me wrong, I'm happy for you and for the many Americans who now see how important you are. I don't remember the first time I learned about you, but I do know Black folks have been celebrating you for generations. What took the rest of the country so long to catch on? Coincidentally, my daughter had a question along these lines, which is the reason for my letter. Why did it take more than two years for folks in Texas to get wind that slavery had ended? I've known the answer intuitively, of course—race is at the heart of just about everything in this country—but I didn't know the details.

You probably get this question all the time. Before the pandemic, I was occasionally invited to speak to schoolchildren for Black History Month. I always had a presentation prepared, a grand scheme toward reconciliation through truth telling, but I'd end up fielding questions like, "Do you think things are getting better?" and "Why is your hair so curly?" I can only imagine the kinds of challenges you must face in getting your message out now that you're being introduced to so many new people. You have to admit, you are a complicated historical marker.

Your name, June*teenth*, absorbs and memorializes the very kind of historical obfuscation that has been used to suggest African Americans have no historical relevance in the life of this country. I'm talking about our pathological ignorance of the central role African Americans have played in building the wealth, prosperity, and security that we all enjoy today, but I'm also talking about the practiced obscurantism around the kinds of clerical data that help us authenticate the stories we tell ourselves about who we are individually and collectively.

Frederick Douglass believed he was "between twenty-seven and twenty-eight years of age" when he wrote his life narrative and lamented that "slaves know as little of their ages as horses know of theirs." This was by design, not merely because there was no column for dates of birth in the livestock ledger. Douglass writes, "I was not allowed to make any inquiries of my master concerning [my birthday]. He deemed all such inquiries on the part of a slave improper and impertinent, and evidence of a restless spirit." What does it mean to be denied, as a matter of principle, anniversaries of any kind? You, Juneteenth, are a brick in the historical foundation on which our country might reimagine its collective future.

This year, we also met COVID-19, which means that my kid, like everyone else's, was homebound for most of the school year. She and I were at leisure to think about you as a historical marker and as a call to reflection—more than just a nod between familiars on the subway. The morning of your arrival found her throwing some plush toy at the door, in my direction. I was trying to tell her about the history of Texas, that the Republic of Texas seceded from Mexico because Mexico had abolished slavery. *Why do I care about Texas?* is all I could pick out from the words muffled by the duvet she'd pulled over her head. I like to think that if you had come on a normal school day, she'd care about Texas.

By that hour of the morning, she would have already made the forty-five-minute subway ride from Brooklyn to the west side of

Manhattan and been sitting in her ninth-grade classroom bursting with questions about Texas. Instead, she had developed a habit of sleeping late and attending—if you count the soundless square displaying her initials as attendance—the optional, late-morning Zoom sessions some of her teachers offered for an hour each day before she drifted off into a miasma of headphones and group chats. Things were not normal.

In the quarantined weeks before you arrived, most mornings, including weekends, a school bell would ring in my mind, and I'd leap from bed in a panic. A combination of climate and virus anxiety made a mash-up with my fear of failing my kids, and together they revised that old nightmare where I walk into a class to discover I'm the only one who doesn't know we're having a major exam. In this version of the nightmare, my performance on the exam will determine the physical, financial, and emotional health of my descendants for the next seven generations. That's enough to drive me to turn every space in our home into a makeshift classroom. My kids now avoid me, and they are not at all subtle about it.

Until this year, my oldest daughter spent her entire educational life at a tiny independent school where she knew every student, teacher, administrator, and in some cases, their extended families. This was her first year outside of the "glass bubble," as she called it. This year, she switched to a public school for multiple reasons, most of them, I suspect, having to do with race. Recently, she told her mother and me that once, in sixth grade, some boys in her class asked her permission to use the N-word. Apparently, they held Black culture in such high esteem that their thirst for Blackness would not be slaked until they could roll that obscenity on their tongues. They called it "privileges," a kind of disposable Blackness that only a Black person could bestow. My daughter alone, as the only person of color in the class, could do the honors. The irony—that these most privileged children would amplify that privilege by leveraging cultural sensitivity against the one person it was intended to protect—may have been lost on the children at the time, but it was a formative moment in their developing relationships to race. The boys learned the importance of preserving the transactional logic that always favors people dependent on generational wealth.

What did my daughter learn? Hers is the only perspective that I care about. I don't want to further privilege the boys and people like them by focusing on lessons in cultural awareness and sensitivity. I want to empower my kid by putting the aggression she will continue to experience into structural and historical perspective. Had she stayed at her private school, she would not have access to resources for understanding her experiences, nor would she learn ways to respond that would be useful to her. As long as she lives in this country, she will continue to have these experiences. Call it systemic racism, call it white supremacy, there's a kind of cultural inertia that will only yield to a substantially opposing force like the one that has risen in response to the murder of George Floyd.

Considering the state's history, it's a wonder news of the Emancipation Proclamation reached Black folks in Texas as soon as it did. You know this, Juneteenth, but I was never taught that Anglo-immigrant settlers, along with the people they enslaved, had occupied the Mexican territory they would eventually call Texas initially at the invitation of the Mexican government. More settlers occupied the territory illegally. When Mexico abolished slavery, these largely—not to paint them with too broad a brush—illegal settlers ignored the law of the land and kept people in bondage. In a move foreshadowing the Emancipation Proclamation, Mexico granted citizenship to free Blacks, and the outraged illegals—the settlers, that is—drafted their own constitution countermanding that citizenship. The settlers were so dependent on slavery that rather than admit to Black humanity for any reason other than to prosecute Black people in courts of law, settlers would rather fight and die to maintain their social hierarchy.

By that time, the Anglo-immigrant settlers had invaded the Mexican territory in such numbers that the Mexican military could not deport them. I'm choosing my words a little facetiously, but slavery thrived in Texas for good (bad) reason. Slave owners in

Texas were not inclined to respect any law that would disrupt the social and economic order. Indeed, in response to the Emancipation Proclamation, slave owners from neighboring states spirited their plantations to Texas to keep profits and the fantasy of their dominion alive. Texas remained a stronghold of slavery even after the Emancipation Proclamation because there had not been a significant enough buildup of Union troops there during the Civil War to enforce it. It took two and a half years for General Gordon Granger to arrive in Galveston with two thousand troops to make the message clear to everyone that slavery had ended.

If there had been no pandemic and classroom instruction hadn't been disrupted, would you have figured prominently in school curricula? Probably not. The idea that Texas was so remote that the news of emancipation didn't reach them for two and half years is deceptive at best. Yet any historical narrative that challenges the image of America as a nation that has always been devoted to fairness and equality gets spun as slander in the larger culture.

If I don't have to practice my special brand of ambush homeschooling next year, it'll be interesting to see how your celebrity holds up in the classroom. Someone will figure out how to Disneyfy your virtues, for sure, but I also hope others will see in you a tradition of resourcefulness in contending with social and economic structures designed to prevent Black people from prospering. That you, Juneteenth, have taken shape enough for me to write to you is proof of progress, I admit. It is also evidence of the challenges we face.

We Cannot Escape History

LOUIS P. MASUR

On March 12, 2020, I began social distancing. Truth be told, doing so was not that difficult for me. I became an academic, in part, because I enjoy time alone. Writing is a solitary act. But teaching is not, and remote education distressed me. I thrived being in the classroom, moving around, engaging the students, hearing them laugh, and helping them learn.

When the pandemic hit, I was teaching my course on the Civil War. It is not a cheerful topic—the near destruction of the nation, the death of hundreds of thousands, the horrors of slavery. But it was a necessary and relevant topic in 2020, made all the more so by a president who embraced racial division and sought to revive Confederate nationalism.

My younger colleagues adjusted more readily than I did to online education. They taped their lectures and had students post comments and interact online. Technologically at sea, I could not do that. I did not want to do that. Instead, I met my students synchronously online at the time of the class. I tried to re-create in that space some feeling of intimacy and connection, but it was hard. Most students kept their cameras off and what questions there were came in the chat. I could not coax a comment from a shy student or sense whether they grasped the lecture by reading their faces.

Somehow, we got through the second half of that semester, and students said they appreciated my effort. But fear was ever present. Fear of getting COVID. Fear of being hospitalized. Fear that loved ones would be lost. And they were.

That fear might have helped us empathize with the dread experienced by those living through the Civil War, but the past is always something foreign, and more often than not we are left confused or unmoved by what people did back then.

If our dire situation did not help us understand the past, could the past help us navigate the treacherous present? I have never believed that history exists to serve the present or any of the hokum that those who forget the past are condemned to repeat it. We remember some version of the past and still we fail again and again.

The best the past can do is to inspire us, offer some models of how to behave in times of crisis. That is where Abraham Lincoln comes in. I love Lincoln. I have written two books about him. I have appeared in documentaries about him. Before COVID, I lectured around the country on Lincoln and during the pandemic I have continued to lecture online about him.

In late March 2020, in the midst of my fear and despair, I turned to Lincoln with my students. Lincoln, who faced a smallpox epidemic with grace and humor. Lincoln, who suffered from deep melancholy, yet managed to tell funny stories. Lincoln, who endured pain and vilification, yet saved the union, issued the Emancipation Proclamation, and preserved democracy. Lincoln, who used education to make himself, much as I hoped my Rutgers students would use their education to approach the world with understanding and humanity.

I ended up writing a piece on Lincoln and leadership that CNN published.[1] Writing that essay helped me get through some long, terrifying days at the beginning of the pandemic. Writing that piece, which appeared online on April 9, helped me clarify how history matters.

Here it is:

"The President quite unwell," reported John Hay on November 26, 1863. On his return from the dedication of Gettysburg National Cemetery, where he delivered "a few appropriate remarks" that would stand to define the war and the meaning of America, Abraham Lincoln had taken ill with varioloid fever, a mild but highly contagious form of smallpox. Even the New York World, a virulent anti-administration newspaper, hoped that "the President will soon be restored to health and strength."

Lincoln handled the illness with humor. He joked that since becoming president, crowds of people had asked him to give them something and now he had something he could give everyone. He also commented, in typical self-deprecating fashion, that being ill offered the consolation that the disease, which could leave scars, "cannot in the least disfigure me."

I have been thinking about Lincoln as the Covid-19 pandemic continues to unfold. Public figures such as Dr. Anthony Fauci, director of the National Institute of Allergy and Infectious Diseases, and New York Gov. Andrew Cuomo have modeled what it means to be a leader in a time of crisis. They have communicated the facts as they know them, have not shied away from telling the hard truth, have offered comfort to the grieving, and have used humor, not to trivialize, but to humanize these most difficult of times.

Part of what made Lincoln such an effective leader was that he never let the gravity of the situation, or his own tendencies toward melancholy, keep him from finding ways to offer solace and hope. In my research on Lincoln, time and again, I return to a letter he wrote on December 23, 1862, to Fanny McCullough, the daughter of his friend William McCullough, who had been killed in battle.

Lincoln had every reason not to reach out to Fanny. The war was not going well, there was opposition to his announcement of a preliminary Emancipation Proclamation and suspension of habeas corpus, and in the November elections Republicans had taken a drubbing. After the Union defeat at Fredericksburg, Lincoln is said to have remarked, "If there is a worse place than hell, I am in it."[2]

But no matter how low he felt personally, even when in February 1862 his son Willie died in the White House,[3] he was able to consider others and their needs. In his condolence note to Fanny, who he heard was suffering terribly from her father's passing, he wrote,[4] "You can not now realize that you will ever feel better, is not this so? And yet it is a mistake. You are sure to be happy again."

Lincoln never stopped preparing for what lay ahead: In the midst of his illness, he formulated his plans for the reconstruction of the Union. He knew whatever actions he took would be judged and remembered. This is what he meant by his comment to Congress[5] in December 1862, "We cannot escape history." He was thinking of future judgments—our judgments—on their actions in the moment.

Lincoln encouraged people to consider how they would want to be remembered and to act accordingly. In a public letter addressed to his friend James C. Conkling, to be read at an Illinois rally of Union men in September 1863, Lincoln scolded those Democrats who wanted peace and objected to the enlistment of black soldiers with this vision of the future:

"And then, there will be some black men who can remember that, with silent tongue, and clenched teeth, and steady eye, and well-poised bayonet, they have helped mankind on to this great consummation; while, I fear, there will be some white ones, unable to forget that, with malignant heart, and deceitful speech, they have strove to hinder it."

Lincoln was in effect telling Americans what Queen Elizabeth[6] said Sunday in her address to Britain and Commonwealth countries: "I hope in the years to come everyone will be able to take pride in how they responded to this challenge."

Even toward those who acted poorly, Lincoln held no bitterness or animosity, and this is what I marvel over most: his refusal to hold a grudge and his willingness to forgive. "With malice toward none; with charity for all," he famously concluded his Second Inaugural, and he meant it. Asked what to do with the defeated rebels, he said,[7] "Let 'em up easy." Vindictiveness was not part of his nature, and he took to quoting the biblical verse "judge not that we be not judged."

That is not to say he did not recognize the meanness and cruelty of others. "Human-nature will not change," Lincoln observed.[8] "In any future national trial, compared with the men of this, we shall have as weak, and as strong; as silly and as wise; as bad and as good. Let us, therefore, study the incidents of this, as philosophy to learn wisdom from, and none of them as wrongs to be revenged."

This is certainly a national trial, and it is a fitting time to look to Lincoln for lessons in leadership, for philosophy to learn wisdom from, and for a reminder that we too cannot escape history.

Readers wrote to say that they took solace from the essay. Lincoln never gave up hope, and I have tried not to as well. In spring 2022, I again taught the Civil War, this time in person. We gathered with masks and examined the ways in which the past is not past. I assigned a lot of Lincoln and sought to empower my students with knowledge and skills that might help them face a challenging future. We looked into one another's eyes, and we got down to work.

Paying Attention

JAMES GOODMAN

I was a high school science dropout. It is embarrassing, and I will not try to spin the story my way by saying that in tenth-grade biology, I objected to dissecting the frog. I was disgusted by the very idea of it, but I did not object, and a close look at the chronology will reveal that I lost interest before we were supposed to gather around the lab table of Mrs. S to see how it was done.

Nor will I remind those who were not around back then (or who were but don't recall) that many of us, when we thought of science thought not of the blessings of antibiotics and vaccines or the thrill of dark matter and gravitational waves but rather the curse of agent orange, napalm, petrochemical pollution, plastics, pesticides, and the atom bomb. Science was the money we wasted racing the Russians to the moon while we cut funds for anti-poverty programs and insisted we couldn't afford the Great Society. That was a blinkered view of science, but it was mine.

Whether I lost interest in biology because I didn't get it or I didn't get it because I lost interest, I can't say. What I can say is that I didn't get it. The words and concepts (eukaryotic, exocytosis, mitosis, meiosis, stomata, stroma) essential to understanding cells, energy, transport, reproduction, and division (explained in diagrams that to this day I struggle to understand) didn't stick the way the Latin words, cases, and conjugations did, or the outlines my history teachers wrote neatly in chalk on the blackboard about

Federalists and Jeffersonians, slavery and abolition, the Civil War and Reconstruction, populism and progressivism. The only thing I remember from biology is the word *permeable*. Yet from world history, I remember many things, including the four causes of World War I: nationalism, imperialism, militarism, and the system of alliances.

My lab partner Heidi could not have been kinder or tried harder to carry me along. With her help, I passed the course. A few marking periods, I may even have earned a B. But on my own, I was hopeless, whereas when it came to translating a paragraph of Cicero or Caesar, I was one of those whose homework classmates were eager to see.

Many of my friends moved on to chemistry and then physics. I took a high school version of physics for poets, which had enough of a lab to fulfill the requirement, all the while loading up on electives like Law in American Society, The 1960s (in 1973), even Speech Arts in which I prepared a "persuasive speech" on the Nixon administration's role in the overthrow of Chile's democratically elected president and a classmate and I conducted a policy debate against two others about national health care. Today, I would need two serious lab science courses beyond biology to graduate.

It took me only a few years to begin to regret it. In college in upstate New York, I fell in love with the rolling hills, glens, gorges, and falls that fed the long, wide, unfathomably deep Finger Lakes. On geology class field trips in the glorious spring of my first year, I learned how, two million years earlier, those lakes, once northward-flowing streams, were carved by the advance and retreat of glaciers. For many of my classmates, Introduction to Geology was a gut course, Rocks for Jocks. Not for me, and when in the fall of my second year I signed up for the next course in the sequence, I quickly discovered that I didn't have the basic skills to complete the first few labs.

Ever since, whenever I have wanted or needed to understand some dimension of science or medicine, I have had to start from scratch. When COVID-19 arrived, I had an enormous incentive to learn, and the lockdown in New York City provided me with time. I read about the virus, the disease, and the development of the vaccines, sometimes following links in newspapers and magazine articles to the studies they were based on. I didn't understand all of what I read, maybe not even most of it, but I did my best, learning bits and pieces of virology, immunology, epidemiology, pulmonology, cardiology, and internal medicine. I learned about viral load, respirators, oxygen diffusion, cytokine storms, spike proteins, mRNA, antibodies, antiviral medicine, and more. When I wanted the latest take on some breaking news or debate about lockdowns, respiratory droplet dispersion, virus spread on surfaces, mask, and then vaccine mandates, booster shots, and variants, I'd search for my favorite doctors, scientists, and public health officials on Twitter. I even followed the debate about the origins of the pandemic: Wuhan seafood market or lab leak?

While I was catching up on my science, many other Americans were doing some catching up of their own, prompted by the uprising that followed the killings of Breonna Taylor, Ahmaud Arbery, Rayshard Brooks, and especially George Floyd, whose murder by a Minneapolis police officer was captured by a young witness on a nine-minute smart phone video. There were thousands of demonstrations involving millions of people, and they led to one more national "reckoning" on race. It seemed as if everyone, at least in the circles that I moved in or kept abreast of—education, arts, media, politics, publishing, mental health, health care, even business and sports—was talking about prejudice, discrimination, explicit and implicit bias, and especially institutional and structural inequality, not just in policing and criminal justice but in every nook and cranny of American life.

I was especially grateful for the attention paid to African American history, including slavery, the Civil War amendments, the promise and achievements of Reconstruction, the terror that overthrew it, the century of Jim Crow, and the century of struggle against Jim Crow that culminated in what we call the civil rights movement. People learned about sharecropping, vagrancy laws, Black men falsely accused of crimes, chain gangs, lynching and the long campaign against it, disfranchisement, white race riots and massacres, the Great Migration, redlining, mortgage fraud, and myriad other forms of housing discrimination and segregation. More and more people came to understand that African American history and American history are one.

Here and there, I had reservations. I've never been comfortable with the idea that racism and race prejudice are in our nation's DNA. Nor am I fond of the characterization, even as metaphor, of slavery as "our original sin." Both have been everywhere in this round of reckoning, and although I understand the reflex and the appeal in light of four hundred years of horrible experience, both are misleading, making race a static, unchanging, and unchangeable thing and (notwithstanding all the talk of intersectionality) isolating it from the existence of and struggle against many other forms of American oppression. But history is argument. There was no chance that with so much history circulating, I was going to be happy with all of it.

One thing made me want to scream. That was when someone, especially (but not only) someone roughly my age, who was learning something new, insisted that they hadn't learned about this, that, or the other thing in school. The first time I heard it, five years earlier, I had screamed or at least yelled. I was listening to public radio. The guest, a Princeton professor, was talking about Woodrow Wilson. This was three years after the murder of Trayvon Martin, two years after his murderer's acquittal gave rise to Black Lives Matter, a year after the police killings of Michael Brown and Eric Garner, and the suicide in jail of Sandra Bland. It was just a few months after the massacre in Charleston's Emanuel AME Church. A group of Princeton students wanted the university to strip Wilson's name from its school of public policy and one of its residential colleges. They staged a sit-in in the university president's office.

The students, the Princeton professor explained, had done their homework. They knew that Wilson had contributed, in word and deed, to the hardening of Jim Crow. In his historical writing, he denigrated the freedmen and women and cheered the violent rebellion against Reconstruction. As president, he allowed most of his cabinet secretaries to segregate their departments: offices, cafeterias, bathrooms. He screened D. W. Griffith's *Birth of a Nation*, the racist melodrama that celebrated the white terror of the Ku Klux Klan, at the White House.

When the professor paused, the host said, "They didn't teach that when I was in college."

"Yes, they did," I said to the radio sitting on the kitchen counter.

Wilson's mixed legacy had been part of undergraduate history courses and a wide range of popular history books for decades. I rushed over to my bookshelf to grab one of the most popular accounts, C. V. Woodward's *The Strange Career of Jim Crow*, published in the 1950s and assigned to countless students since then. The radio host was about my age. I had learned about Wilson when I was in college, as did my mother, who went to college the same years I did and was a great admirer of Wilson's internationalism.

I grabbed my phone in the event the host started talking calls. He did, but before I could get through, he took a call from a Princeton alumnus.

"I learned about Wilson's racism in the 1980s," he said, in a course with the great Wilson scholar Arthur Link.

"They didn't teach that when I was in school." I can't recall if I heard that line again between 2015 and the spring and summer of 2020, but even if I did, I never heard it more than I heard it in the year between the murder of George Floyd in the spring of 2020 and the hundredth anniversary of the Tulsa massacre a year later. I heard it in interviews on the radio and television, read it in opinion pieces, saw it on signs in demonstrations. It was all over social media. On Twitter, one history professor reported how excited she was toward the end of the semester to see that one of her students had produced and posted a list of indispensable books on Black women's history. Excitement turned to frustration when she realized that these were indispensable books that "you have not been assigned in history class." Among them were two books that the author of the list most certainly had been assigned in history class, that professor's class, that semester. Two years later, I still hear or read it every few days.

George Will said it.
Bette Midler said it.
Tom Hanks said it.
Bill Gates said it.[1]

I understand that before the 1970s, "they" didn't teach Black history in most schools. George Will, born in 1941, had an excuse, until he was thirty, fifty years ago. I also understand that in the last fifty years, there has been an enormous variety in what has been taught in grade school social studies and high school history, differences between public and private schools, secular and parochial schools, northern and southern schools, rural, suburban, and urban schools. If red state governors and legislators currently seeking to curtail the teaching of serious history (the history that so many people say they weren't taught) get their way, those differences will grow. College students, meanwhile, choose most of their own courses. I know there are many people who were not taught the Black history they say they were not taught. Just as I am sure there are people who weren't taught about the wars against (and removal of) Indigenous peoples, nativism and anti-Catholicism, the suppression of organized labor, the Chinese Exclusion Act, sweat shops and child labor, forced sterilization of women, the quashing of dissent during World War I, the Immigration Act of 1924, the internment of Japanese citizens during World War II, anti-Semitism, and more.

Sometimes African American history wasn't in textbooks, lectures, or classroom discussions. But even when it wasn't, when it comes to this kind of ignorance, ignorance of an essential dimension of the American experience, present as well as past, "my teachers didn't teach me" is a weak excuse. We never learn all we need to know in school. In suburban New Jersey in the late 1960s and early 1970s, I learned a little bit about civil rights and wrongs in school and much more outside of it, reading newspaper essays, memoirs, and novels, watching television and movies, talking with classmates and friends, especially Black classmates and friends. Everyone can think of something important to them when they were in school, or important to them now, that they learned about (or learned more about) outside of school.

"Race and Reconstruction," said Bette Midler, when asked what subject authors should write about. "The villainy of the impeached Andrew Johnson should be common knowledge, but it is not. Our children should be made aware that we are still living with the consequences of Reconstruction. I'm seventy-five, and it was news to me."

It shouldn't have been. There have been scores of books about Reconstruction and its consequences. In the 1960s, Kenneth Stampp wrote and edited *The Era of Reconstruction* and *Reconstruction: An Anthology of Revisionist Writings*, two elegant books for readers of all ages. Both hold up well today. Eric Foner, among our most prolific and distinguished historians, has written half a dozen books about Reconstruction, several of them specifically for general audiences, one of them, *Forever Free: The Story of Emancipation and Reconstruction*, filled with Joshua Brown's striking visual essays as well as Foner's words.

George Will and Tom Hanks complained that they learned nothing about the Tulsa massacre of 1921. Hanks, calling himself a lay historian, said that Tulsa was not in any of the history books, which he claimed were written by white people about white people. I love Hanks as an actor and as a person. But he is just a few months older than I am, and for most of our lives, that has not been true. There have been articles, oral histories, a slew of books, a special commission study, a *60 Minutes* segment, films, and plays. The massacre is in many textbooks, including John Hope Franklin's 1947 classic, *From Slavery to Freedom*. Franklin's book, now in its tenth edition, has sold millions of copies. If those of us who teach

U.S. history neglected to mention Tulsa one year in the past thirty or forty years, it is only because we focused instead on riots in Wilmington (1898), Atlanta (1906), East Saint Louis (1917), Chicago, or a half dozen other cities and towns in the Red Summer of 1919.

Bill Gates, also my age, was asked to recommend a book that would help explain our politics. He chose Jill Lepore's recently published one-volume history of the United States. "The book is long, but it makes it clear how a lot of what we learned in school is simplified and ignores the less savory parts of American history."

Sure, it was simplified. It was high school. The primary contribution of Lepore's book is its breadth, five centuries, and its synthesis of politics, culture, law, technology, mass media, organized around a few ideals Lepore takes to be our national truths. You would be hard-pressed to find one unsavory thing in those pages— nearly one thousand of them—that people who grew up when he and I grew up have not been talking about for decades.

I don't know exactly what courses Bill Gates took in high school or his two years at Harvard. Most accounts focus, sensibly, on his computing. He wrote his first programs, traded his already formidable debugging skills for corporate computer time, and automated his school's class scheduling system. (He and Paul Allen then hacked it to put Gates in a class with mostly girls.) Unlike me, he was a terrific student, a national merit scholar, with near-perfect scores on his SATs, at a prestigious private school. He probably couldn't avoid history and English as easily as I could avoid advanced math and science. But I bet his head was probably not in the former the way it was in the latter.

No one can know everything, or even be interested in or engaged by everything, whether at a particular moment in their lives or ever. The chasms of my own ignorance, even about the subjects I study and teach, are wide and deep. It's great that Gates and so many others are catching up on some of the less savory parts of our history now.

I would simply encourage people, when they learn something new, something they are surprised, frustrated, or embarrassed that they didn't know before, to pause before blaming it on their teachers and schools. And when you hear someone say, "They didn't teach us that when I was in school," don't take their word for it. Ask a few questions. Do some research. Remember me and biology. My teacher tried her best. I was not paying attention.

A Reckoning with Names

Signs, Symbols, and the Meanings of History

DAVID GREENBERG

Social turmoil made 2020 a banner year for renaming: of streets, cities, schools, buildings, parks, bridges, sports teams, food products, and innumerable other things. One could start the list practically anywhere. The groundbreaking anthropologist Alfred Kroeber's name was expunged from a University of California, Berkeley, building because he was latterly judged insensitive to the Native Americans he studied. The great philosopher David Hume's name was wiped off a University of Edinburgh building. The State of Rhode Island and Providence Plantations became the State of Rhode Island—what everyone called it anyway—even though its plantations weren't the "Gone with the Wind" kind. Uncle Ben's Rice and Aunt Jemima became Ben's Original Rice and the Pearl Milling brand. The Washington Redskins finally ditched their offensive name, and the Cleveland Indians conceded that theirs, too, might need to go. The Dixie Chicks reappeared as the Chicks so no one would get the wrong idea, though calling women "chicks" today seems pretty problematic as well.

As busy as 2020 was on the renaming front, however, it would be wrong to imagine that this sort of sweeping revision was somehow new. History abounds with examples of place names getting retooled and for countless different reasons. How and why we choose to relabel has always been a strange process—subject to changing social norms, political fashions, historical revisionism, interest group pressure, the prerogatives of power, consistent inconsistency, and human folly.

Think about place names. In 1924, the Bolsheviks saddled splendid Saint Petersburg with the chilling sobriquet Leningrad—"after the man who brought us seventy years of misery," as tour bus guides tell their passengers in what is again Saint Petersburg. After Franklin Roosevelt was elected president, the U.S. government cleansed federal public works of any association with the most hated man in America, and the Hoover Dam became the Boulder Dam. In 1945, as Manhattan was emerging as the global capital, Mayor Fiorello LaGuardia and the city council rebranded Sixth Avenue as Avenue of the Americas, though a survey ten years later found that by a margin of eight to one, New Yorkers still called it Sixth Avenue. With independence in 1965, Rhodesia ditched its despised eponym to become Zimbabwe. Saigon, when it was overrun by the Viet Cong in 1975, was made to bear the propagandistic moniker Ho Chi Minh City. On Christmas Eve 1963, Idlewild Airport became JFK. In 2000, Beaver College, tired of the jokes, chose to call itself Arcadia University. Even old New York was once New Amsterdam.

So why was renaming such a big deal in 2020? What seems different about the nomenclature battles this time around is that they (mostly) turn on a highly specific set of questions, sometimes about gender but mainly about race. Every day—starting before 2020 and continuing after but peaking in that turbulent year—new demands arise to scrub places, institutions, and events of the designations of men and women who were once judged heroes but whose purported complicity in racist thoughts or deeds is now said by some to make them toxic. Not only Confederate generals, upholders of slavery, and European imperialists are having their time in the barrel. So too are figures with complex lives and legacies that contain both good and bad, as diverse as Christopher Columbus and George Washington, Andrew Jackson, and Woodrow Wilson,

Junípero Serra and Charles Darwin, Margaret Sanger and—even though it sounds like a parody—Mohandas K. Gandhi.

For too many years, American society failed to pay sufficient attention to its historical treatment of nonwhite peoples, including by some men and women we judge admirable or heroic for other reasons. So when the reckoning of 2020 came, it was to be expected that it would sweep up some estimable figures, along with the flagrantly reprehensible ones, in its dragnet. Still, many people, surveying the hasty and wholesale iconoclasm, wondered if there aren't ways to make the decisions about renaming more thoughtful and nuanced. Can we develop criteria and practices to bring some consistency to what has been a slapdash undertaking, some consensus to what has been a divisive process?

The criteria being invoked for effacement are not always articulated, but it helps to look at those that are. One body that in 2020 spelled out its renaming standards was a Washington, DC, mayoral committee with the ungainly label DCFACES. (An ungainly name is an inauspicious quality in a body tasked with retitling.) That acronym stands for the equally ungainly District of Columbia Facilities and Commemorative Expressions. In setting out its criteria, DCFACES decreed that historical figures would be "disqualified" from adorning a public building or space in Washington, DC if they had participated in "slavery, systemic racism, mistreatment of, or actions that suppressed equality for, persons of color, women and LGBTQ communities." The result was to make some sensible changes but also a number of dubious ones. For example, they changed the name of Washington's Franklin School because Benjamin Franklin—though a magnificent patriot, politician, democrat, diplomat, writer, thinker, inventor, publisher, and abolitionist—also owned two slaves, whom he eventually freed.

DCFACES botched its assignment, at least in part, because it didn't think through criteria. On close inspection, its list of disqualifying sins seems both too broad and too narrow. It was too broad because some of the fouls it cited, such as "support for oppression," are so vague and subjective that they could implicate any number of forgivable actions. It was overly broad, too, because it made a single offense wholly disqualifying so that someone like Hugo Black or Robert Byrd (both of whom joined the Ku Klux Klan as young men, only to repudiate their actions and go on to distinguished careers) could never be honored. Each of us is more, as Bryan Stevenson says, than the worst thing we have ever done. Besides, if, as it is now stipulated, everyone has prejudices and blind spots—if everyone is a little bit racist—then by this logic we're all disqualified.

Even as it was too broad, the DCFACES lens was also too narrow. The single-minded focus on sins relating to race and sex, after all, in no way begins to capture the rich assortment of human depravity. A robber baron untainted by racist bias but tyrannical toward his workers would pass muster. So would a Supreme Court justice with a clean racial record but a poor one on civil liberties. Dishonesty, duplicity, and cowardice are nowhere mentioned as disqualifying. Neither are lawlessness, corruption, cruelty, any of the seven deadly sins, or scores of other disreputable traits we might easily list.

If the wholesale elimination of anyone with racist taint led to unsatisfying outcomes in many people's eyes, others in the renaming business tried to establish some consistency by focusing on the secessionists who founded the Confederate States of America. Here, by 2020, it was easier to find broad agreement. Over the years, Americans have learned that Southerners imposed their Lost Cause nomenclature and iconography not out of naive tribute but as part of a rearguard racist project of reinforcing Jim Crow. By 2020, partial defenses of even a once-romanticized figure like Robert E. Lee, of the sort that David Brooks earnestly mounted in *The New York Times* a few years before, sounded ridiculous ("As a family man, he was surprisingly relaxed and affectionate. . . . He loved having his kids jump into bed with him and tickle his feet"). Were *The New York Times* to publish a piece like Brooks's today, the whole masthead might well be frog-marched out of the building.

Still, as the far-right protests in Charlottesville in 2017 showed, even Lee retains his champions. Plying his demagoguery that summer, Donald Trump warned that if Lee were to be denied public commemoration, George Washington ("a slave owner") and Thomas Jefferson ("a major slave owner") would be next. "You have to ask yourself, where does it stop?" he asked, not unreasonably. To this, there was a ready answer: Lee, Jefferson Davis, Stonewall Jackson, and the others were traitors; Washington, Jefferson, and the founders were not. That logic made sense. Yet it has only very limited application. Outright traitors are a tiny subset of those who have come under fire of late. The founder/traitor distinction, valid so far as it goes, says nothing about Theodore Roosevelt, Winston Churchill, John Muir, Kit Carson, Voltaire, and countless others.

And the distinction doesn't satisfy everyone. Lost Cause devotees reject it, but so does the far left. If Trump and the right want to keep all names, today's Jacobins wish to expunge them all—Washington, Jefferson, and many more. (This, too, has been going on for a while. In 1997, New Orleans struck George Washington's name from a public school. In 2015, University of Missouri students marked Jefferson for erasure on the oversimplified notion that he was a "rapist.") Some 2020 activists targeted Abraham Lincoln, Ulysses S. Grant, and Frederick Douglass.

Which brings us back to criteria and consistency. If Woodrow Wilson's name is to be stripped from Princeton University's policy school because he implemented segregation in government, why should the name of Franklin Roosevelt, who presided over the wartime Japanese internment, remain on other schools? If the geneticist James Watson's name is scratched from a graduate program because of his noxious views on race and IQ, why should that of Henry Ford—America's most influential anti-Semite—remain on the Ford Motor Company or the Ford Foundation? In what moral universe is Andrew Jackson's name scratched from the Democratic Party's "Jefferson-Jackson" dinners, but Donald Trump's remains on a big blue sign along the West Side Highway? How can the District of Columbia go after Benjamin Franklin but leave untouched Ronald Reagan, whose name adorns the downtown trade center? It's not a close contest as to who made life worse for the city's Black residents.

A first step toward achieving consistency in deciding when renaming is appropriate would be to create a process of education and deliberation before decisions are made. Our public debates about history unfold in a climate of abysmal ignorance. How much is really known about the men and women whose historical standing is being challenged? What matters most about their legacies? Were they creatures of their age, or was their error evident in their own time? What harm is perpetuated by the presence of their name on a street sign or archway? The answers are rarely straightforward.

The undergraduates I teach tend to know about Andrew Jackson's Indian removal policy and that he owned slaves. But they know little of his role in expanding American democracy. Millions of young people read in Howard Zinn's now-hoary bestseller about the horrors that Columbus inflicted on the Arawaks of the Caribbean. But Zinn was rebutting heroic narratives from historians like Columbus biographer Samuel Eliot Morison, and how many students read Morison? How many have a sound basis for understanding why so many places in North America bear Columbus's imprint in the first place? They were not meant to honor genocide. Without efforts to educate the young—and the public in general—about the full nature of these contested figures, our debates will devolve into a simplistic crossfire of talking points.

On this score, we at Rutgers University might indulge in some introspection. In the centennial of the birth of one of Rutgers' most esteemed graduates, Paul Robeson, the university and New Brunswick named a plaza and a street for the man. And rightly so: Robeson was a magnificent athlete, singer, and actor who shattered many color lines. A civil rights activist, he fought for labor rights, civil liberties, and the State of Israel. Yet no less than Jackson or Wilson, Robeson possessed unpardonable flaws—notably his apologias for Joseph Stalin. "Glory to Stalin," he said in an infamous eulogy in 1952. "Forever will his name be honored and beloved in all lands." This blight on his record isn't a reason to strike Robeson's name, but the Rutgers community should have been more fully taught about his failings during that centennial year, full of events and commemorations. We should never forget that no hero is without blemishes.

A similar challenge confronted Princeton University in 2015, when a campaign began to remove the name of Wilson—the university's onetime president—from its policy school and other campus institutions. Princeton president Christopher Eisgruber convened a multiracial, multigenerational committee that included trustees, historians, higher education leaders, and social justice advocates. It weighed the evidence—both the segregation of federal agencies and his immense legislative achievements; both his far-sighted wartime leadership and his intrusions on liberties—and turned in a thoughtful report. Princeton decided to keep Wilson's name on the buildings but to add plaques to provide frank accounts of his career and beliefs. More important, the university would, it said, take tangible steps to address the underlying grievance: that many Black Princetonians do not feel they are treated as equal members of the campus community.

There the matter rested—until 2020. After the killing of George Floyd, protests erupted nationwide calling for police reform and other forms of racial justice. This time, Eisgruber launched no deliberative process, appointed no diverse committee, convened no searching conversation. He simply declared that the board of trustees had "reconsidered" its verdict. His high-handed decree, more than the ultimate decision, violated the principles on which a university ought to run.

Around the same time, Yale University also performed a banishment—of John C. Calhoun—from one of its residential colleges. Calhoun, of course, is far less admirable than Wilson.

He made his reputation as a defender of slavery and a theorist of the nullification doctrine that elevated states' rights over federal authority, providing a rationale for Southern secession. Yet just as important were the procedural differences in how the two universities behaved. Princeton jettisoned a deliberative decision to implement an autocratic one. Yale did something like the reverse.

After the Charleston massacre of 2015, Yale president Peter Salovey announced that the university would grapple with its racist past. Then, after much reflection on his part but no deliberative process, he announced that Calhoun's name would remain. He explained that it was valuable to retain "this salient reminder of the stain of slavery and our participation in it." To erase Calhoun's name, he suggested, would be to take the easy way out.

Students and faculty rebelled, and Salovey backtracked. He now organized a committee to tackle the naming question. He populated the committee with faculty experts on history, race, and commemoration. Even more than the Princeton report, the final document was judicious and well reasoned. When Yale eventually dropped Calhoun's name from the residential college, no one could say it did so rashly.

Importantly, the Yale committee spelled out its reasoning. Unlike the DCFACES group, which went looking for sinners to crucify, Yale sought out the "principal legacies" of the person under consideration, the "lasting effects that cause a namesake to be remembered." That is to say, we honor Wilson for his presidential leadership and vision for international peace—not for his racism but despite it. We honor Margaret Sanger as an advocate of reproductive and sexual freedom—not for her support of eugenics but despite it. Churchill was above all a defender of freedom against fascism, and the context in which he earned his renown matters. Of the recent efforts to blackball him, one Twitter wag remarked, "If you think Churchill was a racist, wait until you hear about the other guy."

Principal legacies can evolve. They undergo revision as people who once had little say in forging a scholarly or public consensus participate in determining those legacies. Still, as the Yale committee noted, our understandings of someone's legacies "do not change on any single person's or group's whim; altering the interpretation of a historical figure is not something that can be done easily." As frequently as we discuss Jefferson's slave owning, his principal legacies—among them writing the Declaration of Independence and articulating enduring principles of human rights—remain unassailable. We will have to learn to live with all of him.

The Yale committee also rightly asked whether the criticisms of a historical figure were shared in his or her own time, or if they are a latter-day imposition. The difference matters. Values change, even in a short time. As late as 2012, when Barack Obama endorsed gay marriage, most Democrats did not. Today, same-sex marriage is a constitutional right. It might be fair to condemn someone in 2022 who would overturn the court's decision, but it would be erroneous to label as homophobic everyone who had doubts about gay marriage in 2012. Historians judge people by the values, standards, and prevailing opinions of their times. No doubt we, too, will wish to be so judged.

Then, too, a person's name can be a useful reminder of a shameful time or practice. In 2016, at Harvard Law School a committee met to reconsider its seal, which came from the family crest of Isaac Royall, a Massachusetts slave owner and early benefactor of the school. While the committee voted to retire the seal, Professor Annette Gordon-Reed and one law student dissented, arguing that keeping the seal would serve "to keep alive the memory of the people whose labor gave Isaac Royall the resources to purchase the land whose sale helped found Harvard Law School." A concern for history is what warns us not to hide unpleasant aspects of the past.

Context can promote tolerance or pluralism or other noble principles better than erasure. Plaques, panels, and displays at historic sites can educate visitors about the faults and failings (as well as the virtues) of the men and women whose names appear on their buildings and streets. Addition—more information, more explanation, more context—teaches us more than subtraction.

Above all, renaming should be carried out in a spirit of humility. The coming and going of names over the decades might inspire a presumptuousness about how easy it is to remake the world. Instead, it should induce a frisson of uncertainty about how correct and authoritative our newly dispensed verdicts truly are. "We readily spot the outgrown motives and circumstances that shaped past historians' views," writes the geographer David Lowenthal; "we remain blind to present conditions that only our successors will be able to detect and correct."

Our understandings of our history must be refreshed from time to time with passionate challenges to hardened beliefs. There are always more standpoints than the ones we already possess. Yet passions are an unreliable guide in deriving historical understanding or arriving at lasting moral judgments. In light of the amply demonstrated human capacity for overreach and error, there is wisdom in treading lightly.

The COVID States Project

Empowering a National Response

KATHERINE OGNYANOVA

The COVID States Project was launched in March 2020 by a multiuniversity group of researchers with expertise in computational social science, network science, public opinion polling, epidemiology, public health, communication, and political science. Its inception was driven by concerns about the lack of detailed real-time state-level and local information about COVID-19, its impact on communities, and the public attitudes related to the disease. The project seeks to help practitioners as well as local, state, and national governments to make informed decisions and allocate resources more effectively.

We are collecting large-scale longitudinal data from all fifty states and Washington, DC, to produce a stream of timely and relevant information aiming to improve the national response to the pandemic. Network-based survey questions allow us to assess the impact of COVID-19 not only for our participants but also for their households, their personal networks, and their local communities.

Since April 2020, we launched a new survey every six weeks, recruiting about twenty thousand respondents per wave. We have completed eighteen large-scale fifty-state waves, as well as three smaller national surveys. In all, over the life of the project, we have conducted more than 350,000 surveys with close to 250,000 Americans. In addition to public opinion polling, we are also collecting social media data from a panel of more than 25,000 consenting respondents and from a larger pool of more than a million Twitter users.

Combining online information with self-reported data allows us to better understand the spread of the virus as well as its health-related, social, economic, and political consequences. We also seek to evaluate how well the information and communication needs of Americans are being met during this crisis. Among other factors, we examine the sources of information and misinformation used by our respondents, their knowledge of critical health guidelines, and their trust in social and political institutions.

The fifty-state COVID-19 project has three major goals:

1. Providing data and insights to practitioners and policymakers in near–real time, allowing them to make informed decisions.
2. Providing data to epidemiology researchers modeling the spread of the disease over time.
3. Conducting academic research so we can learn from this crisis and improve the national and local responses to future emergencies. The comprehensive data collection will allow us to study individual and group behavior, differential information access, knowledge, and trust during a crisis.

The project has been supported by Rutgers University, Northeastern University, Harvard University, and Northwestern University. It has also received funding from the National Science Foundation, Russell Sage Foundation, Knight Foundation, and the Peter G. Peterson Foundation.

Since its formation, our project team has published more than eighty reports, currently available online at covidstates.org. Our research seeks to identify links between social behaviors and virus

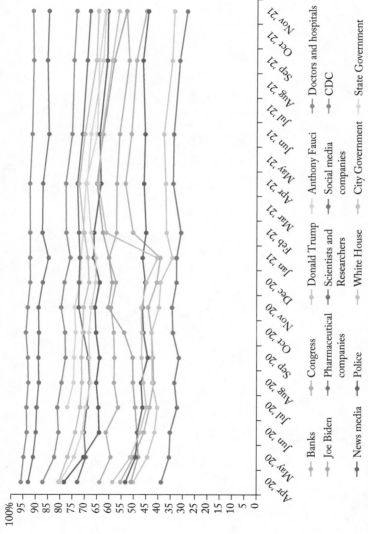

COVID-19 Trust Tracker. Source: The COVID-19 Consortium for Understanding the Public's Policy Preferences across States (a joint project of Northeastern University, Harvard University, Rutgers University, and Northwestern University).

transmission as well as the impact of messaging and regulation on individual and community outcomes during this crisis. We are sharing our data and insights directly with collaborators and decision-makers as well as making our findings public online.

I've Missed You (2021)

DIDIER WILLIAM

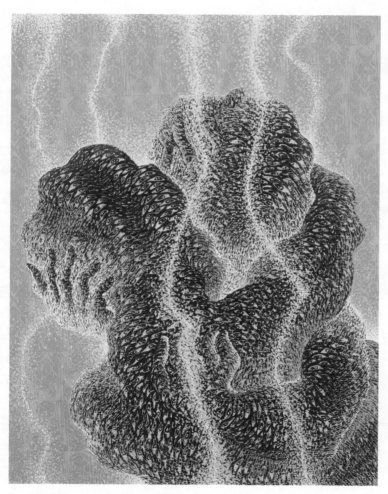

I've Missed You, 2021, by Didier William, Haitian American, born 1983 in Port-au-Prince, Haiti, acrylic, oil, wood carving on panel, 40 × 30 inches. © Didier William. (Courtesy of the artist and Altman Siegel, San Francisco.)

Burning Bologna, 2021

SUSAN L. MILLER

Frying bologna in a cast iron pan, I watch the meat hump up
in the middle, making

a hill with crispy edges. My daughter
has just come in from the yard, where

she made friends with two snails, one
that came out of its shell, and one that

did not. She was careful to wet the skin of her palm to hold
them, naming them

Mary and Joseph, though Mary was the larger, shy one. *Girls
don't always have to be smaller,*

she said. And if they have a baby snail? I asked. *I will name
it Daisy.* The past few weeks

she's been concerned about animal life, getting up from bed
to check on our elderly cat,

defending worms from her playmates.
She wants to be a vegetarian, although

she loves chicken nuggets, so we strike
the bargain that she's vegetarian until dinner.

She won't take a walk outside unless it's with her father, though
some days she cries because

she misses the playground. Some days she just cries. Some days
she goes out back and screams

I hate coronavirus at the top of the stairs
so the whole neighborhood can hear it, but
not today. She turns her bright face up to mine, hands me a
fistful of poppies and mint.

I sweep the hair from her eyes, kiss her, and send her to wash her
hands before she'll eat.

I flip bologna, watching the edges smoke and spit a little. Smell
the Unmistaken

scent of salt and fat blackening, and
if I close my eyes I see it: the story

someone's grandma told about the time when, as a child, a
hundred years

ago, she walked out the front door
of her house and saw so many neighbors

in their yards, just lying there, all down the lane, one after
another in the grass. How strange,

she thought, how many people decided to take a nap outside all
at the same time,

and with their sheets.

Pandemic Theology

"Bliss and Grief"

SUSAN L. MILLER

No one/is here/right now
reads a whole, late poem by my teacher Marie,
two years gone. But from our back porch, where we step out

for charcoal for the bases of my
new terrariums, I can see a garland of sunflowers
two doors down, flanking Gerard and Edy, our neighbors,

marrying each other by the back fence.
We can hear their laughter, someone yelling
"We have champagne!" and Edy calling, "*We* don't!"

We can only see a flash of her tattoos,
Gerard's black Irish hair and his white shirt collar.
"Well, this is a weird thing I never expected to do," he says,

then, laughing, "Shit," and "I probably shouldn't
curse on the wedding Zoom." The afternoon breeze
        is cold, but the sun's warm. My yard is still brown, pots
            of dead flowers

arrayed where I left them last summer, some
broken by ice or wind. A week ago they were buried
under two feet of snow, and afternoons, when the shadow

of the house creeps over the wooden planks
of the back patio, we're still chilled—but spring
comes on in the buds on the lilac, the jonquils and hyacinths

raising their green heads. Just this week
the neighbor kids were digging and found a worm,
which made Ophira scream, but Ethan looked and said,

"Worm! I love you, worm," though when
I held it in my palm to see, they ran. And I had
just received a shot that spread into my shoulder muscle,
brought fever, and made me glad to have
a headache, since this year, two of our neighbors died too young.
      Marie did say one can't feel both

bliss and grief, but since most of life
is grief, why not get married, drink champagne,
dig, plant the seeds I've bought—coreopsis with its gold

profusion, black petunias, black-eyed
Susans, cornflowers, five-inch zinnias, and
six-foot-tall sunflowers: russet, yellow, honey brown.

We wave and cheer from the back porch,
closer to evening, and now the guests have started to go indoors.
My husband and daughter go back inside as well,

too cold to stay out longer, leaving me,
before that long shadow falls, to watch
the late light on the rowhouses changing color.

Kid's Cloth Face Mask from Cat & Jack™

BELINDA MCKEON

Dove gray
with black stars

Like a hood for a tiny sorcerer,
Like a slingshot from the Prepper Pre-K.

Wired like an A cup
Reversible for efficiency
Stained like her brother's breakfast bib.

Crumpled from my pocket
Tattered from traveling steerage in my tote bag
Underused, is the truth of it—
We barely go anywhere.

Authorized by FDA
under an EUA
by use for HCP
only for the duration
of the declaration
that circumstances exist

under section 564(b)(1) of the Act,
21 U.S.C. § 360bbb-3(b)(1)
unless the authorization is terminated or revoked sooner.
Not FDA cleared or approved.
Not for medical or surgical use.
Made in China, and I wonder how that person is today,
And what they will sew today and tomorrow and Wednesday,
And what they might shape,
With their hurried fingers,
For the time into which Cat and Jack
have yet to lead us
and yet to style.

Call the Midwife

LEAH FALK

"This is the thalidomide episode," I said to my husband, as onscreen Sister Julienne cradled yet another baby born with defects, this time without any limbs or discernible sex organs. The monitor in Josh's hands flickered slightly, picking up street noise as our perfectly healthy baby snoozed upstairs in her crib.

My mother and I had watched this episode of *Call the Midwife*, the long-running British drama about midwives working out of a convent in mid-century, impoverished East London, long before there was a chance of me becoming pregnant or her becoming a grandmother. We'd probably watched on the kind of evening we took mostly for granted: me visiting Pittsburgh from one of the lives I was trying on in Boston or Ann Arbor, lying with my feet up on her couch, the garden she'd shepherded visible through the glass door. The grape arbor and forsythia bushes and peach tree, the string beans and morning glories trawling the deck rail. My mother had lived through that time in the 1960s when pregnant women could take a morning sickness pill that left their babies with abbreviated, disabled bodies. It was an entry in the ledger of the many forces of chaos circulating in the universe, the bad things that could pin you, randomly, in their sights. Difficult for my mother to watch that, or any, misfortune unfold without uttering a prescription against it, like an amulet: better to have locked windows or not drive too often on freeways or steep hills. Better not to skip the test even if your doctor says it's okay. Better to walk every day, and eat plenty of fruit, and keep your mind active.

Now, just as our child was born, the forces of chaos she tried to circumvent with those cautions had enveloped the world. With travel on the list of things that could kill you, no family had arrived to welcome our daughter. Instead, friends hovered on our stoop with lasagna in foil pans or dispatched delivery drivers with steaming cartons of Thai food. All day and sometimes all night, my husband and I passed our daughter back and forth between us in a slow dance of survival: our bodies were the only ones she knew. In bed, my exhausted muscles braced for the moment when she would cry out for food or comfort; after she'd finished eating, we would both drift off to sleep.

Sister Julienne, taking the dying infant from the counter in the hospital refuse room, murmured a few words of blessing before the breath went out of its body. No amount of calculated caution or recreational walking could have staved off the traumas the show's mothers-to-be endured either. The emotional abuse and the dangerously high blood pressure, the postpartum psychosis and the racism, the occasional baby born dead—these were the accompaniments of poverty, the understudied country of pregnancy, and sometimes just being a woman. When my mother and I had watched together, we'd been drawn to the drama in a sanguine way. Here were ordeals of the pregnant body, the childbearing body. We felt solidarity—hers borne of experience, mine then anticipatory—as a new mother hollered through her labor pains each episode, felt calmed by the no-nonsense older nun maneuvering a breech baby, by the younger midwife tying her hair back with a kerchief before she listened expertly to the fetal heartbeat.

At first, revisiting the series after I'd given birth was a chance to play at diagnosing the pregnant women's symptoms since during my pregnancy I had gorged on medical information out of anxiety disguised as preparation. "Preeclampsia," I would say triumphantly to the screen as though solving a crossword puzzle. As the pandemic wore on, though, I looked forward to Vanessa

Redgrave's soothing voiceover, the voice of an older nurse recalling her youth, that bracketed each episode. I watched with a little envy, too: Britain's National Health Service, new during the period when the show was set, dispatched these midwives to the homes of every pregnant and postpartum woman in the East London district. In Philadelphia in the twenty-first century, I saw the midwife who had delivered my daughter once at six weeks postpartum, accepted her prescription of birth control pills, and disappeared from the patient rolls for another year. The young *Call the Midwife* nurses with their set hair, jaunty caps, and bicycles or the nuns with kind faces framed by wimples seemed as close to thorough postpartum care as I was going to get.

I could never bring myself to watch television while my daughter was nursing, even during the extended cluster feeds of late-summer afternoons—the movement on the screen sometimes distracted her from the breast—so the show was my post-bedtime reward. After my husband's parental leave ended and he went back to working the late shift at a coffee shop, it became a solitary one. At those times, hurrying to cook myself dinner, the show became a strange mirror. To watch the fictional bodies of other pregnant, birthing, and postpartum women was to reexamine my own, to compare it with others' torn vaginas and deflating bellies and shedding hair. I wanted someone, even someone on a screen, to scrutinize these things and tell me they looked normal, that what was happening to me matched millions of iterations of what humans had done and been for millennia. Other times, I looked at no one else but my daughter, and she at me, as if there was no one with whom to compare ourselves, as if we were each the first to be us.

Call the Midwife seems engineered to elicit crying in people who have borne, or might ever bear, children. In the first few weeks postpartum, my emotions were unpredictable—I once fell apart while nursing because I just wanted to go for a run—and watching a show that almost always ended with a sweaty woman holding a new baby felt like a reliable way to regulate the tears, the way driving a car regularly keeps its battery in good shape. They never felt manipulated in the way of big Hollywood blockbusters, when close-up shots and carefully chosen music can manufacture emotions that feel a bit unearned. Instead, the tears felt released as if from a hidden cache deep in my internal organs, one that I seemed to have been hoarding throughout my pregnancy every time I made a list of baby names in the Notes app on my phone or lip-synced to Linda Ronstadt's 1980s hit "All My Life" during a twilight run.

But watching an hour-long episode—okay, sometimes two—every night, I gradually felt the waterworks dissipate and began to notice something else. In addition to her midwifery duties, every young nurse or nun took on some sort of additional civic responsibility: playing the piano for the local choir or leading a rowdy Scout troop. A midwife who was also a vicar's daughter taught the local Sunday school. The show did not present these duties as the kind of pandering extracurriculars they might be for a high school student gunning for a place at a competitive college, nor as the kind of work an AmeriCorps volunteer might sign up for to establish trust in the community they hoped to serve. Taking on these additional roles seemed, instead, to be just how people passed their leisure time.

At about the time my *Call the Midwife* obsession crested, I was also reading *Bowling Alone*, Robert Putnam's famed sociological study of how American civic engagement has declined since the mid-twentieth century (revised and updated in 2020). By "civic engagement" Putnam doesn't only mean the petition signing, canvassing, and protesting that we associate with politically active individuals, although he does include those actions; nor does he only mean the soup kitchen and neighborhood clean-up volunteerism that many engage in a few times a year. The sections that struck me most were those on belonging: that the decrease in Americans who were members of churches and synagogues, neighborhood associations, brother- and sisterhoods, leagues and clubs constituted a major entry in the decline of overall citizenship activity.

I could see myself in the downhill graphs: I, like many other young people I knew, had spent years unaffiliated with a religious institution, volunteered most often on a one-time basis, and couldn't speak of any associational memberships, least of all those in which I had any kind of leadership role. To be a member of something didn't seem particularly significant, especially when many of the memberships promoted to me seemed, as Putnam notes, to constitute little more than being on a list for regular fund-raising. I rarely thought of membership as being synonymous with real belonging, with making up the responsibility one undertakes to be counted as part of a community.

When, just before our daughter was born, we joined the progressive West Philly synagogue we had attended inconsistently, we repeated the true-seeming line that it was for the sake of her future Jewish education. But when we held a naming ceremony for her over Zoom, wrapped her in a friend's tallit, and watched the faces of our family members and friends from across the country appear on the screen, it was clear that this belonging was also for us. With the click of a button, we had become connected where we were once isolated. Synagogue members who barely knew us delivered food to our doorstep for weeks after her birth, just because we said we needed it. Almost as quickly as we'd felt the warmth of that generosity, someone else in the congregation had a new baby and we reciprocated by sending takeout. To belong, suddenly, was not just to be a passive limb on a larger body; it was to comprise a cell among many cells, to be in a constant state of energy exchange, investing and being invested in.

The additional roles the midwives take on have a direct impact on their work with patients: directing the local choir, one is present at the crucial moment when a young mother, who has given birth alone out of shame, passes out from a dangerous postpartum infection. In this way, their work, and their civic and personal lives—their entire identities—become seamless in ways I couldn't imagine for myself. But perhaps more importantly, they view the resources they put into the community as renewable ones.

Beginning to think of myself as a member of something constituted a paradigm shift. Critics of American upper-middle-class cultural norms, such as Matthew Stewart, author of *The 9.9%: The New Aristocracy That Is Entrenching Inequality and Warping Our Culture*, point out that for those families, personal resources are often seen as finite. Parents prioritize investment in children and the nuclear family; any additional giving to society is seen as an altruistic extra, not a necessity. I had grown up watching my father, who had himself grown up working class, write annual checks to soup kitchens and other charities; I dutifully carried fifty cents for tzedakah to Sunday school each week. But these gifts, although they contributed to the weekly and annual rhythms of our lives, didn't quite feel interwoven with our relationships to others; the help they offered was distant, somewhere outside the realm of our ordinary days.

As I watched the exchange of money, energy, and time buzz around me during the pandemic, I began to see my family's resources the way the midwives seemed to see theirs. In crisis, the margins of survival seemed ever narrower, as they must have for the poor community the midwives worked in; everyone's chances, from restaurants to public institutions to individual families, depended more and more on everyone else's willingness to contribute. If I wanted my local library branch to be there after the pandemic, I had to start attending volunteer meetings again. If I wanted this organization that gave groceries to people with food insecurity to pull through, I had to give them twenty-five dollars, whether I was sure I could spare it. If I was astonished at the generosity of my friends when my husband contracted COVID, I could show my gratitude by jumping at the chance to send someone else a meal while they convalesced. Eventually, I had realized something that I knew was obvious to many poor and working-class people: what I gave to my community, I didn't lose for myself but rather earned back in the currency of community.

During the nights my husband was working and I was alone in front of the television, or during the long days when I lived from nap to nap and craved adult conversation, I at first thought *Call the Midwife*'s seamless portrait of civic engagement was a window: that I was watching something bygone, the results of a kind of cultural training in selflessness and kindness that just didn't exist anymore. We'd been driven away from each other and toward ourselves, it was easy to think, especially in the isolation the pandemic demanded. The show didn't necessarily encourage this kind of nostalgia, but neither did it work to dismiss it: even as the 1960s march on, even as individual midwives make mistakes and have professional and personal crises, the moral compass of the house points northward. The engagement I saw in the streets and in my community seemed different—one borne of reflection and reinvention and design. An involvement constructed by questioning. But the models had a basic belief in common: that the energy one provides with one's body yields equivalent energy, if not immediately, then somewhere down the line. For Shelagh, a nun who leaves the order to marry the local doctor, directing the choir means it has a chance at a big regional prize, which boosts everyone's spirits; having a semiorganized Scout troop means that the district has a group of eager boys to lean on the night of a frightening blackout.

I have worked for mission-driven organizations my entire career and know as well as anyone that such outcomes—that return of the energy you've put in—aren't always visible to the frontline workers, the ones delivering the babies and administering the vaccines and running the after-school programs. That they almost always come full circle on *Call the Midwife* is a tidy trick of good television. But that doesn't mean they aren't coming, like a huge wave you can see building itself far out at sea, one that appears gentle but whose crest you know will knock you out if you remain standing still. I've learned to sit with the view of that gentleness, to wait patiently for the deafening return.

George Floyd was killed just ten days after my daughter was born, and the flexible network of Philadelphians who had been invisibly holding each other up throughout the first weeks of the pandemic suddenly seemed to emerge above ground. During the summer's protests, I put my daughter in the stroller and walked out to our neighborhood's main thoroughfare where marchers, dutifully masked, filled the streets like mortar. Still fearful of exposing my child's new, fragile body to crowds, heat, the virus, everything, I stood at the edge of the march where three women were handing out extra water to protesters. I told myself that despite standing apart, I was showing my daughter something important by being there. What was it? "There is no such thing as standing; there is only being held up," our rabbi wrote in a weekly newsletter months later, quoting Franz Rosenzweig. I'd been afraid that my daughter would enter the world alone, that my husband and I would be the only witnesses to her life beginning—her only, inadequate guides to the world's complexities. The people around me had, as best they could, seen to it that she did not, that we were not. Those friends and neighbors had helped convey her into a world raging against itself, the same one the protesters shook as they insisted on a different ending to the stories of men like George Floyd, as they insisted on bearing him out of the world as he had been borne in. On 13th Street in South Philadelphia, a man carrying a Black Lives Matter sign and carrying a gallon jug of water passed us closely, his brow soaked with sweat. The heat bore on us from all sides, insisting we feel our bodies, insisting we see. And I wanted my girl to see, as if her seeing could make it always true: no one must leave the world alone either, not if the living can help it.

Slap Roti and the Story
of New York City

MARC ARONSON

Thomas Wolfe, the 1930s novelist, called New York City "the place of everlasting hunger" where "the one permanent thing is change itself."[1] I spent a good part of the first COVID year finishing a many-year-long project of writing a history of Manhattan and what I called the New York idea. What happens when everyone from everywhere is pressed together on a small island? You get a place of change: confrontation and mixture—of people, cultures, ideas. COVID reversed Wolfe's apt phrase and my abiding theme. Instead of being the city of connection, the universal mandate was to separate, mask, keep at least six feet of distance, work, socialize, shop, and teach remotely, through screens. How did this present, and an unknown future, change the story? What ending would be true to the COVID-ravaged city and the themes I had traced from the city's beginnings in 1609?

The answer came with a recipe.

I knew from the start that my book would be thematic, not encyclopedic. The two great volumes of *Gotham*, one by Mike Wallace and Ed Burrows, the other by Wallace himself, are miracles of deep scholarship and clear writing and bring readers from pre-colonial days through post–World War I. It will be decades, if not more, before anyone needs to attempt anything similar. I saw the rationale for my book in concision—I am exploring places and themes in the city's history, rather than covering every important person, event, or topic. I got at themes two ways—by centering the book on five specific spots in Manhattan and by tracing fault lines and bridges that emerge and reemerge over the four-hundred-year span. The five locations are in turn Wall Street (colonial era), Union Square (nineteenth century), Times Square, followed by West 4th Street and 125th Street (twentieth and twenty-first centuries).

In 1688, as England experienced its Glorious Revolution, New York was in chaos. No one knew who was in charge in London, leaving local factions to battle it out in Manhattan. Amid the uncertain days, James Graham saw a way to protect himself no matter who came out on top and in doing so, gave the city a motto: "Money makes the man." That is the city's blessing and its curse. Blessing because over time, money would become a solvent, allowing those who would be rejected elsewhere to find a place. Yet money was strangling the city. Early on in my writing, I thought the ending of my book would talk about expensive Manhattan: the wildly overpriced apartments and whole buildings purchased by the international super wealthy to park cash. Manhattan was becoming a very safe desert where young people, artists, and new immigrants were largely shut out. High prices ensured residential segregation (by income), which, in turn, led to some of the most racially segregated public schools in the country. This was precisely the opposite of my argument for the city of mixture. How could I end the book in a way that was true to this reality and yet matched my ongoing argument?

The High Bridge linking upper Manhattan and the Bronx was built in the 1840s to hold tubes that brought upstate water into Manhattan. By 1848, a walkway was added to allow pedestrians to enjoy the view over the Harlem River. But in the 1970s—in a period of crime and neglect—the walkway was closed. I was there the day it reopened in June 2015, and I thought that was the ending of my book. Even if Manhattan froze into a museum of money, the city would thrive in its other boroughs. The High Bridge represented a hope for the city as a whole: safe, emptied-out, pretty Manhattan might serve as an event location for people who lived elsewhere. That is where I stood as 2020 began.

COVID-19 changed everything—Manhattan real estate crashed. Instead of articles about hyperwealth ossifying Manhattan, there were warnings about the death of the city. Restaurant owners announced they could make more money in Florida and shut down visible spots in the heart of the island. Sages wrote about the irreversible shift to remote work, which was certain to strangle the city of corporate headquarters, taking down all the small businesses on surrounding streets with them. Families who could fled for houses upstate and beyond. The city of change seemed about to become the emptied-out ghost town relic of a prior age. And it was worse: The very people who had been marginalized by the wealthy city—people of color, working people, immigrants—were dying at accelerated rates, even as they were often the frontline workers dealing with the pandemic. Nurses, EMT staff, and transit workers cannot work remotely. Those the city had neglected were being forced to face fatal danger to keep it alive.

And yet in this moment of threat, I found my ending—and the proof of Wolfe's phrase. What I have seen throughout the city's history is how challenge and decay breed new life. In the mid-nineteenth century, the Five Points in Lower Manhattan was such a notoriously dirty, dangerous, brothel-filled slum that Charles Dickens ventured there to describe its lowest depths. Historians have since found evidence that his nightmarish descriptions were more a testament to his novelist's skill than accurate renderings. And just there in the heart of the slum, William Henry Lane, known as Master Juba, combined Irish clog dancing and African American invention and gave birth to tap dance.

Throughout the city's history, you see the possibilities that were born when lives that would never touch elsewhere—or, certainly, be visible elsewhere—took shape. Read carefully and you see traces of mixed-race families and integrated neighborhoods from the 1600s on. By the 1920s, mixed families were joined in the Village by visible same-sex couples, some of whom stepped out in glory in well-publicized Harlem drag balls. For all its conflicts, the city really has preserved a place for difference and mixture.

In the 1960s and '70s, when Times Square became the Deuce—theaters filled with porn, hustlers on the street—first Beat poets and then filmmakers turned rot into creativity. In the '70s, rappers and graffiti artists created new art forms out of ominous streets and failing subways. The city finds ways to turn damage into art, into new life. And so again in the pandemic.

Every night at seven, when the shifts changed at the hospitals, New Yorkers leaned out of their windows or stepped onto balconies to serenade their heroes. Broadway stars lent their voices while shower singers banged pots. Those who remained in the city recognized how much they needed one another. That too is part of the city's story.

Brown and Black New Yorkers fared better than their peers in many other places because of the social services the city had already put into place. In the 1950s, New York tried to be the home of big business and of unions—the city of corporations and of free universities, cheap subway travel, and rent control. That vision had been partial—many unions were segregated or filled with women and people of color yet led by white men. Still, the city was the first place in the nation to pass laws against housing discrimination (the Fair Housing Practices Law, 1957) and job discrimination (a decade earlier, with the Ives-Quinn anti-discrimination bill in 1945). COVID provided an X-ray of the city and a clear path forward—if New York is to thrive, it must fulfill its promise of inclusion.

That lesson came to me directly in an unexpected way. One of the largest groups of recent immigrants to the city hails from Guyana—a Caribbean nation on the coast of South America. My father-in-law was a pioneer of that cohort back in the 1940s. Because he was in New York, he and his Russian-Jewish wife found a place to live—in the planned community of Parkway Village in Queens that was created for the United Nations, international, and interracial families. My wife had recently discovered a missing branch of her Guyanese family living, by coincidence, very close to Parkway where she had grown up.

Helen, the grandmother of the family, had made a cookbook of Guyanese recipes, and Nellie, one of her daughters, is an accomplished cook and caterer. In the COVID silence, our newfound relatives taught us to cook from that family recipe book and especially to make "slap roti." Rotis are a flatbread popular throughout the Caribbean. You sift together flour, water, and salt to make a simple, smooth, soft dough. You let the mound rest, covered with a cool cloth, then roll out the dough into a thin circle. Brush the circle with vegetable oil or clarified butter (ghee). You make an incision with a knife from the middle to the edge and start folding over the oiled dough into cones. The tip of each cone is pressed down to make a little divot. You dip your finger into the oil and press down to seal and to add a bit more oil. The cones rest again under a damp cloth. When ready, use your rolling pin to roll out new semitranslucent circles and turn the heat under your baking stone (or *tahwa*). Once the oiled *tahwa* is lightly smoking, put on your thin roti sheet until you can see big bubbles, then flip it (with your hand if you can), rub the cooked side with oil; once big bubbles form, reverse once again, and oil again. With both sides oiled, lift to a colander over a sink, fold the circle twice, throw it up and smack it with your hands, at least five times, until you see flakes. Flaky, soft, absorbent roti are your reward for slightly scorched hands.

Our sixteen-year-old son worked patiently through kneading and folding the dough and letting it rise, always looking forward to that key moment when, perched over a hot stove, he would be the slap master. Soon we invited my cousins, who had fled Benjamin Netanyahu's increasingly reactionary rule for Park Slope, to Zoom, slap, and eat along with us.

Zoom allowed us to watch and learn, to bring our far-flung relations directly into our home. We did not need to be together physically to connect. So many of us have had similar experiences. But our delicious rotis were possible because of Parkway, because of the mixed school where my Israeli niece gets to sit alongside children of every faith and color she would never meet at home.

As soon as vaccines became available, you saw life again on the streets. The need to serve people out of doors, combined with the lack of traffic, allowed restaurants to fill streets with extensions—creating new vibrancy, especially in areas frequented by young people. Someday, I hope Nellie can open a Guyanese place, and in summers, Rafi will come to help. He will be there in the kitchen creating mounds of slap roti to feed a new set of "hungry" New Yorkers.

From *The Journal of a Therapy Cat*

JOYCE CAROL OATES

> In the end all you can do for them is purr.
> —Therapy Cat Handbook

Under the best of conditions, the lot of a therapy animal assigned to a writer is not an easy one. In quarantine, every difficulty you can imagine is magnified.

For it seems that my (solitary) writer human is in the grip of a collective malaise that has settled upon her like toxic mist. Where under ordinary conditions the therapy cat might coax her human out of a depressed mood by the usual stratagems—purring seductively, brushing against her legs with soft silky feline fur, settling warmly in her lap, mewing tenderly, "kneading" with claw-retracted paws—in this case, since the malaise isn't private but public, virtually worldwide, and since the human lives alone without a (human) companion to console or distract or commiserate with her, there is little to be done except navigate each day as cautiously as possible.

Each day in this perilous late-winter/early spring 2020, which, so far as any one of us can guess may be our last, my human passes through moods like a downhill skier—bumpy patches, smooth patches, sudden jolts, frissons of panic, small bursts of serenity, even euphoria; sudden, hard thuds, a near-fall. . . . New York City and New Jersey have begun to go into "lockdown" (a term usually associated with prisons, not private households). My human's life, normally so predictable, steadfast, and enjoyable, has become precarious, unfathomable.

She is frequently unable to work, or rather to concentrate in preparation for work, unless forced by a prearranged schedule to participate in such outlandishly named activities as FaceTime, Skype, Zoom. She is at the mercy of emails, text messages, telephone calls; where in the past these were usually welcome, bringing the possibility of good news, now my human stiffens in dread at receiving them. Ominously named "breaking news" is a continuous, pounding, annihilating surf that rarely brings with it a promise of hope, only more dread—the horror of deaths mounting with each day, news of another friend, or a friend of a friend, succumbing to the mysterious coronavirus of which no one had heard before January. . . . I see her struggle between hope and despair, activity and passivity, the will to persevere and the sinking-down sensation of gravity that is depression—this constitutes life in quarantine, as life in quarantine is a magnification of life itself.

In this pandemic quarantine, in effect now for what seems like eight months and not merely eight weeks at the time of this writing, when COVID-19 deaths are calculated in just five figures—20,000, 30,000—astonishing statistics already, my human is more likely to contemplate her work than to actually do it. Indeed, her brain overheats, rehearsing work, circling it warily, advancing, retreating, and advancing until it is too late: the "workday" is over. For work demands concentration, and a reasonable expectation that the next hour will not bring devastating news; work requires uninterrupted periods of time that, in theory, should be guaranteed in a lockdown situation but is not.

In quarantine, the existential question arises, how is one to *be*?

As a novice therapy cat, less than one year attached to my writer human, I was slow to register danger signals in her behavior after the start of the shutdown: a morbid addiction to "breaking news" where formerly TV news was avoided, out of revulsion at the sight and sound of the minority president whose voice seemed to her unbearable in its oleaginous insincerity; a morbid attentiveness to the internet and social media (notably Twitter, a Babylon of voices usually at full pitch, quivering with moral indignation, outrage, juvenile humor, and a plethora of kitten/puppy videos) where the awfulness of breaking news is amplified; a reluctance to go to bed at any hour but never before 1:00 A.M., out of a morbid fear of lying paralyzed in insomnia until dawn; a reluctance to get out of bed in the morning (at any hour) out of a morbid fear of confronting an anxiety-ridden day endless as the Sahara if the Sahara had no horizon.

At such times the therapy cat is most needed. Kitsch as it is, purring is probably the best remedy, though simply to *exist* as a warm, living body in an otherwise empty household is of much value, for human beings require someone, or something, to talk to, if only to hear the sound of their own voices, to reassure them that they too, in turn, *exist*.

Under normal conditions, or what passes for normal conditions in the Trump dark age that has devastated the United States since January 2017 like a toxic malaise, or indeed a wildly proliferating viral invasion, the lot of a therapy animal is not an easy one. Service dogs are professionally trained and licensed, widely respected through the world—"seeing-eye" dogs, usually handsome German shepherds, at the top of the hierarchy; smaller and less ostentatious dogs for persons less showily incapacitated; cats of all breeds, sizes, and temperaments for persons whose "challenges" may be entirely mental, thus not visible or measurable, prevailing beneath the radar of legal protections and continually at risk of being exploited for our stoic and tractable feline natures.

The typical therapy cat is likely to lack formal training of the kind required of seeing-eye dogs. Thus, we lack formal licenses, certificates, and contracts; we belong to no unions or brotherhoods; we are held hostage indoors under the pretext that we might hunt birds—as if cats hunting birds is something radically new and perverse! More than the therapy dog, the therapy cat is likely to be required to sleep on, or even in, the same bed with her human, however insomniac and restless her human might be and however badly the therapy cat might wish to spend nocturnal hours prowling in secrecy, not tending to a human on the brink of nervous collapse. Nighttime no less than daytime, the therapy cat will be expected to purr loudly and continuously as a sort of comforting "white noise" for her human charge, likely to be, in this time of social quarantine, in terror of her own thoughts, which purring is believed to somewhat supplant.

It should be impressive to humans that *Felis catus* is uniquely suited to self-isolation and, if neutered and well fed, quite happy to dwell alone, while *Homo sapiens* is obviously ill-equipped for seclusion under even the best of conditions.

No wonder that in the United States at present, there are reportedly as many as five hundred thousand service dogs and two hundred thousand "emotional support" animals, legally registered with healthcare authorities. Added to these is a vast unknown number of unofficial "therapy animals" like me, a gorgeous "tuxedo" female Maine Coon cat adopted from a rescue shelter in May 2019, named by my whimsical human, "Zanche," after the fiery servant in John Webster's *The White Devil*.

Indeed, to the neurasthenic among us, very likely a rapidly increasing group in quarantine, purring has become the white noise of comfort, replacing even human commiseration.

The irony is that purring may not be natural to cats but a tactic cultivated by their feral ancestors to seduce, disarm, and domesticate *Homo sapiens*, the only fellow mammal species that could be manipulated to cats' advantage.

As days and then eventually weeks pass in the stasis of quarantine, a miasma of the soul that will be (I predict!) virtually forgotten when the pandemic subsides, my unhappy human is barely able to sit in one place for more than a few minutes. She looks back with appalled nostalgia at a time not long ago, in fact as recently as February 2020, when she could happily lose herself in work for ten or twelve hours at a spell. Now she stares out the window blank-brained, in a sort of trance, assailed by seemingly random lines of oracular prose or poetry drifting through her mind like skeins of algae as she paces about the house even during nocturnal hours as time has melted as in a Dalí landscape and life has become a careening run-on sentence with no natural stops or starts: "All the unhappiness of men arises from one single fact, that they cannot stay quietly in their own chamber" (Pascal, *Pensées* #139). "Nothing gold can stay" (Robert Frost). Henry David Thoreau, whom my human has admired since adolescence, now sounds boastful, arrogant to her in his declaration in *Walden*:

> I wanted to live deep and suck out all the marrow of life, to live so sturdily and Spartan-like as to put to rout all that was not life, to cut a broad swath and shave close, to drive life into a corner, and reduce it to its lowest terms.

My human thinks, *What naivety!* In forced isolation one is apt to wonder why anyone would ever wish to reduce the richness and variety of life to its "lowest terms"—a luxury wholly dependent on a stable world to be repudiated. At Walden Pond, Thoreau lived just a brisk walk from his loving family in Concord and visited whenever he felt lonely, wanted a good meal, or needed his laundry done.

Man is not a very rational animal, but man is certainly a social animal. We humans take our social cues from other people: their smiles, frowns, scowls, sorrow, laughter. Even silence, amid others, has a meaning it cannot have when we are alone. As William James observed, each individual has as many social selves as there are people who know him and interact with him; conversely, if our social selves are not continuously established by interaction with others, do we exist? In mid-March 2020, as the outer world became a teeming Petri dish of contagion and the number of deaths rose hourly, a stay-home policy was decreed in New Jersey, establishing our essential estrangement from one another in the face of possible—probable!—infection of one another. Dazed observers are propelled past astonishment into numbed horror. An aura of unreality creeps through our lives causing us to doubt our very identities: Have these identities been, all along, social constructs and not durable entities? *Are* we "real" in such estrangement? It's as if our very bodies are on the cusp of melting into ectoplasm, as in those absurd but unsettling early twentieth-century "spirit photographs."

For what, after all, *is* identity—and what is sanity, when we are alone for too long, hiding from a raging but invisible non–life form called a virus? And what is the proper tone to use at a time when many are suffering terribly?

As the nightmare pandemic continues through April and into May, each day bringing more illnesses, deaths, and an astonishing failure of leadership, even of common humanity, in the public response of Trump and his cohort, there begins to emerge a sort of contest in our household: to see *how little* a writer can accomplish in a single day, like a bicyclist testing how slowly she can pedal before toppling over.

With millions of people quarantined, there is a great demand for books, as for films and TV series, but the prospect of future creative projects, how they will be produced when the workforce is in quarantine, how they will be brought into being (as "virtual" or "real"), and who will even survive to receive them is uncertain.

As for those luckless novelists, like my human, who have books soon to be published in the spring of 2020, prospects for the success of these projects are not promising even as the injunction not to speak of such trivial matters in a time of catastrophe renders them speechless, gnawed at from within.

For the first time in my human's experience, news of a friend's sudden, unexpected death (by stroke, in her sleep) stirs in others not only surprise, sorrow, grief but envy—"She never woke up! My God."

It may require a while for the meaning to sink in. Some of us have arrived at the point at which we think the best we can hope for is a merciful death.

Gentle assonance of *passing away.*

Cease upon the midnight with no pain.

And none of this is the least fictitious—none of it is allegory or metaphor (realms of being in which the writer feels most comfortable)—none of it may be reduced easily to "revelations" or "epiphanies." It's the writer's curse to imagine that meaning can be gleaned from the most terrible circumstances and that it is within the writer's power to express it.

Storytellers who conjure up dystopias and hellish landscapes have long taken for granted the relative normality of the "real world." If the real world has become the hellish landscape, to replicate it in prose seems redundant. There may be some grim satisfaction in being a prophet of the current dissolution of liberal democracy in the United States, but it is certainly a bitter satisfaction—the inclination is to think that having imagined a disaster should be enough. We wonder about the fates not only of future creative projects but also of the people who might be their audience.

Zoom. At first, there is disapproval and distrust, cautious experimentation, fairly rapid acceptance, even gratitude. Suddenly in March 2020, there is a new term in our vocabulary: "remote instruction." Soon we come to appreciate a certain perverse intimacy in this new means of communicating with others via a computer screen. Through a technological sleight of hand, we are empowered to see the faces of others close up, yet without violating what is called social space. And there is an added bonus: names are supplied beneath pictures, as, in actual life, names are never so supplied. No need now to memorize student names and attach them to the proper faces, for overnight that challenge is banished.

Having been a university instructor for many years, my human is always happily involved in a teaching situation in which her truest, most authentic self emerges in conjunction with students. Though online teaching can be awkward, lacking those metalingual features that ease communication, it has been a godsend for instructors in schools and universities, if not a substitute for what has come to be quaintly called face-to-face or in-person instruction.

Though my human could not have anticipated anything like the situation in early 2020, she managed to teach six "remote" courses, at Princeton, New York University, and Rutgers. Though it sounds difficult to believe, students in all these courses did very well; perhaps isolation and quarantine can be inspiring to some. Classes via Zoom can be as lively as classes in person, particularly since, on Zoom, no one is required to wear a mask, as one must otherwise.

In each Zoom session was, without a doubt, my presence on screen: gorgeous Zanche peering at the mysterious little squares containing human faces, most of which expressed delight at seeing *me*.

Once a Zoom session is over, it is indeed *over*: no lingering after class or straggling out of class, not a backward glance. In an instant, the screen dissolves as if it had never been. Like a time traveler or one who has been teleported to a remote place, the individual is expelled from an intensity of human interaction, finding herself back again in quarantine, alone with her therapy animal.

Of course, the best cure for insomnia isn't a cure but a nullification: books.

Sleepless nights so bereft of hope, so miserable with dread of the future that they can't be redeemed, are transfigured by switching on a bedside lamp, reading.

There is a particularly cherished category of book, the bedside book, often read sporadically, rarely finished, and even if finished, only reluctantly shelved. On my human's cluttered bedside bureau are many books of this type, several of which have been there for (literally) years, for my sentimental human does not want to put them away just yet. Such books are ideal quarantine reading. What follows is a list of the books that saw my human through the worst of the quarantine in 2020:

Weatherland: Writers and Artists under English Skies by Alexandra Harris is a wonderfully eccentric compendium of prose involving weather over the centuries—skies, clouds, landscapes, "moods"—in works by Shakespeare, Milton, Spenser, the Romantics, the Brontës, Woolf, Constable, Turner, Millais, Ted Hughes: "In the years to come, which may be the last years of English weather, our experience will be determined by memory and association, by the things we have read and looked at, by the places we have been to or imagined" (389).

Adam Nicholson's kindred *The Making of Poetry: Coleridge, the Wordsworths, and Their Year of Marvels* is a chronicle of the young poets and the idyllic English landscapes through which they walked together, their routes replicated by the intrepid author more than two hundred years later.

Ideal too for late-night reading are Robert Hass's weighty *A Little Book on Form: An Exploration into the Formal Imagination of Poetry* and Don Patterson's even heftier *The Poem*, as well as the massive treasure troves *The Work of the Dead: A Cultural History of Mortal Remains* by Thomas W. Laqueur (so abundant with fascinating detail one might peruse its more than six hundred large pages for years) and *The Invention of Nature: Alexander von Humboldt's New World* by Andrea Wulf, which begins with the description of a harrowing mountain climb by the great visionary naturalist Humboldt, particularly attractive to those reading in bed beside a slumbering animal.

Add to these the online book club selection *War and Peace*, Tolstoy's monumental epic of love, death, disillusion, and idealism in the age of Napoleon, the great nineteenth-century novel whose near-interminable length and its vast array of characters (including the charismatic Napoleon, in more than just a cameo role) makes it the perfect choice for obsessive quarantine reading.

As Tolstoy's corpulent, gentlemanly, ultrawealthy nobleman philosopher Pierre says at the conclusion of the long, long march that is *War and Peace*, "Let those who love good join hands, and let there be but one banner—that of active virtue."

Addendum: February 2022. As life swings back to a diminished and wary sense of "normality," it may be that the therapy cat is best equipped to understand how fragile "normality" has always been. Her human may be feeling some relief, that the pandemic appears to be subsiding; only the therapy cat understands how fragile human equanimity is and how swiftly, in a world in which environmental determinism seems to be the rule, everything can change.

Black and Gray

TERESA POLITANO

Cello is batshit.

Cello, my son said, is like that guy from the eighth-grade scare video, the guy who does one hit of bad acid and never recovers.

We were lurching down the steep driveway. Not so fast to cause alarm but fast enough to break free. In the back seat, my son was bouncing, hyper. Cello, he said, receives messages from Kanye.

The day before my son's scheduled release—and I say *release* and not *discharge*—he phoned us his list. His Nike sneakers with the long laces, his silver necklace with the cross charm, a razor so he could shave. Items not permitted in the psych ward.

Once home in his bedroom—which we had cleaned, my husband and I, removing every threat and every perceived threat, rummaging through each drawer and every backpack pocket, reading private notes, and throwing out candy wrappers and soda cans—my son sat on the floor like a child and painted his fingernails black. His pinky first, then the ring finger, then the middle finger. My heart jumped in optimism. Such whimsy. I dared not comment. I doubt my son was pursuing adorable.

None of us believed my son's box cutter threat. I doubt even my son believed. Yet if we dismissed him again, would he prove us wrong just to make a point?

Overnight in the emergency room, the beds had filled with suicide threats, each teen assigned a personal guard and each guard keeping a log—this much sleep, this much food, this much anger. The emergency room was cold, then hot, and four separate times they announced a code blue and four separate times no one could be heard scurrying.

Sixteen hours later, after a ten-minute consultation, they said my son belonged in the psych ward, where they could feed him limp chicken sandwiches, where nurses with flashlights would bed-check him every fifteen minutes, where the echoes of adolescent anguish bounced off the cement walls. Where he could meet Cello, who had been in the psych ward many times before.

Sixteen hours later, after a ten-minute consultation, they said the psych ward was my son's only safe option. No one believed that either, but if my son were sent away, the emergency room overnight crisis team representative could cross her arms and shake her head and repeat phrases such as *abundance of caution* and *you can't be too safe*. The emergency room overnight crisis team representative was not a psychiatrist or even a therapist. When we asked about other options—my son already had a therapy session scheduled for the very next Monday—she licked her lips and suggested parental neglect. She curled her brittle overdyed blond hair behind her ears, and she called Child Protective Services.

In the psych ward, they gave my son Prozac and cut the strings from his sweatpants.

In the psych ward, where the social workers and the therapists and the psychiatrists told us that teens in particular are suffering deeply from the isolation wrought by the pandemic, they took away my son's phone and his laptop. Family visits were forbidden. In the psych ward, every door that opened set off an alarm, and the waiting room hammered with election fraud updates from Fox News. In the psych ward, they did not permit my son his pillow from home.

From the emergency room to the psych ward, each person— therapist, psychiatrist, social worker—expressed surprise that our stories were the same, mine and my son's, as if we are not locked together in the same world, as if he is not the boy I know and as if I am not the mother he knows. From the principal's office to the pediatrician, each expert expressed deep concern about his lack of academic motivation, yet all of us know that my son's schoolwork is makeshift busywork—watch this video, complete this online quiz—and still we deem him lazy when he calls us out. *The New York Times* tells us that teen mental health visits to the emergency room amid the pandemic are up 31 percent.[1] Our youth are imprisoned, and we are surprised that it is not going well for them. And when the pandemic ends, my son will return to a world of active shooter drills and climate change.

In the psych ward, my son talked Cello down, reminding him that Kanye takes his meds even though they tell us that Kanye does not take his meds. In the psych ward, my son's favorite nurse was Cedric; they played chess for hours. "He's the bomb, Ma." In the psych ward, Cello and the girls on the fourth floor cheered when they learned that my son could leave. He had speedrun the game. My son promised to stay in touch, even though he is not permitted to contact the people who shared the most harrowing week of his life. By the time he left, one girl no longer thought my son was there to kill her. "That's a real compliment, Ma, from someone who's paranoid."

Once home in his bedroom, my son turned up his music, Frank Ocean and Otis Redding. Downstairs, listening to the yearning, the pain, the romance, and the tragedy, I typed nonsense and sent emails and I could not stop crying. Downstairs, listening to the music and the yearning, I thought about a rosary wrapping a wrist, of fingernails smooth and buff like a pearl, painted a subtle gray, the color of a winter sky. I thought about my son's grandmother, who had died just a few weeks earlier. My son, who had been a pallbearer. My husband, who nearly broke watching his baby carry his mother.

I thought about the funeral, where family and friends turned from her, the matriarch, removing their masks, laughing and deal-making and slapping backs. My son, angry and appalled, who left the room. Death is not a country club, he said.

At night, I worry that my son's grandmother wants to take him with her. During the day, I worry that he must deal with the world we gave him.

Playing with Anxiety

CHRISTIAN LIGHTY

September 2019

I decide to take another risk. I apply to Rutgers as a transfer student. My grades are up to par; my GPA is higher than 3.0.

My father died in 2012 from a self-inflicted gun wound. I deal with anxiety and depression. I press "Submit" on my application, and my anxiety goes through the roof. I almost have an anxiety attack in that moment. I'd been denied admission before. I had toured the campus and met with an admissions advisor. She said she was excited that I'd taken another chance. I asked, "Why did I get rejected in the first place?" She said Rutgers doesn't accept students who take pass/fail courses. The university, she said, expects actual letter grades. I completely understand. I'm nervous waiting for the email.

November 2019

I'm driving to the car dealership to get my car serviced. I receive an email from admissions. I'm in. I call my mom immediately. I'm happy to point my life in the right direction after all I've been through.

January 1, 2020

I am sick. I have a constant fever of 102 and higher. I'm throwing up. I have body aches and I can't get out of bed.

January 13, 2020

I'm still sick. My fever is still high. "That's it," my mom says. "We're going to the hospital." All the tests come back negative. No flu. No strep. No mono. "Sometimes your body just comes up with weird viruses," the doctor says. They give me flu medicine. Two days later, I have no fever and no aches. I feel good to go.

January–March 2020

I move into my off-campus house on Easton Avenue, on the College Avenue campus in New Brunswick. I have never lived off campus. I am more than excited. I go to classes. Some of my classmates are from my hometown. I'm having the time of my life. I don't think much of the news about COVID; as a nation, we've been through Ebola. But then Rutgers goes remote. And then NBA All-Star Donovan Mitchell tests positive. Donovan is my friend. I consider him a big brother. The NBA season ends. The state is on lockdown.

My anxiety escalates. I feel as though we are living in a movie. My thoughts go everywhere. A deadly virus, highly contagious, no cure. My whole family could be affected. I review the list of symptoms; I had all these symptoms in January. I wonder if I already gave COVID to my mom. I wonder if she has the antibodies. My mom works in a hospital, and my stepdad drives a delivery truck. They're both at high risk. They both see new people every day. I wake up anxious. I can't lose them. I already lost my dad. I can't lose my mom. I can't lose my stepdad.

April 2020

I manage to get through each day. School isn't easy. Most classes don't meet by Zoom; the assignments are posted online. I'm expected to do the work and figure things out myself. I miss a lot of assignments. I have my worst semester. I don't fail any classes, but I have only one A. I get Cs otherwise. I'm in a hole. It's my first semester at Rutgers, and I feel like maybe I'm not cut out for school here. I tell myself I'm good enough to do this. I tell myself no one will hire me with these grades. In quarantine, I lose myself every day.

May 2020

I am blessed to see my friends after a month of lockdown. We all promise to see only each other. We go to Andrei's house because he has a pool. We go to Tony's house because he has the nice deck. We play drinking games but with water—water pong, dice, and cards. We go home and sometimes play video games with each other until 5:00 A.M. I feel like a kid again, playing video games with my friends.

June 2020

I celebrate my twenty-first birthday. My closest friends—we've been friends for more than ten years—throw a surprise party. We meet around 6:00 P.M. I can't even tell you when the party ended because I had so much fun.

I work out five days a week, by myself or with friends, which helps with my anxiety. Still, life is not easy. Sometimes I think I'm having the best summer of my life. Other times, I leave the world and don't know how to get back.

September–December 2020

I return to school. I don't like online classes. I like to be in person to ask questions. All my classes are asynchronous. I never meet my professors. I have a subpar semester. Am I good enough for Rutgers? I snap out of it. I can't put myself down after one bad semester.

I don't want to live in fear all my life. I can't protect my mom and my stepdad. When life knocks you down, you need to get back up.

February 2021

I tell myself I dealt with a pandemic. I tell myself I'm learning and growing every day. I'm ready to take on life. I'm ready to stand tall.

I go to my desk and start producing music. I turn off my phone. I don't want to get distracted. I want to stay in my zone. I choose my music according to my mood. If I'm sad, I look up dark piano melodies that are 85–115 beats per minute. Once I find the sample that fits my mood, I get straight to work. I get lost in the music. Every worry in the world is out the door and I'm focusing on making the best beat possible for an artist who is in my same mood. I'm not always sad. When I'm in a great mood, I go through guitar melodies, faster piano melodies. Sometimes I sample an old-school song and make it modern. When I find a few seconds I like, I chop it up and add a new drum pattern, feeling like I'm the greatest in the world.

Once I finish the beat, I might remember that my friends have stopped over. I might go outside and see the poker table. I might sit at the table and announce, "Deal me in." Sometimes we play for money. Sometimes we play for fun. Most of the time, you just got to throw in $20 and work from there.

Virtual Class #219, March 2021, 2:50 p.m.–4:10 p.m.

MACKENZIE KEAN

yesterday, the screen was a container—
a square of my world, of my everyday,
so many squares of the self—
all in one moment, with pixels and light,
I saw you, I saw them, I saw me.

four walls around me made it clear
I was on my own, pressed into
the folds of my loneliness—

my only company: a cup of tea,
the way it consoled me without
a hand or a mouth or an ear.
it sat there inside of itself looking

for something to call a sun or a moon
or a cloud—finding only my face,
your face, their faces.
look up! look up! it said.
there are so many things to open for.
look up into the sky of the face.

my face. your face. our faces.

It's Harder for Extroverts

KELLY-JANE COTTER

We splashed color on the gray days of March 2020. We hung a rainbow drawing on our front door. My daughter, then fifteen, saturated our sidewalk with chalk drawings, and when they melted away, she drew more. I brought out the good china for ordinary dinners. I sowed seeds on the windowsills.

Daffodils emerged, their buds still tight but with a sliver of yellow visible, promising sunshine and heat.

To be clear to future generations, we never had a "lockdown" or even a full "shutdown." I don't know what we should call it. We were allowed to drive wherever and whenever we wanted. There just wasn't much to do once you got to wherever you went. My E-ZPass statement reflected this in mid-2020. No trips up or down the parkway. My world was whittled down to my backyard and my computer screen. I couldn't complain about this, especially as my essential-worker husband was out in the germy world six days a week, and our daughter had to switch to remote learning just as she was finding her footing as a high school freshman. It felt okay not to be doing anything. In early spring, at least, it was okay. Everything in nature seemed to be on standby, trees still bare, birds still quiet, colors muted.

But after the daffodils opened and faded and the backyard vibrated with the hum of new growth, there was no denying that summer was on its way. I grew restless and itchy for celebrations that would not come. No parades or parties, no festivals or fireworks.

I have a friend who, more than two years into the pandemic, still hadn't left the house for much more than veterinary appointments and other quick, curbside errands. She still gets her groceries delivered and doesn't expect that to change, even post-COVID. She likes the convenience.

But I like going to the supermarket. I like choosing my produce and listening to the '80s music over the sound system. I like waiting in line at checkout, peeking into other people's carts and imagining what they're going to have for dinner. I don't need to strike up a conversation with my fellow shoppers, although sometimes that's exactly what I do. I like the busy-bee feeling of pushing a cart and seeing other bees doing the same.

"It's harder for extroverts," my cooped-up friend acknowledged.

During the semi-shutdown, I took walks around the block every day and realized I lived in a neighborhood. I'd been friendly with my immediate neighbors but rarely saw anyone else on the block except on Halloween or after a snowstorm. But here they were, even on ordinary days! I started small-talking with these newly discovered people, and I started long-talking with the neighbors I already knew. One told me he and his wife had to cancel an anniversary getaway. Who knew when vacations would be feasible again?

"Are we going to LBI this year?" my daughter asked, as the pandemic took hold. Every summer, we rent a house for a week on Long Beach Island, coordinating with three other families and an array of other day-tripping friends and overnighting relatives. We stake claim to four or five rentals, creating a temporary neighborhood of close friends. This tradition long preceded the births of any of our kids. We've been doing this since the mid-1980s, when we spent most of our waking hours together as Rutgers undergraduates, working at the student newspaper, *The Daily Targum*. Back then, we all fit into one house. Most of our inside jokes, many of our collective memories, have their origins in these trips. One friend says he works all year for the reward of "opening night," the moment when we're all together on a rooftop deck—dinner finished, dishes done—popping open a cold beer, clinking wineglasses, with a week of beach days stretched out before us. We never skipped a summer in more than thirty years. My daughter wasn't the only one wondering if we'd be able to make it to Parkway exit 63 in 2020.

In the spring of 2020, when Zoom parties were still fun, my Targum shore trip friends and I spent an hour or so hanging out in our Brady Bunch squares, making each other laugh. The guys all had shaggy hair, and I realized I never gave thought to how often men need to get their hair cut. My mood lifted just by seeing them. Even if the beaches and barbershops remained closed for the summer, we decided we needed to go to LBI. Everything was being done in "an abundance of caution," so we defied that. I sent our deposit to our realtor with "an abundance of hope."

Now, I'd like to tell you that we had a fantastic week together, but in truth, it was not one of our better times. We had a week of oppressive heat and intense rain. Our cat was very sick, and my husband and I had to return home twice that week to care for her. On the way back from one trip, the transmission on our car failed and we had to wait for a tow truck. Plus, you know, the pandemic. I felt awkward and inhospitable, not being free to hug my friends or hang out in each other's houses. But at least we were there.

It would take another year, until the vaccinated summer of 2021, before we had a more typical week with our friends, with paddle ball on the beach and last call at Kubel's, jumping unreasonably chilly waves and laughing until we were breathless.

My overriding memory of the summer of 2020 is from a few weeks before our LBI trip.

"Happy Weird Fourth of July!" texted another friend that morning. She came over with her son and we all sat on the deck, chairs far apart. It wasn't a long visit, and it certainly wasn't a party, but it gave me a feeling of festivity and anticipation. That evening, I took my walk around the block. Lightning bugs surrounded me as if

I were a Disney princess. Suddenly, the neighborhood lit up with amateur fireworks. It seemed every house had someone in the backyard, presenting an unchoreographed solo performance, a relentless barrage of smoke, noise, and sparkle. It was dangerous and it was dazzling, and each boom made me laugh to myself. There was no place to go, so everyone was home, and this was a percussive symphony of isolation. I was the audience, and so, I applauded, though no one could hear me. It was a lonely kind of joy.

The Old Has Passed Away, Behold, The New Has Come

(2 Corinthians 5:17)

STEPHEN MASARYK

I was driving to my wedding, tuxedo in the back seat, when I received the phone call from Human Resources. My position had been approved. The pandemic actually became the wind in the sail.

Chela and I had been friends for four months. We dated for seven months, were engaged for eight months. I proposed on her twenty-first birthday. I took her to Asbury Park, imagining we would spread a blanket on the beach and drink champagne. It was a dumb idea since it was so cold. Instead, we had dinner at an Italian restaurant and walked the boardwalk. At Convention Hall, we climbed the stairs, and with the ocean as my backdrop, I took a knee. Chela thought I was kidding. "Seriously?" she said. "Seriously?" She must have said seriously fourteen times. She also said yes.

The date was February 28, 2020.

Chela is a ball of sunshine. Zealous. Joyful. She's the bright colors—I'm the dark colors. Chela is yellow and bright blue. I'm burgundy, navy, forest green.

When I proposed, I was working part time as an operations coordinator at Rutgers University. I was part of the space and facilities management team in the School of Arts and Sciences. It's a two-person team. We manage seventy-seven buildings. We deal with everything from mold to clogged toilets, from furniture to technology. We are the liaisons between faculty and maintenance; we track projects and work with managers. The job paid $9 an hour less than my previous job. But here I had an opportunity. I had the possibility of full-time work, with benefits and tuition remission.

When the pandemic hit, our responsibilities changed. Before we knew what the virus was, we were gathering gear—blue surgical masks and gowns. We were ready to have everyone dress like surgeons to come back to work. Later, we distributed personal protective equipment and masks with the university logo. I did walkthroughs of the empty buildings, looking for evidence of a break-in or a leak, the kinds of problems that would be caught if people were in the buildings. I helped prepare for our return to campus; the plans were always changing. Often, I was the only one in the office. I could get coffee whenever I pleased, walk around with my shoes off.

My supervisor had said that she wanted a full-time assistant. But that was before the pandemic, and my contract was set to expire in October.

Chela and I went ahead with our wedding plans. It was the middle of a pandemic, and I was about to get married. Chela's mother works as a risk analyst in a financial institution. I was a big risk to her. "The Lord will provide," I told her. "You can't just say that," she replied. I promised I'd find work elsewhere if necessary. I was willing to bust my butt. I'd worked as a cook, in an auto parts store. I'd work three jobs simultaneously.

As the wedding date approached, I continued to be hopeful. Maintenance is always necessary; some of the campus buildings are hundreds of years old. I heard that a full-time position had been approved, but they were still ironing things out. I wasn't sure what that meant. In my view, things were still up in the air. I was heading west on Route 78 when I got the call from a woman in HR:

she conferenced in my supervisor. The question they asked was simple: Do you accept this position? I tried not to scream my answer. I'd never made a salary. On the job application, I had requested the minimum—I had to be realistic; I knew I was starting from the bottom. On the phone, they offered me $4,000 more.

Think about this. I'm heading to my wedding. By this time, my mother-in-law has become accustomed to the idea that her daughter is marrying me. But now I can tell her I have a salary. Now I can tell her my salary is even higher than I expected.

I did feel guilty. Lots of people lost work. I took the job that was offered to me. If God wants you somewhere, he'll get you there. I'm still the low man on the totem pole. I absorbed a lot of responsibilities. I restock coffee. I order water. It keeps me humble.

Our wedding ceremony was outdoors; we invited a hundred people to Barnesville, Pennsylvania. The weather was spectacular, 75°F in October. "I'm so shook we even made it," Chela wrote in her pre-ceremony letter to me. The bridesmaid's dresses were the color of sunflowers. Chela and I were married in a stream of sunlight and autumn leaves. I would be lying if I said I didn't cry during my vows.

People thought we were too young to get married. How old are you? How old is she? Are you ready?

My answers were simple: "I'm twenty-five. She's twenty-one."

But was I ready? How could I be ready? I'd never been married. The longer I pondered that question, the more I became aware of my insufficiencies. I was ready to learn.

Chela and I, we're learning together. And we're totally fine with it just being us—going on road trips and hikes. Every so often, we're gently reminded, it's not just you guys.

I think I'm okay with saying that 2020 was one of the best years of my life.

Rutgers Spit Test

NICK ROMANENKO

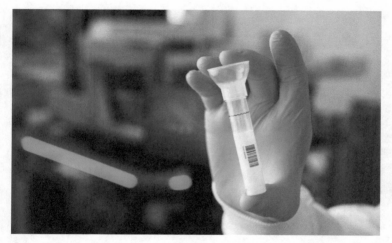

The university's groundbreaking saliva test received emergency-use authorization from the Food and Drug Administration in April 2020. (Photo: Nick Romanenko / Rutgers University.)

Connectivity, Connection, and Care during the COVID-19 Pandemic

VIKKI KATZ AND AMY JORDAN

We are scholars of communication and media who research the ways that technology can reduce or exacerbate educational disparities. So when the pandemic hit and courses were rapidly moved online, we shared a set of worries. We were both teaching large lectures with more than two hundred undergraduates. In addition to trying to reimagine those courses when neither of us had ever done anything but face-to-face teaching, we had grave concerns about whether our students could make the transition with us. Rutgers serves large populations of first-generation and low-income students. We feared that many lacked the resources needed for a smooth pivot to remote learning: stable Wi-Fi, a working computer, physical space and time at home to focus on their schoolwork, and access to assistance when they got stuck navigating unfamiliar learning platforms and programs.

We surveyed our own classes to uncover issues our students might run into during what, at the time, we thought would be a few weeks of remote instruction. Some reported that they had to rely on their phones to access online learning management systems, and they were quickly maxing out their data plans. Some had to return to countries many time zones removed from Eastern Standard Time. Others were moving back into chaotic home

187

environments, with parents who were designated as essential workers and younger siblings who were left in their care. Soon, they began reporting that they or a family member had contracted COVID-19.

As it became apparent that the COVID disruption was going to last longer than a few weeks, we decided to conduct a larger, more systematic study of undergraduates' experiences. Our goal was to identify which students were managing to confidently pivot to remote learning and why others were facing greater challenges in doing so. Once we had Institutional Review Board approval, we reached out to colleagues at Rutgers and across the nation.[1] Between mid-April and mid-May 2020, nearly three thousand undergraduates learning remotely at four-year colleges and universities in nineteen states and the District of Columbia participated in our survey.

We were not surprised to find that the two-fifths of students who had struggled with inconsistent internet access and inadequate digital devices prior to the pandemic had a harder time managing the sudden pivot to remote learning. We found that three-fifths of students had inadequate internet access in the early weeks of the pandemic, making it harder for them to feel confident understanding what instructors were expecting of them, keeping track of deadlines and due dates, and effectively using digital platforms and programs required for remote coursework.

What *was* surprising to us, however, was finding that students' inability to communicate with their professors explained more of the variance in their remote learning efficacy than the technology challenges they experienced. Student comments in our survey highlighted the many obstacles they felt in establishing communication in online courses. One said, "I feel that speaking up [in Zoom class meetings] distracts from the conversation rather than adds to it," noting that it was hard "having to unmute myself, get the professor's attention, and [making] sure everyone can hear me." Another felt "uncomfortable attending online office hours." And yet another (probably correctly) observed that "some of the professors get tons of emails a day, and my email can get buried in that."

It may be that students' casual opportunities to chat with instructors before or after class, or by passing by their instructors' offices, could not be adequately replicated in remote instruction. Our findings suggest that students needed two kinds of connection to confidently transition to online learning: consistent high-speed internet and devices to connect to it and feeling a sense of connection to their instructors. The latter plays a pivotal role in whether students develop confidence that they can be successful remote learners. Instructor encouragement and outreach were essential not only for clarifying content but also for boosting students' morale.

From this survey, we also learned that students were craving connection: to their instructors, to their peers, and to campus itself. They struggled with losing the routines and rituals that made university life not just manageable but also pleasurable. They were frustrated by trying to keep track of too much information. Nearly two-thirds said they did not have a clear idea of what was expected of them or had trouble remembering due dates because the familiar classroom structures they had relied on to support their learning had suddenly vanished.

What was most surprising (and perhaps most resonant) to us were the answers students gave to open-ended questions about their remote learning experiences. Students often blamed themselves for not being motivated enough, saying they felt "lazy" and "unfocused." The early months of the pandemic were a period of acute crisis on multiple fronts. The pandemic forced a rapid reorganizing of everyday life amid daily, deeply disturbing reports of how many people were being hospitalized and dying. Simultaneously, the news was filled with the racial reckoning following George Floyd's murder in May 2020, ongoing political polarization, the effects of climate change, and other compounding personal and global crises. It was heart-wrenching to read how hard students were on themselves amid such chaos. By and large, they took personal responsibility for struggling to maintain their attention on their coursework when the world required exhausting levels of vigilance.

The pandemic laid bare societal inequalities at all levels—and the necessity for empathy at every level as well. We, like our colleagues, have been overwhelmed by students' disclosures of what they have had to manage to remain in school. Students continue to experience difficulties with inadequate internet access and digital devices. They face financial stresses related to lost employment or having to take on extra work shifts to cover mounting expenses. And let us recognize that New Jersey has been one of the states hardest hit by the pandemic: many of our students have become ill, had family members become ill, and have lost loved ones to this virus. We recognize and respect their incredible perseverance against these odds.

For many students, however, these burdens have simply been too great to persist in higher education, a trend Bill Conley and Robert Massa have called the great interruption. A 2022 report from the National Student Clearinghouse Research Center reports that 5 percent fewer students enrolled in college from high school compared with 2019—a decline of nearly one million students nationwide.[2] Community colleges and less selective public universities have been particularly hard hit by admissions declines, suggesting that lower-income students are more likely to be diverted from a college-bound trajectory. These students are, according to Sarah Brown's reporting in the *Chronicle of Higher Education*, disproportionately first generation, Hispanic, and male. These trends suggest that without rapid intervention, decades of hard-won gains in equitable access to higher education are at risk.

The multiple crises of 2020 and 2021 also disproportionately affected the most vulnerable faculty, including those in contingent and pre-tenure positions. A 2020 *Chronicle of Higher Education/Fidelity Investments* survey of university faculty found much higher levels of stress and burnout compared to the previous non-pandemic year.[3] Female faculty were harder hit than their male counterparts, reporting greater workload and work-life imbalances resulting from the pandemic. Likewise, many faculty have faced inordinate pressures to maintain scholarly productivity and pedagogical excellence as they pivoted between remote, hybrid, and in-person teaching. These changes came while having to navigate their own pandemic stresses and caregiving responsibilities, duties that have been disproportionately assumed by women.

The pandemic experience has required a great deal of empathy. We needed to suspend cynicism and believe students and faculty when their vulnerabilities have not been immediately visible. Faculty needed to be sympathetic to students who asked for more time to complete assignments and more flexibility in how they receive their instruction. In our own classes, we found that students whose attendance suddenly dropped off explained with embarrassment that their family had not been able to pay their internet bill that month or that their absences were due to their own or family members' hospitalization with COVID-19. Students also had to be sympathetic to faculty who were struggling with inadequate internet access or learning how to use new features of their course management platforms. And administrators had to trust instructors to use their best judgments about how to create safe learning environments for themselves and their students, especially once the university began transitioning back to in-person instruction while the virus raged on.

Empathy requires energy and imagination, both of which are hard to muster amid fatigue and burnout. But we must find that energy and imagination for the sake of our collective well-being as we (hopefully) enter a "management" phase of the pandemic. It is evident that there cannot be a return to "normal." The pandemic has identified disparities, and it is incumbent on faculty and university leadership to address them. The sudden pivot to remote learning highlighted the ways that campuses provide access to fundamental learning resources—including Wi-Fi and digital technologies—that, when no longer available, disproportionately impact our most financially precarious students. We must ensure that all students have access to high-speed internet access and high-quality digital devices. Digital equity is imperative whether or not remote learning is necessary again in the future. Succeeding in college requires full access to digital opportunities now more than ever. The two of us continue to work on understanding how digital inequality has affected students' learning and development throughout the pandemic via new interviews and a large-scale survey at Rutgers–New Brunswick.

Empathy is also crucial for developing new infrastructures for learning and work that balance students' and faculty's professional commitments with full recognition of the diverse pressures and demands on their lives beyond the classroom. Caring for each other as well-rounded human beings first does not take away from academic excellence. Prior research is replete with evidence of how students' motivation is fueled by feeling that their instructors are invested in their overall development, not just their success in a course. Likewise, faculty flourish when they feel supported not only for their professional achievements but as whole people. These new infrastructures of care can anchor university-wide efforts to realize the potential of all members of our beloved community.

The Faculty Parent

Juggling Parenting, Teaching, Research, and Writing in Uncertain Times

PATRICIA AKHIMIE

The Faculty Parent, a blog chronicling pandemic parenting, "the highs and lows of juggling parenting, teaching, research, and writing in uncertain times," began in summer 2020, as I worked late from the basement of my in-laws' home in the suburbs, with a ten-month-old baby sleeping by my side and a four-year-old sleeping upstairs. I had joined the Rutgers-Newark P3 Collaboratory, a center devoted to professional development, as the 2020–2021 Chancellor's Scholar in Residence with a specific project in mind:

Letter to the P3 Collaboratory, April 23, 2020:

As the 2020–2021 academic year approaches, I find myself at a pivotal moment in my career. I have been recognized for my scholarship in the best possible ways. . . . Yet in the wake of COVID-19 I find myself without childcare for two small children, living far away from home while the city is unsafe for the immunocompromised members of my family, slated to teach classes online for summer 2020 and design whole new online courses for fall 2020, and feeling very far from the routine of research, teaching, and writing to which I am accustomed. I don't want to lose ground in my research or in my teaching, and I want to continue as best I can to feed my pipeline of publications. I don't believe I am alone in facing this challenge. I propose to reimagine my work-life balance for this new academic landscape and to help others do the same. I would like to use my time while virtually "in residence" to build and support a cohort of other RU-N faculty parents—especially junior and midcareer faculty . . . to serve as a sounding board for those facing the kind of constraints I am facing now, asking how to build a career and a life in a time of uncertainty.

Taja-Nia Henderson, dean of the RU-N Graduate School and director of the P3 Collaboratory, suggested that a blog, a communiqué that would reach faculty parents wherever they were, might be one important way to establish and nurture such a cohort. When I sat down to write the first entry, the prose came out so easily and the conversational tone felt so right that I was startled. I don't know how much the monthly blog posts helped others, but for me, it was a relief to speak some kind of truth into the void.

September 17, 2020

"Calling all Rutgers Newark Faculty Parents"

Dear Fellow Faculty Parent,

How is your **pandemic parenting** experience going? I find myself deeply grateful for extended family and yet still overwhelmed by the realities of juggling teaching, research, and writing with parenting under these unprecedented conditions. I have a 15-month-old son and a 5-year-old daughter who has just started kindergarten. My daughter is returning to school in person after six months of living in our "bubble." And here begins my story, which I imagine will be all too familiar to many of you.

When my daughter's preschool shut down in early March we moved out of our small (really, really small when there is nowhere to go and not much to do) apartment and into the basement of her grandparents' suburban home where we stayed for six months. My summer research and writing plans came to a screeching halt. My "workday" shrank to a mere two hours or so after both kids were down for the night. From about 8 P.M. to 10 P.M. I answered emails, planned fall classes, drafted fellowship and grant applications, corrected footnotes, postponed major deadlines, listened to the nightly news with growing horror and deep sadness, and produced precious little new writing. Pre-pandemic, I was poised to launch into the most crucial and productive year of my newly post-tenure career. Under contract to produce an edited volume, a scholarly edition of a play, and at work on a second monograph, I had planned to soar to new heights of scholarly achievement! I was fired up, having finally left the haze of newborn-care behind. Instead, I found myself struggling to keep up with the absolute bare minimum.

I learned that my preschooler does not like video conference calls. She curled into a ball and hid under a table whenever we tried to use Zoom with her preschool classmates. Remote learning was a bust and the non-stop, 24/7 baby care was beyond grueling. In the meantime, my infant turned into a toddler with increasingly obvious gross motor delays, and we found ourselves scrambling to get him assessed and to get him some kind of appointment for early intervention, a developmental pediatrician, and physical therapy. He took his first steps this month to wild applause from parents and grandparents and mild interest from his sister. I was humbled by his determination to move forward, and I learned a lot about my own limitations as a parent and as a scholar this year.

I wanted to share my pandemic faculty parenting story because I have learned that talking about what I have been experiencing is restorative. I realized this slowly as I began blurting out things I would never normally say in work meetings, like, "I have to go now! I have to give my toddler a BATH!" and things I shouldn't have had to say, such as, "No, I cannot meet on Sunday morning at 9 A.M.," "No, I cannot join you for Zoom cocktails at 6 P.M.," and "No, I cannot stay on this call for an extra 15 minutes to talk about Ron's agenda item." I realized I needed to be able to vocalize and share my new reality because it is a huge part of who I am and what I bring to my work life now. The segregation that had always been implicit to me in "work-life balance" has been replaced by something altogether messier and more honest—a change I'd like to keep even when things "go back to normal."

As the fall semester dragged on, I found that the voice I had found in the blog posts took on a strident tone. By December, my communiqués had become somewhat manifesto-like. With no end in sight to the pandemic and school and day care closures ongoing, it became somewhat imperative to begin to imagine what life might be like if things never got back to normal. Or rather, it became possible to imagine that what had once passed for "normal," pre-pandemic—the impossible juggling act of so-called work-life balance—was no longer going to be acceptable.

December 14, 2020

"Parenting 2021: Hitting the Reboot Button"
Looking ahead to the New Year I am reflecting on some of the biggest changes in my professional life as a faculty parent. Perhaps one of the strangest is that I have been to more speaking events, conferences and symposia in the last few months than I have been able to attend in the last few years. Without the hassle of having to leave my partner to parent alone for several days or (gods-forbid) travel with a toddler to Des Moines or wherever, I can show up. And when I can't be there for the live session, I can often watch the recording later. I can be there and not be square—amazing! In a profession in which being

there and being up to speed on the latest research is essential, this change is a game changer.

I am hoping that, even after this pandemic is behind us and the toilet paper aisle is full of toilet paper again, we can keep some of these changes. I would gratefully transform my conference travel schedule to an 80% online and 20% in-person attendance ratio, instead of 10% in person and 90% hear about it from a friend or forget about it altogether ratio.

And that's not the only thing I'm hoping to take with me when this pandemic ends and the schools reopen, and my work schedule is un-upended someday, somehow. If nothing else, this past year I've learned how to shut everything down and try something completely different, to hit the reset button, no, **the reboot button**, on, for example, writing:

This year I threw absolutely everything at the wall to try to eke out a bit of writing. I hung in there with my weekly writing accountability group. I worked with a writing coach to develop a master plan for my long- and short-term writing projects, a process which included weekly check-ins. I reconnected with a former writing partner (also a Rutgers faculty parent) who watched me like a hawk via Zoom in 45-minute intervals to keep me on task. With this hefty lineup of supports I managed to make the most of the extremely limited amount of writing time available to me each day. Knowing how effective this souped-up writing support machine has been, I don't want to step it down even when my childcare worries are lessened (if there is such a world).

And what about family:

I knew it would be hard to raise kids in the city (New York and then DC) but never dreamed it would be as hard as it was this past spring. After a few disastrously stir-crazy weeks in a tiny apartment with a baby and a 4-year-old we moved: out of the city, away from campus, into my in-laws' basement. Not wanting to lose the support from nearby family, we moved again, into a rental down the street from my in-laws, complete with a back-yard, a spare room I could use as a home office, and a nearby school that was open for (mostly) in-person learning. It was not the ideal time to make a big move and then another one with a family, BUT yesterday my toddler got kisses and graham crackers from his grandparents after breakfast. Last week my daughter played with her cousins in between remote kindergarten learning sessions. I ate a hot dinner (at actual dinner time) made with love by someone other than me or my husband. I leaned on my spouse and coparent, my mother- and father-in-law, my sister- and brother-in-law, my other sister- and brother-in-law, my nephews and niece, my little brother, my dad, and it was wonderful, and maddening, and wonderful. Having had this taste of the good life, I don't want to give up living near extended family.

And there's more:

I dug deep and hired a grader; I hired a babysitter for three hours on the weekend so I could do my teaching prep and take an honest-to-god nap; I tested local services to find the best and most cost-effective way to get groceries delivered; I found a great Pilates class that meets via Zoom. All these unexpected resources have become as familiar and irreplaceable to me now as my old routines. I'm not planning on letting them go.

In the spring of 2021, the wear and tear of the past year was apparent in every aspect of life at home for parents and kids alike. I was not prepared for the new challenges that began to pile on top of existing ones. I was regularly supporting students and extended family members facing academic, financial, and mental health crises of all kinds, having become skilled at referring folks to free resources that might best meet their changing needs. But I was truly at a loss when my own child began to suffer.

April 26, 2021

"Spring, Breaking: Kids, Mental Health, and the Darker Side of Being Home Together"

Perhaps you are one of those parents who bundles kids into cars or planes and hoists sail for exciting destinations during spring break. Perhaps you outwitted the pandemic by trundling in an RV to a campground, avoiding crowds, mass transit, and shared bathrooms altogether. If so, good on you. You may, however, have spent your spring break the way I spent it: holed up with—guess who?—those same cherubic monsters. We did come up with a few small adventures. We went to the nursery and bought some flowers, which we hung from the side of the deck. We made a deep-dish pizza from scratch (or "out of scratch," as our five-year-old says) or at least we *tried* to make one; in the end we ordered in. We even braved the clothing store with our matching masks, forgetting that the five-year-old, who lived in the city pre-pandemic and went a whole lot of nowhere during the pandemic, had never actually had a full-on Old Navy experience. She quickly approached sheer frenzy at the sight of racks upon racks of spring-themed sparkle jelly shoes and rainbow unicorn dresses. We left relatively unscathed only because we threatened that we would *never* return if she didn't put *down* the armfuls of fluffy bunny socks.

For some, spring break means gearing up for a hard push of grading, research, and writing. For those with full-time caregiving responsibilities, spring break means doing a whole lot less of those things. But this year spring break was not just a "break" filled with even more responsibilities. In fact, it was all about **breaking**.

Our happy-go-lucky five-year-old has not been so happy. Despite our efforts to find a school where she could attend in person, and our efforts to make sure she was surrounded by extended family to shower her with love and attention, the combination of regular kid anxiety and unlimited unknown pandemic-related factors had culminated in something that looked like depression. She started saying, regularly and with conviction, "I'm a terrible person"; "I'm a terrible daughter"; "I don't deserve any dessert"; "Nobody likes me"; "I'm not a good artist"; "I'm not smart"; and on and on. Our spring break was spent launching a plan to refocus attention on a kid clearly crying out for . . . something. Not knowing what's wrong or how best to help has been perhaps the worst part of this worrying.

In our case, at least for now, things seem to have stabilized. For others, maybe for you and yours, things are not so stable. We've heard a lot lately about mental illness, depression, and suicide in adults. We've heard how isolation, job loss, financial worries, and the constant threat of infection has exacerbated existing mental illness or triggered new symptoms. I nearly lost an extended family member to suicide just before the winter. Receiving a suicide note and calling the police is one experience I never want to repeat. In our roles as faculty members, we know a great deal about how students are suffering and about the added burden on BIPOC, LGBTQ+, low-income, and undocumented students. We've been the ones to gently direct students to the mental health and other resources they most need.

We've heard less about how these same stressors have affected children, whose situations vary depending on their age and other factors, including their parents' responsibilities, siblings' lives, access to schooling, level of interaction with other children, their geographical location, living accommodations, access to spaces for play and expression, and (crucially) their access to medical and mental health resources. This constellation of variables has meant, for some families, kids with serious depression and anxiety, kids with suicidal ideation, kids who make suicide attempts; in short, kids pushed to their breaking points. And if the move from in-person to virtual schooling wasn't hard enough (against the backdrop of racial reckoning and a rising COVID toll), the transition back to the classroom brings new challenges. It can be difficult to find and access mental health supports for children even at the best of times.

Today I am following the advice of a friend and faculty colleague whose ten-year-old recently survived a suicide attempt (yes, ten years old). Reach out now, my friend advised, to your pediatrician and parent network to find highly recommended

pediatric mental health professionals—psychologists, psychia-
trists, support groups—in your area and to learn about costs,
wait times, and whether they are covered by your insurance.
Find out which hospitals provide in-patient care for children
facing mental health issues. Save this information for a rainy
day, or a rainy pandemic. If things take a turn for the worse, you
will have the information you need to get reliable help quickly.
And remember this, you are not alone. Parenting, kids, and
mental health may not be the top story on the nightly news, but
it's the top story in every household. I see you, and I share your
concerns.

It felt important to put this story out into the world, and readers
reached out to say they shared a similar experience. *The Faculty
Parent* was an experiment in building community at a time when
isolation was almost impossible to escape. The blog was the begin-
ning of something bigger, something that I hope will last a good
long while. Following the spring 2021 semester, *The Faculty Parent*
blog continued but with a growing number of authors, other scholar
teachers with caregiving responsibilities for young children, older
kids, aging parents, and other family members. As the blog began
running, I established a listserv for faculty caregivers, and a work-
ing group of Rutgers-Newark faculty parents, which was eventu-
ally recognized as a task force reporting directly to the RU-N
chancellor on policies and issues affecting caregivers on campus.
That these things—structures to foster community and dispel
isolation—did not exist before the pandemic still surprises me.
That the conditions of the pandemic spurred me and others to cre-
ate and to share them inspires me still.

Resiliency, Resourcefulness, Responsibility, and Reinvention

DAVID DREYFUS

Recently, we have all received a crash course in supply chain management. I like to think that supply chain management is having a moment. I no longer have to ask, on the first day of class, "Who has heard of supply chain management?" For decades, we have grown accustomed to ever quicker deliveries with increasing methods of tracking. Two-day deliveries, free returns, and omnichannel retailing have become the norm.

Supply chain management is defined as a series of events that are required to source, make, and deliver goods and services. In other words, it entails managing the risk of a business. We usually take for granted the orchestra of activity that comprises the processes of how we receive, interact with, and consume our goods and services. However, supply chain management is where this orchestra is tuned.

So what happened during this pandemic that caused our supply chains to play out of tune? You may remember that we ran short of ventilators, personal protection equipment, toilet paper, and computer chips. As the world shut its factory doors and workers were asked, or chose, not to come in, goods and services were not manufactured or delivered. Instead of an isolated disruption, as is usually the case amid a natural disaster or war, this pandemic occurred almost simultaneously around the world. Issues that are normally invisible to the consumer, as they typically occur and are resolved behind the scenes, started holding our attention.

After the first early weeks of the pandemic, demands for goods escalated. This renewed demand ballooned to extreme levels in many industries. With greater demand and fewer workers, businesses and suppliers could not keep up. The complexity and structure of our supply chains were working against us. Suppliers could not obtain enough raw materials or make enough components. Drivers were in demand. Finding alternative suppliers is not simple in normal times; the process is far more difficult during disruptions.

The toilet paper shortage offers a good example. At the onset of the pandemic, consumers hoarded toilet paper as they prepared to stay indoors for an unknown length of time. And toilet paper businesses shut down. Demand had surged, but production had halted. Eventually, loggers returned to their forests and machines. Lumber mills reopened to process the trees. Paper mills started making the raw materials into paper, and finally, the toilet paper manufacturers ran their manufacturing lines again. At each step, logistic providers were needed to transport the goods from one entity to the next. Finally, once the toilet paper was made and packaged, it had to be transported to distribution centers and retailers. The shortage of workers and drivers at each step made this journey slow and expensive. Additionally, many protections were put into place to keep people further apart, thus slowing down existing processes and communications.

To support the goals of business, the supply chain management team must ensure that it has the internal capabilities to produce a good or service. This includes physical constraints, like the size of a building or the speed of a machine, but also the number of people needed to run the business. Looking up the supply chain and beyond the walls of the business, suppliers must be obtained and approved to provide raw materials or components, along with logistics providers to move everything around. Looking down the supply chain, distributors and customers require additional logistics and services to ensure successful delivery. Each step requires a relationship and trust. During the pandemic, these relationships were put to the test.

The pandemic revealed the level of globalization and complexity of our modern supply chains. And the fragility. When any part of this chain breaks, disruptions are likely to follow. To limit risk, several options are available to businesses. Each contains trade-offs. These may include having multiple suppliers, which limits economies of scale, or stockpiling inventory, which increases inventory costs. A business could vertically integrate—controlling more aspects of its supply chain. But that choice demands movement from a core capability; in this scenario, the business is no longer focused primarily on what it does best. Regardless, businesses should map processes to better understand the movement of products and information through their supply chains. Mapping allows a business to see and address problems more quickly, but mapping is time consuming and requires expertise.

At Rutgers Business School, we have a culture of resiliency, resourcefulness, responsibility, and reinvention. Many businesses are now adopting a similar culture due to needed changes exposed by the pandemic. The understanding that everything is a process that can be mapped and standardized has taken on a more important meaning as colleagues are regularly absent and the need for others to step in and fulfill duties persists. The connections and relationships built over years between businesses have been put to the test as solutions had to be found for the frequent supply, labor, and transportation shortages.

By the end of the first year of the pandemic, many businesses had adopted new practices and found new suppliers, if needed. Strategies were shifting within companies to bolster supply chains. Companies were building stronger relationships, formalizing processes, adopting new technologies, developing new suppliers. Yet we still faced regular shortages of goods, logistic challenges, and a backlog at our ports. Not everything was back on track.

Similarly, consumer spending remained skewed toward durable goods, which left many service industries struggling.

Businesses will not revert to the strategies of the past, nor should they. Online shopping remains popular. Shortages continue for some goods and services. Service spending on hotels, airlines, and more is returning. Labor shortages continue to plague certain industries and businesses, many of which were begun before the pandemic, such as those in health care and trucking.

Looking ahead, what can we do? A business can hide many of its problems by carrying extra inventory. However, no amount of additional inventory is enough to last years. Furthermore, new challenges have emerged as we try to put the pandemic behind us. War and inflation offer new disruptions. Better and more robust supply chain management principles should be adopted. Ultimately, our quest to manage the risk within businesses continues.

Globalization has led to supply chains crisscrossing the world. To unravel these paths completely would be unwise. These paths have integrated nations on a scale never before seen. This integration has led to some of the most peaceful years in recorded human history. Businesses are run by people. When people work together, relationships are built. These networks create a powerful force, which should bring us all closer together. In the future, we will solve these challenges so that our supply chains are not as fragile and ensure that the next disruption is not as painful. To do this, we must remain resilient, resourceful, responsible, and continue to reinvent.

COVID-19 and Spaces of Confinement

ULLA D. BERG

At the onset of the COVID-19 pandemic, some described our newfound collective experience of confinement at home as equivalent to being in jail. Nothing could be further from the truth. Here's why.

It was a strange week that first week. I remember deciding to drive my daughter on Thursday to her high school in Manhattan from Brooklyn where we live and wondering if it was safe for her to even attend. The following day, I didn't send her or her younger brother to school. Over the weekend, the city shut down and families and individuals isolated at home as we best could. Our new lives in confinement evolved around maintaining kids engaged without the option of going outside, wiping down groceries with a variety of Clorox products, obsessively monitoring the number of coronavirus cases at coordinates and in communities dear to us, reminding each other that we were running out of toilet paper, and zealously checking the news for national and global developments on all things COVID. Sitting at the computer refreshing numerous internet sites in hopes that a grocery delivery slot would materialize became part of my nightly routine.

After the first two weeks of pandemic-style staycation, the realization that being confined at home would be the new normal began to settle in slowly. As public schools in New York City reopened online, Google classrooms became part of my everyday life as a parent. More weeks went by, and discussions were had, especially among female colleagues, about how we were supposed to continue our scholarly work given all the logistical difficulties of just getting through the day. It even felt irrelevant and unjustified to worry about research agendas and publication plans given the illness, death, hurt, and loss going on in our local communities with dismal and disproportionate effects on immigrants and communities of color. And then there were the sirens. I will never forget those sirens tearing constantly through the silence of the night.

For many, being confined at home that long was a first. The term *confinement*, according to standard dictionary definitions, means the temporary and generally imposed isolation of a person, group of people, or population for health, safety, or disciplinary reasons. This is where the comparison with being in jail and being confined at home seemed logical to some. To others, such a comparison was a sign of cluelessness or lack of awareness of privileges and class status and disrespectful to the incarcerated.

By the time the pandemic hit, I had been working for a couple of years already on a book manuscript about the detention and deportation of South Americans from the United States. As an anthropologist working on migration, (im)mobilities, and confinement in the Americas, I immediately tuned in to how COVID-19 had major ripple effects not only on people on the move but also on those stuck in transit or currently in immigration detention in the United States. Then on March 24, 2020, the inevitable happened: A thirty-one-year-old Mexican national held in immigration detention in Bergen County Jail became the first federal immigration detainee to test positive for the virus. By April 10, 2020, New Jersey had sixteen of fifty confirmed COVID-19 cases among immigrants in detention—more than any other state in the nation at the time.[1] By the end of 2020, 8,455 cumulative COVID-19 cases had been confirmed among detained noncitizens across the United States, and the hotspot for infections among people in detention had moved to other parts of the country.[2]

When Governor Phil Murphy declared a state of emergency in New Jersey on March 9, 2020, Rutgers University had already created an institutional hub for COVID-19-related research activities, which included intramural funding opportunities for members of the Rutgers community to work in interdisciplinary teams on COVID-19-related issues.[3] Social science proposals were particularly encouraged at the time, given the overrepresentation of the biomedical sciences in COVID-19-related research activities at the university. Together with my two colleagues, K. Sebastian León (LCS/criminal justice, RU–New Brunswick) and Sarah Tosh (anthropology, sociology, and criminal justice, RU-Camden), we proposed a project that would examine the role of immigration detention in the attempted containment of COVID-19 and the effects of the pandemic response within carceral institutions on detained migrants and on immigration system processes.[4] Our project, titled "Migrant Detention, Deportation, and COVID-19 Transmission: Public Health and Safety Challenges in New Jersey," was part of the first round of funded proposals.

Pandemic-related protocols and restrictions made it impossible to do in-person ethnographic research, and we instead designed our project to be carried out remotely and structured explicitly around the ethical and logistical constraints of the coronavirus pandemic. We focused on four detention facilities in the state of New Jersey—Bergen County Jail, Essex County Correctional Facility, Hudson County Correctional Center, and the privately owned Elizabeth Detention Center. In these four facilities, an average of two thousand migrants were confined awaiting adjudication of their cases in New Jersey and New York City immigration courts. From prior academic and activist work, we already knew that conditions in detention facilities and migrants' experiences of them varied greatly, even though facilities must abide by the same federal standards. We were now interested in understanding how local best practices and idiosyncrasies affected how the outbreaks were managed in each facility and how these practices and protocols, in turn, were understood and experienced by different stakeholders including jail administrators, immigration lawyers, detention activists, and migrants recently released from detention.

Doing carceral ethnography without setting a physical foot in the jail or detention center was challenging and required taking ethnographic contextualization to new levels. We conducted all but one of our interviews via Zoom and also relied on secondary sources and analysis of media accounts and on participant observation at various online events and public hearings.[5] Furthermore, we were fortunate to draw on each team member's prior research and activist commitments with immigration detention, deportation research, and carceral systems to contextualize our research findings with pre-pandemic carceral contexts. Our findings made clear that migrant detention and deportation present distinct challenges that undermined local attempts to contain the spread of COVID-19. Some of these challenges were associated with physical aspects of the detention infrastructure, including the presence or absence of windows, appropriate ventilation systems, and lack of access to outdoor space. For example, detainees in the Elizabeth Detention Center, located in a converted warehouse in the port area of Elizabeth, New Jersey, have no windows, outdoor recreation areas, or access to fresh air and sunlight. Other challenges had to do with the spatial arrangements for eating, sleeping, and using common areas within the facilities. Detainees voiced in no uncertain terms the challenges they faced to get timely and adequate access to medical care and reported that sick calls were sometimes left unanswered for several days or even weeks. This had already been an issue before the pandemic but was exacerbated by the public health crisis. Finally, we found that broader immigration system processes, including transportation systems used to transfer detainees between facilities and immigration courts, were also potential vectors for transmission of the novel coronavirus as court dates for the detained docket, transfer between facilities, and deportations were ongoing during the pandemic. These movements also contributed to spreading the virus from U.S. detention centers to countries in Latin America and the Caribbean.[6]

The hardest part of our work was to emotionally process ourselves the fear and trepidation of detainees worried about getting sick and even dying from COVID-19 during their lockup. Their fears were not unfounded: Fiscal year 2020 had the highest annual death toll of migrants in Immigration and Customs Enforcement (ICE) custody in fifteen years—eight out of twenty-one deaths reported by ICE were attributed to COVID-19.[7] Harrowing stories of entire dormitories full of people sick from the virus; guards coming and going, sometimes without masks, putting detainees at risk; a scarcity of sanitary cleaning products and personal protective equipment; and a lack of consistent testing were frequent complaints in the early months of the pandemic. The mental health crisis had also deepened, with more detainees spending longer periods in isolation and solitary confinement. Some told us that they had only half an hour daily out of their cells to shower, call their families, and talk to their lawyers.

Yet migrants in detention are not just passive spectators to their own immobilization. They organized as they best could to protest the profoundly unethical practice of confinement during a public health emergency. Hunger strikes were organized at all three county jails in our study at some point during the pandemic. These were often coordinated with advocates on the outside to bring attention to the dire circumstances of migrant detention during COVID-19. In some parts of the United States, detainees managed to use the contact-free communication tools to tell the world about the scary conditions they endured inside the prison walls. One such video recorded by women in the Irwin County Detention Center in Georgia on the app GettingOut circulated widely over the internet, reminding us that even though detained migrants are physically confined, their words and testimonies can travel beyond the walls of the prison. Their message was loud and clear: The only way to reduce COVID-19 transmission is to get people out of detention.

The pandemic surely evidenced—as did our research—just how senseless and dangerous it can be to lock people up in immigration detention with insufficient oversight and an acute lack of accountability structures. Many commentators described ICE detainees as "sitting ducks" waiting for the worst to happen. This image was not lost on local and state elected officials in New Jersey for whom the human drama of immigration detention in the state had become a growing burden. In June 2021, Governor Murphy responded to mounting pressure from activists and local communities and signed historic legislation banning localities in New Jersey from entering, renewing, or extending contracts with ICE.[8] In a span of less than six months, Essex, Hudson, and Bergen County Jails ended their contracts with ICE. Unfortunately, this historic win did not result in ICE detainees being released to return home to their families and communities. Many were instead transferred to facilities in other states, some in the middle of the night and without notifying their families and attorneys, gravely interfering with due process and increasing the likelihood of the migrants getting deported.[9] Transfers do not resolve but only displace the problem of detention.

Doing research on confinement while in confinement in my home in Brooklyn during the long year of 2020 and beyond taught me many things about the different meanings and experiences of the term *confinement*. For some, like me, pandemic confinement meant a welcome opportunity to work from home and spend more time with my family, whereas for others, it was a dangerous, isolating, and violent experience that had little to do with just staying home. The main lesson I learned is that release from detention is the best, safest, and cheapest option to protect both public health and the human and legal rights of migrants. Most ICE detainees have not committed any serious or violent crimes, yet they are subject to mandatory detention laws in existence since the late 1980s and 1990s, which are hopelessly out of sync with today's global mobilities, with the reality of a public health emergency but also with contemporary social and racial justice agendas. The pandemic thus also revealed the urgency of working toward the abolition of immigration detention and other oppressive carceral systems and undo the "crimmigration" agendas of successive U.S. governments. This would include eliminating the criminalization of all steps in the immigration enforcement system—from arrest and detention to hearings and deportation—and stop locking people up, risking their health and even their lives in the process.

Stephanie Boyer, *STOP!* 2021. Graphite and oil on canvas. (Courtesy of the artist.)

STOP! (2021)

STEPHANIE BOYER

On September 1, 2021, the remnants of Hurricane Ida hit New Jersey, bringing record-breaking rainfall. Flash flooding along the Raritan River caused significant damage on the university's New Brunswick campus.

The Climate Crisis and the University

ROBERT E. KOPP

One way or another, the choice will be made by our generation,
but it will affect life on earth for all generations to come.
—Lester R. Brown, Rutgers College of Agriculture '55[1]

On March 11, 2020, I had dinner in a nearly empty restaurant in Manhattan. The next morning, I led a small breakfast seminar on sea-level rise and its economic costs. I rode back to New Brunswick on a train with an eerily low occupancy, then picked up a few items from my Rutgers office. It would be about a year and a half before I next returned to campus.

For my toddler son, that week marked a major shift. For the previous year, on most workdays, his mother and I had left him in the care of his babysitter, while we headed into our offices. For most of the next two years, we would alternate between remote work and childcare over the course of every day. Our son would almost always have one parent playing with him and another working just a few rooms away.

I'm a climate scientist. I study the planet's past and future and how the choices we make today as a global civilization and in our local communities shape how we will experience that future. And since my son was born—and particularly since March 2020, when I've had many days where my wife and my son are the only other humans I see in the flesh—he's become an increasingly important lens through which I look at the past and the future.

In the early 1980s, when I was the same age as my son was during the pandemic, Ronald Reagan was president, and Al Gore was convening some of the first congressional hearings on climate change. Each year, humans were pumping about nineteen billion metric tons of carbon dioxide into the atmosphere by burning fossil fuels. Since the start of the Industrial Revolution, humans have emitted a total of about six hundred billion metric tons, raising global average temperature by about 0.4°C (0.7°F).[2]

If Al Gore's hearings had led to climate action right then, humankind might have had about a century to eliminate its net carbon dioxide emissions while still keeping warming below the 1.5°C (2.7°F) threshold that nations of the world targeted in the 2015 Paris Climate Agreement. That would have been Future A, but Future A did not happen. Instead, by the time the Paris Agreement was signed, fossil fuels emissions had nearly doubled, to about thirty-six billion tons.[3]

Between the time of those first congressional hearings and the start of the pandemic, fossil fuel burning dumped another trillion tons of carbon dioxide into the atmosphere. As COVID-19 spread across the planet, global average warming was approaching 1.2°C (2.0°F), and the impacts of the heating climate were obvious throughout the world.[4] The hot, dry American West saw record-breaking forest fires, while the Northwest saw deadly heat waves. The warmer, wetter atmosphere led to more intense rainfall—including during Hurricane Ida, which caused devastating and deadly flooding in New Jersey in September 2021. Sea-level rise was making coastal flooding increasingly common: along the Jersey shore, high-tide floods that were rare events in the 1950s were occurring several days every year by the 2010s.

In 2030, as my son enters middle school, global warming will be approaching 1.4°C (2.5°F).[5] Irrespective of efforts to limit emissions, heat waves will continue to grow more frequent and extreme.

Rainfall will continue to become more intense, and the ocean will continue to rise at an accelerating rate.

But by 2030, it will also be clear whether we have managed to turn a corner. In Future B, the urgent calls for climate action from scientists, youth activists, and even politicians, businesspeople, and diplomats will have made an impact. Massive infrastructure changes will have led global emissions to fall substantially, and the climate benefits of these changes will start to be felt in the 2030s. With net emissions on a clear downward trajectory toward zero, there will be a good chance of limiting warming to well below 2°C (3.6°F), another marker set out in the Paris Agreement.[6] In Future C, on the other hand, policy inertia will keep emissions stalled at their current levels. Clean energy technology will continue to progress but not fast enough to drive systemic change. The Paris Agreement goals will become increasingly out of reach.

As I write this, I am forty years old. By the time my son turns forty, the two climate futures will markedly differ. In Future B, large-scale investments in a booming carbon-free economy will have led to near-zero net carbon dioxide emissions. Since 2020, about 750 billion metric tons of carbon dioxide will have been emitted into the atmosphere by burning fossil fuels; but going forward, very little more ever will be.[7] Global temperature may be stabilizing. Heat waves, flooding, and wildfires will still be worse than in 2020 or 2030, and the oceans will still rise for many centuries to come, but we will be able to develop the systems to manage the elevated risk.

In Future C, emissions will have continued at around their 2019 levels; about 1,500 billion tonnes of fossil carbon dioxide will have been added to the atmosphere, and temperatures will be blowing past 2°C with little slowdown in sight. The impacts of climate change—on health, on agriculture, on energy demand, on economic growth, on violent conflict, and on many other aspects of life—will continue to worsen and will fall disproportionately on the poorer parts of our country and the world.

In 2100, the horizon that has long defined the end of many climate projections, my son will be in his eighties. In Future B, growing prosperity will have made climate change impacts in a stabilized climate increasingly manageable. We might even be working to reverse climate change, drawing carbon dioxide out of the atmosphere by expanding forests, improving soil management, and using new breakthrough technologies. In Future C, with emissions continuing, warming will be closing in on 3°C (5.4°F). If we are unlucky, collapsing ecosystems and melting permafrost might augment human-caused carbon dioxide emissions and further boost temperatures. In this future, my great-grandchild will be born into a world of continued and growing climate instability—with extreme weather events growing exponentially more common as the planetary thermostat continues to rise.

> Saving civilization is not a spectator sport.
> —Lester R. Brown, Rutgers College of Agriculture '55[8]

Like all parents, I worry about my son and his future. But unlike most parents, I spend a lot of my day job scientifically analyzing what that future may be like over the course of his life. And so, I worry in a highly quantitative manner.

I worry because I know we have the technology and the means to pursue Future B, and yet it's not clear that we will. It's not clear, in significant part, because the climate crisis isn't the only crisis we are facing. My son is also growing up amid a democracy crisis. Inequality, polarization, misinformation, and short-term attention spans have made the United States' constitutional structures rickety. In the middle of the pandemic, the U.S. Capitol was invaded by Confederate flag–carrying insurrectionists seeking to overturn a democratic election. The machinery of disinformation that brought them there was a turbocharged version of machinery that had been aimed at climate scientists for decades and that was turned on medical scientists over the course of the pandemic. And I don't think it'll be possible to get to Future B without functioning and democratically responsible governance in the world's richest and most powerful country. So I worry.

But I don't just worry. In part because of my son, I've become increasingly focused on how I can act in my communities to help build the future I want for his generation. One of my most important communities right now is Rutgers.

Rutgers is a land-grant university. As such, it is heir to an institutional tradition of collaboration to solve real-world community problems: a tradition rooted—as Liberty Hyde Bailey, the founding dean of Cornell's agricultural college, stated in 1915—in advancing "real democratic expression on the part of the people."[9] In 1907, the land-grant pioneer Kenyon Butterfield, who served as president of what is now UMass-Amherst, envisioned partnerships of land-grant universities, rural schools, and farmers' organizations advancing the democratic and economic development of rural communities.[10] And it's a tradition that can be ideally suited for a time of democratic and climatic crisis—if we make real investments to scale up collaborative, participatory scholarship that advances climate action and democratic engagement.

At Rutgers, we have our own pioneers who have been building these sorts of partnerships. For example, over the last decade, my indefatigable colleagues Marjorie Kaplan and Jeanne Herb built the New Jersey Climate Change Alliance—a network of governments, nonprofits, and businesses working together on climate adaptation and mitigation, not unlike a small scale of Butterfield's vision. Building on their work, the legislature established the New Jersey Climate Change Resource Center at Rutgers in 2020. It charged the center with providing usable information to guide climate decision-making by communities, businesses, governments, and organizations across the state.

With National Science Foundation support, in 2016, Rutgers scientists, engineers, and urban planners launched a new graduate training program in Coastal Climate Risk and Resilience that teaches students to work across disciplines and with communities to develop climate-resilient land use and hazard migration plans, as well as to conduct innovative research guided by community needs. Leveraging this program, the Climate Change Resource Center is creating a new Climate Corps—a team of advanced graduate students who help municipalities plan for climate hazards.

In 2021, Rutgers was chosen to lead a new, twelve-university National Science Foundation–funded "hub" focused on science that supports community climate risk management in dense coastal regions like the New York–New Jersey–Philadelphia megalopolis. The Climate Change Resource Center is playing a key role in linking researcher and community voices.

In 2019, the year before the pandemic, student climate strikes swept the world. At Rutgers, responding in part to climate strikers, President Robert L. Barchi asked supply chain management professor Kevin Lyons and me to lead a task force looking at how Rutgers could match its academic climate strengths with operational climate leadership. The President's Task Force on Carbon Neutrality and Climate Resilience was charged with coming up with a plan to get Rutgers to carbon neutrality and make our campuses more resilient to climate impacts. Leaning into our land-grant tradition and our role as an anchor institution, it had an additional charge—to advance "climate-positive, equitable economic development" across the state.

After a process that involved hundreds of students, faculty, staff, and alumni, carrying on despite the obstacles posed by the pandemic, Kevin and I delivered the task force's report—the university's first Climate Action Plan—to Rutgers' new president, Jonathan Holloway, in the summer of 2021. The plan, which Holloway adopted in his September 2021 University Senate address, lays out a pathway for Rutgers to eliminate its net greenhouse gas emissions by 2040, around when my son will be graduating from college. But Rutgers' Climate Action Plan isn't just about getting our own, on-campus house in order. In the words of the plan, its overarching goal is to "mobilize Rutgers' academic, operational, and economic capacities to advance just, equitable climate solutions and help achieve national net-zero greenhouse gas emissions no later than 2050."[11]

With nearly one hundred thousand students, faculty, and staff, an annual budget of nearly $5 billion, and a footprint across the entire state, Rutgers is a major economic and political force capable of serving as a laboratory for a broader societal climate transformation. Central to doing so is recognizing that we must be one university: the staff who operate our physical facilities and administrative systems working in equal partnership with the faculty and staff who drive its academic mission. To leverage the full strength of the university, climate action requires integration of academics, operations, and planning. To ensure that happens, President Holloway asked Kevin and me to set up a new University Office of Climate Action, charged with oversight and accountability for the implementation of the Climate Action Plan.

What does such integration look like? Imagine students and faculty partnering with operational staff to use the university's facilities across the state as testbeds for 24-7 clean electricity and low-carbon building materials. Imagine staff and students expanding the university's role providing emergency support to communities in the aftermath of a disaster. Imagine a scaled-up Climate Corps, partnering teams of students at every level with communities across the state to advance climate action—from developing hazard mitigation plans to helping households figure out how to disconnect from fossil gas. Imagine a university budget system that integrates the social costs of greenhouse gas emissions, university policies that incentivize faculty to build community partnerships into their research and teaching, and systems of distributed governance that engage faculty, students, and staff across the university in leading climate action. Imagine Rutgers allying with public universities across the country to ensure that no community is left behind in the climate transition.

Universities have a special role to play in tackling the climate crisis, rooted in their natural long-term time horizons. Many of our alumni will have careers and civic lives that stretch for half a century beyond their graduation, and it is the university's role to prepare them not just for their first jobs over the next five years but for their lives over the next fifty. Universities are also loci of research innovation: the birthplaces of ideas that will transform technology and society, not just over the next few years but over the next generation. At the same time, we are also large economic and operational entities that must exist and thrive in the world today. By more tightly integrating our operational and academic missions—infusing the multidecadal perspective of our teaching and research into how we operate—we can serve as what one great American innovator, Walt Disney, called "experimental prototype communities of tomorrow." Universities can become laboratories of long-term thinking, where the systems of human governance needed to justly navigate the climate crisis are created and tested.

In March 2020, the pandemic began with urgency and united action to flatten the infection curve. The American response dissipated in the face of our democratic crisis, leaving the world's wealthiest large country with one of the planet's highest death rates. But the differences in the severity of the public health crisis across the country ought to remind us that acting in our communities matters. The national government, even absent the democratic crisis, can do less than many people think; cities, states, and civic institutions—including universities like Rutgers—can do more. These communities must become laboratories where democracy is renewed, the climate crisis is controlled, and a healthy, just future is built for my son and all his generation.

2020

A New Jersey Economy Reinvented

JAMES W. HUGHES

The year 2020 was always expected to be a milestone year, as it marked the beginning of the third decade of the twenty-first century. What was not anticipated was a year engulfed by a once-in-a-century pandemic event, one that would send us on nothing less than a wild, often terrifying, economic roller-coaster ride.

When 2020 unfolded, both New Jersey and the United States were riding the crest of a record-long economic expansion—often called the Great Expansion—that had started in 2009, more than a decade earlier. Total employment levels reached record highs while unemployment rates hovered near fifty-year lows. Yet inflation remained in hibernation, nowhere to be found. It was a "Goldilocks economy"—not too hot, not too cold, just right—a condition that seemingly ensured an ebullient 2020. Although many economic inequities and disparities were prevalent, in aggregate terms, our economic stars were seemingly in full alignment.

But two months into 2020, Goldilocks completely unraveled as a seismic economic reversal took place. The Great Expansion ended not with a whimper but with a resounding bang. Coronavirus-driven economic disruptions quickly ravaged New Jersey. Historically, long expansions rarely die of old age—they seldom pass away in their beds. Instead, they are usually murdered by the Federal Reserve sharply increasing interest rates to combat inflation. However, in February 2020, as the Great Expansion reached a record 128 months in length, it was done in by an unforeseen assassin: COVID-19.

New Jersey was hit with unprecedented fury in March, precipitating a series of convulsive and staggering economic events that ultimately changed the ways we live, work, shop, and play. A draconian economic shutdown precipitated a fundamental breakdown of life's everyday rhythms as the "world of work" was subjected to unprecedented shocks in both scale and scope. The economy swung on a "great pivot" with economic indicators plummeting at a pace and to an extent never experienced before.

For the preceding thirty years, my close Rutgers colleague Professor Joseph J. Seneca, who contracted COVID-19 and passed away in November 2020 after a lengthy illness, had partnered with me in producing the Rutgers Regional Report. This project produced more than one hundred economic, demographic, and housing market research reports focusing on New Jersey and the New York region. In February 2020, along with Connie O. Hughes (GSNB '76), we had just produced the latest report: *"Urbs," "Burbs," and the Immigration Locomotive.* Shortly thereafter, pandemic-driven economic effects caused the three of us to pivot sharply in research direction.

With the encouragement of then–executive vice president for academic affairs Dr. Barbara Lee, we embarked on a new monthly project, "Fast Track Research Notes," monitoring pandemic-driven economic conditions. This became the intense focus of what we immodestly called the "Fast Track Dream Team" throughout 2020, with economic data mining and analysis completely dominating our research lives. Ultimately, seven reports (totaling approximately 250 pages) were produced, each intensively detailing the cyclical status of the economy and the long-term structural transformations underway. This essay is drawn from that work.

The Great Contraction

According to the Business Cycle Dating Committee of the National Bureau of Economic Research (www.nber.org), the 2020 downturn officially lasted just two months—comprising March and April 2020—the shortest U.S. recession on record. Nonetheless, due to its severity, it was labeled the Great Contraction. It became the final member of what can be called the infamous "economic trilogy"—the three worst economic downturns of the twentieth and twenty-first centuries: the Great Depression of the 1930s, the Great Recession of 2007–2009, and the Great Contraction of 2020.

The Great Contraction was unique in that it was the first deliberately engineered recession. Parallel public policy and private market decisions were made to purposely shut down economic activity—a necessary and painful sacrifice of livelihoods to save lives. Everyday life was placed on indefinite pause.

The draconian lockdown led to an off-the-scale employment collapse. New Jersey's two-month employment loss (–732,600 jobs) was almost double the entire employment gain of the preceding ten years (+388,900 jobs).[1] Economic commentators were "staggered" and left speechless. But our Fast Track Dream Team soldiered on, searching for historical analogies to explain the severity of our economic condition.

For example, most (–699,100 jobs) of New Jersey's total employment loss (–732,600 jobs) occurred in April 2020, a month that will live in economic infamy (to badly paraphrase President Franklin D. Roosevelt). This loss was nearly seven times greater than that (–98,500 jobs) of September 1945—the previous record holder—when the federal government abruptly and totally shut down the Arsenal of Democracy. That sharp transition from an arms manufacturing juggernaut to a peacetime economy disproportionately impacted legions of wartime women production workers personified by Rosie the Riveter. But April 2020 now stands as the cruelest economic month in history as employment fell off a much steeper cliff, and women again were disproportionately impacted. Female job loss rates due to COVID-19 were nearly double male loss rates. Black households were also extremely hard hit.

Disparate Impacts

There was not a single downward recessionary job-loss path. The Great Contraction essentially took a K shape, graphically depicting a bifurcation into separate divergent paths or sectors—for example, a fortunate upper leg of the K versus a struggling bottom leg of the K. Like any recession, 2020's Great Contraction widened the gulf between those able to navigate its effects and those who could not. Many successfully coped (upper leg)—such as the elite-credentialed, knowledge-based professionals working remotely at home—while others suffered (bottom leg)—such as the ranks of low-wage lesser-credentialed (but essential) frontline or support workers who bore the brunt of the economic shock. A new dual "Zoom and gloom" economy emerged.

The Reemployment Surge

Just when the Fast Track team was fully convinced that we were irretrievably sliding into the economic abyss, something happened, something that shocked us: the world neglected to come to an end! Throughout March and April 2020, the U.S. government introduced unprecedented stimulus and relief packages, while the Federal Reserve rolled out innovative policies aimed at preventing financial and economic meltdowns. With this assistance, the two-month freefall ended abruptly, and the economy reopened in May.

To the surprise of most forecasters, employment bounced back sharply. A record-setting monthly gain (+131,400 jobs) in New Jersey was achieved in July. To put that in perspective, the average annual employment gain for the entire decade of the 2010s—the Great Expansion—was approximately 40,000 jobs per year. Mirroring the sharp economic roller-coaster ride down, the scale of the ride up also had no historical precedent.

At year's end, New Jersey had recovered more than half (+408,600 jobs) of the 732,600 jobs lost in the Great Contraction. Substantial progress was made in climbing out of a deep economic hole. However, the cyclical upswing did not mean a return to pre-pandemic normals. Vast structural shifts were initiated in 2020, promising to change everything.

2020: Reshaping the Next Normal

The maelstrom that was 2020 expedited the future—the "next normal." For example, by necessity, four years of digital cultural adaptation took place in a matter of weeks. Zoom went from little known to ubiquitous. COVID-19 was a "gasoline on the fire" accelerant, vastly increasing the pace of structural change that was already underway: accelerating remote work practices, with both organizations and individuals forced to rapidly boost their technology game; accelerating the surge in e-commerce; accelerating the evolution of bricks-and-mortar retailing; accelerating millennial (Gen Y) residential suburbanization, sparking the biggest housing boom in more than a decade; accelerating the pace of baby boom retirements, which aggravated labor shortages and knowledge retention problems of organizations; and accelerating the importance of Gen Z (post-millennials), the new entry-level digital workforce. Embedded change in each of these areas was transformed into hyperchange.

Work Processes, Workplaces, and Office Markets

The year 2020 was nothing less than a watershed moment in the world of work. The coronavirus shock exposed an outmoded white-collar workplace structure and outmoded ways of working. It also revealed that the office ecosystems of many organizations were being run as relics of the twentieth century. It was probably a major market failure that work as a place remained the dominant mindset for so long.

A pandemic that causes changes in ways of working is not unique. In 1666, Isaac Newton developed his ideas on gravity, optics, and calculus while isolating himself in the English countryside to avoid the Great Plague of London. In 2020, the process of redefining work was kickstarted by the coronavirus outbreak.

As a result, it is now recognized that work is more of an activity than just a physical place. A significant proportion of white-collar work has been decoupled from presence in the office. A signature transformative event of 2020 was the initiation of remote, out-of-the-office, work-from-home protocols. It taught us that many forms of work, especially high-end knowledge work, can be done effectively and creatively away from the traditional workplace. At the end of the day, this could rank as one of the great work and office-market disruptions—and advances—of all time.

Thus, 2020 began a massive rethink of the traditional knowledge-based workplace and launched fundamental organizational resets. The shelf life of many pre-pandemic assumptions and certainties began to expire. The primary purpose of the centralized office hub may no longer be a place to get actual work done but rather a place for periodic organizational culture building, collaboration, networking, connecting, and socializing—the "hub as a club." Another central office function may be as a "god pod"—inhabited daily by top organizational leadership and their attentive support staff. Suffice it to say, 2020 precipitated a significant rebalancing of the entire office and work ecosystem, exploring and testing a range of different hybrid work models and flexible distributed work networks.

The year 2020 also spawned an additional rethink: the blind acceptance of long commutes guided by rigid nine-to-five schedules. What may now be an endangered species is the ritual of commuting five days per week to centralized offices. Work-from-home and hybrid work models launched major changes in daily travel patterns.

Moreover, 2020 also initiated fundamental labor market shifts, particularly worker bargaining power. Unprecedented levels of churn and turmoil have led to a new phenomenon now known as the Great Resignation, or the Great Reshuffle. Pandemic-driven labor shortages and record unfilled job openings have provided an expanding set of economic opportunities for workers—and a power dynamic shifting from employers to employees. There is now greater recognition by all organizations of the needs and preferences of their workforces.

Consumption and Lifestyle Changes

Prior to the pandemic, online shopping growth had already started to fundamentally change retail conventions. Clicks were rapidly displacing bricks, upending the historical retail order. The pandemic in 2020 quickly accelerated e-commerce's rise.

New Jersey's economic landscape became increasingly inundated with massive distribution and fulfillment centers. As an aside, what could sound more virtuous than a "fulfillment center"? What marketing genius came up with the term *fulfillment* replacing *warehouse*? Fulfillment suggests happiness delivered, just what the Garden State ordered. And to speed up the delivery of happiness, e-commerce started to produce many smaller last-mile delivery stations. Shipping times that used to be measured in days are now counted in hours. Delivery speed is of the essence and a new consumer ecosystem is continuing to evolve.

The combination of the exponential rise of e-commerce, the shift to remote work, and COVID-19 restrictions changed consumption patterns: more spending on consumer goods and less on out-of-the-home services and activities. This quickly exposed supply chains to crushing demands and major disruptions. Such events in 2020 initiated what may become an era of long inflation. The inflation-free decade of the 2010s is a distant memory.

Generational Disruptions Intensified

The pandemic of 2020 also intersected with the demographic and generational disruptions that had been remodeling New Jersey. The relentless changing of the demographic guard—the greatest age structure transformation in history—stood as an immutable force as 2020 began. Even though COVID-19 was not able to alter the aging process, it did accelerate changes in generational behavior, decision-making rationales, and lifestyle choices and desires.

Four key generations—age-defined population cohorts—are shaping the future: baby boomers, Gen X, Gen Y (millennials), and Gen Z (post-millennials). Each successive younger generation is more diverse than its predecessor, continuously remaking New Jersey.

The fabled oversized baby boom (1946–1964) produced people who were between fifty-six and seventy-four years of age in 2020 and had a median age of sixty-five. Prior to the pandemic, every four and one-half minutes another baby boomer retired in New Jersey, or 320 per day. But the new pandemic-altered reality caused many boomers to accelerate their workforce departure. Their retirement plans were rescripted, adding to the problems of labor shortfalls and the exiting of topline organizational leadership. This is the first example of COVID-19 affecting generational behavior. Consequently, the acceleration of the baby boom out of the workforce represents the greatest experience and brain drain in the state's history. All dimensions of economic and organizational activity are being impacted.

Born immediately following the baby boom, Gen X (those born 1965–1980) is an undersized population cohort initially labeled the baby bust. It is New Jersey's neglected "middle child" sandwiched between two noisy behemoths—the baby boom and Gen Y/millennials. By 2020, the Gen X cohort was between forty and fifty-five years of age, furiously raising families and trading up in the housing market. Gen Xers were poised to assume the leadership ranks left open by exiting and retiring boomers, but this process was greatly accelerated by the pandemic. Organizational leadership composition and styles are being rapidly transformed.

Gen Y/millennials (born 1981–1996) comprise the first population cohort born and reared in the digital age. It was the first digitally savvy generation and the most diverse labor market entrant. During the 2010s, it transformed the workforce. For all organizations, it became the prized labor force commodity, often labeled the digerati. At the same time, much of their pre-pandemic geographic residence shifts could be described as "sprawl withdrawal"—exiting the suburbs and heading to fashionable 24-7 live, work, play environments such as Jersey City and Hoboken. Many millennials viewed suburban single-family living as yesterday's boring obsolete lifestyle.

But like each of the generations, millennials were not immune to aging and movements through the household life cycle. By 2020, the oldest millennials had turned thirty-nine years of age and had already begun to raise families. They had tepidly, just tepidly, begun their suburban odyssey. Many had been sitting on the fence, but pandemic shocks and fears pushed many of them off it, accelerating their move to the suburbs. This may have been the most visible demographic disruption caused by the pandemic: millennials supercharging the housing market. The result was a Garden State suburban housing boom, soaring single-family home prices, and intensifying concerns about housing affordability. New pandemic-driven life and work choices began to revitalize suburban communities, with many "zoom towns" emerging. The new 2020s housing model was both an apocalypse bunker and a finished machine for living—a place providing not only shelter from the elements but also a live, work, learn, and play environment.

The fourth generation was originally called post-millennials, but the term *Gen Z* has steadily gained favor. Born between 1997 and 2012, it is the first post–World War II cohort born in two different centuries. While millennials comprised the first generation raised in the digital age, Gen Z is the first generation raised in the mobile era of smartphones and social media. Its members have grown up with access and hyperconnectivity to everything, every-where, instantaneously. In 2020, the leading-edge members of Gen Z turned twenty-three years old, having just graduated from college, and comprised the new entry-level workforce.

In the emerging era of labor force shortages, Gen Zers are the source of diverse fresh digital talent—the next-gen digerati—eagerly sought by all expertise-seeking organizations. For many leading-edge Gen Zers who are currently working from home, the central office is a remote concept. They may have a significant aversion to pre-pandemic work lifestyles. Much faster than expected, all organizations must be prepared to repeat (albeit differently) the labor market adjustments and disruptions that accompanied the coming of age of millennials.

So 2020 further escalated the generational changes and disruptions already underway: the accelerating retirements of baby boomers, the accelerating movement of Gen Xers into leadership positions, the accelerating suburbanization of family-raising millennials, and the accelerating dependence on Gen Z for the entry-level workforce. Overarching these generational movements and pandemic-linked behavior transformations is the accelerating search for easier and more affordable lives by all demographic sectors.

A Restructured Future

Let's speculate on the possibility of a long-term restructured future—a future potentially shining brighter. There is a possibility—perhaps an over-the-top possibility—that the full decade of the 2020s could encompass a technology-driven "super cycle" like that of one hundred years ago. This would be a super cycle resulting from the transformation of the engines of economic disruption and other transformative forces unleashed by the pandemic in 2020 into the engines of economic innovation and advances propelling us through the balance of the decade.

A century ago, in 1921, the nation had exited a severe eighteen-month-long recession, a downturn that had followed several socioeconomic disruptions, including the 1918–1920 Spanish flu pandemic. But the end of the 1920–1921 recession unexpectedly marked the start of a transformative social and economic period—the Roaring Twenties—a decade driven by vast technological innovations that restructured the foundations of the economy.

Fast forward a hundred years to today: Will history repeat itself? Will a "Roaring 2020s" emerge out of the coronavirus pandemic and the structural upheavals it spawned? Certainly, while an era of supercharged growth remains only a possibility, the reality is that COVID-19 has unleashed technological and economic megaforces. As they relentlessly move forward, they should produce innovative—perhaps monumental—advances that would provide new economic opportunities alongside never-before-seen challenges. And it all started in 2020.

Work in the Pandemic and Beyond

ADRIENNE E. EATON

Many people point to the NBA decision to pull teams off the court on March 11, 2020 as the moment those of us in the United States knew that life as we knew it was about to change. Most of us view the NBA as a source of entertainment, but the league is also an affiliation of workplaces. Basketball players are workers, even if well-paid ones. As shutdown after shutdown followed—in sports, transportation, hotels, and restaurants, whether voluntarily or by mandates—some sectors pivoted to the provision of services, and therefore work, from home. Rutgers, a large public research university and my employer, shut down research labs and sent students, faculty, and white-collar workers home. Some workers remained on campus, taking care of the physical plant and the hundreds of students who could not simply go home. Healthcare workers employed by Rutgers or working in our partner facilities also could not work from home. Over the longer term, with the loss of customers to serve, many dining hall workers were laid off.

Rutgers, then, was a microcosm for the three pathways most workers faced early in the pandemic and continuing in many cases even today. Workers suddenly found themselves either working at home, continuing to go to a workplace but with grave concerns about safety, or having lost employment altogether. Each path presented challenges to workers and those who employ and manage them and the governments responsible for creating a social safety net.

Healthcare workers from hospitals to long-term care. First responders including ambulance drivers and police. Food supply chain workers. These workers, and others, were put in harm's way. A study from the University of California–San Francisco, using California data and looking at deaths from March through October 2020, identified food/agriculture as the industry with the highest death risk, followed by transportation/logistics and facilities. The occupations with the highest risks were cooks, packaging and filling machine operators and tenders, and agricultural workers.[1] This study also points out that the death rates were even greater for people of color. "For example, while white people working in the food or agriculture sector saw a 16 percent increased risk of death during March 2020 through October 2020 when compared with pre-pandemic times, Black people in the same sector had a 34 percent increased risk of death and Latino people had a 59 percent increased risk of death."[2]

A Massachusetts study using data from March 1 to July 31, 2020 had similar findings. The occupations with higher-than-average death rates were, in rank order, healthcare support; transportation and material moving; food preparation and serving; building and grounds cleaning and maintenance; production; construction and extraction; installation, maintenance, and repair; protective service; personal care and service; arts, design, entertainment, sports, and media; and community and social service. This study reported racial and ethnic disparities similar to those in California.[3]

The level of danger remains contested terrain. Many workers felt strongly—to the point of conducting work stoppages—that they were insufficiently protected. Some demanded hazard pay. Many employers denied that they were failing to protect workers. There seems little doubt that there was a serious shortage, early on, of adequate personal protective equipment. We know from healthcare workers themselves that the most protective masks were often not available and that workers were forced to reuse or overwear masks. It's also hard to forget the photos of nurses wearing garbage bags in spring 2020.

The World Health Organization estimated that between 80,000 and 180,000 healthcare workers died from COVID in the first year or so of the pandemic or 2.3–5.2 percent of world deaths at that time.[4] A *Kaiser Health News/The Guardian* investigation reported 3,600 U.S. healthcare worker deaths during the first year but noted that the federal government was not tracking these data. Two-thirds of those deaths were of people of color; lower-paid direct care workers were more likely to die than physicians.[5] As a manager, those times when I had discretion to require people to come back to work or not weighed far more heavily than past decisions given their potential life-and-death consequences.

Many of us remember the news of COVID hot spots in the meat processing factories. In fact, a U.S. House Select Subcommittee on the Coronavirus Crisis investigated the meatpacking industry's practices. The committee made public data from the industry showing that almost 60,000 workers at Tyson Foods, Smithfield Foods, JBS, Cargill, and National Beef caught the virus in the first year of the pandemic, with at least 269 of them dying.[6] Reuters, doing its own investigation, reported that 218 of the 246 facilities of those companies had outbreaks.[7] As any nonvegetarian grocery shopper will have noticed during the omicron surge, meatpackers were hit again—this time, along with government meat inspectors—leading to staffing shortages and supply chain problems.

The federal agency charged with protecting the safety and health of most workers in the United States, the Occupational Safety and Health Administration (OSHA), did essentially nothing to protect workers during the Trump administration. In New Jersey, Governor Phil Murphy stepped into that void, issuing an executive order establishing new COVID-related protocols for the workplace (including cleaning requirements, notification of workplace exposure, etc.), a complaint mechanism, and a training program. The School of Management and Labor Relations at Rutgers, of which I am dean, partnered with the state to provide that training, reaching more than five thousand workers, most of them low-wage workers. Under the Biden administration, OSHA issued a mandate requiring businesses with more than one hundred workers to vaccinate or test their employees. In January 2020, this mandate was blocked by the U.S. Supreme Court, though vaccination rules for healthcare workers, promulgated by a different federal agency, were allowed to stand.[8]

Not Working

According to the Congressional Research Service, 22.1 million jobs were lost between January 2020 and April 2020. Official unemployment rates (14.8 percent) soared in April 2020 to levels that were the highest since the Great Depression.[9] In New Jersey, the rate was even higher: 16.3 percent.[10] These rates were unevenly distributed across racial and ethnic groups. For instance, the peak unemployment rate in the United States as a whole in the first pandemic year for Black workers was 16.7 percent compared to 14.1 percent for whites.[11] Of course, unemployment as measured and reported by the federal government is not an adequate representation of who was not working. Many workers "voluntarily" pulled themselves out of the labor market, bringing the labor force participation rate (60.2 percent) to the lowest levels in many decades.[12] The federal government responded with increased unemployment insurance monthly payments, longer eligibility, and broader coverage, with many "gig" workers eligible for the first time.

The money that was plowed into this expanded safety net— along with programs for small businesses—was important. It is also key to note the shortcomings. Most states did not have the technology or a sufficient workforce to handle the volume of new unemployment claims. Many people did not receive their checks in a timely way or ever. Some states continued to restrict eligibility. Many undocumented workers could not take advantage of official government programs. Immigrant organizations struggled to simply provide the communities they serve with food and to help protect families from eviction. An immigrant organization in New York City, Make the Road, issued a report in May 2020 that documented these challenges and fears:[13]

> Well, in the case of my family, we are very scared, because we had the loss of my brother who died from the cv. And everyone is scared by this pandemic that we have had to live in isolation, without work, without money and with great fear.

> It is impacting us financially, emotionally—there is sadness, worry, fear, and anguish among my children because of the fact that we, their parents, could die. We as parents are concerned about financial insecurity and not knowing when we will return to work.

Working from Home

The third major category, working at home, happened abruptly. A Pew survey tells us that of the 38 percent of workers who can do their jobs from home, 20 percent reported telecommuting before the pandemic versus 71 percent in October 2020 (or roughly a quarter of all the workers surveyed). Interestingly, 54 percent said they wanted to continue the practice after the pandemic.[14]

There were (and remain) challenges in getting adequate hard- and software, quiet spaces to work, and ergonomically sound workstations, challenges that affect workers with lower incomes and less living space and those with families, especially children, differently. (In my own unit at Rutgers, we let people take computer equipment home but not chairs; there was a logic behind this decision, though I'm not sure I can explain it now.)

Two groups of at-home workers were hit hard: new hires and workers (especially women) who were providing care for family members, especially young children. The same Pew study mentioned above found that half of telecommuting parents with children under the age of eighteen reporting difficulties in getting their work done.[15] The best evidence of the struggles of working mothers probably comes from the 865,000 women who left the workforce in September 2020, with another 300,000 in September 2021 (and more in between). Not all these women were telecommuting, but wherever women were working, they found it difficult to manage work and childcare. These burdens again fell differently on low-wage workers. Higher income families were better equipped to create cooperative learning pods or to buy their way out of the difficulties. Young workers just beginning their careers struggled with a lack of social connection, the inability to learn organizational culture, and an absence of mentoring. Indeed, my Rutgers colleague Jessica Methot's research has identified how important "water cooler talk" is for most workers for emotional well-being and connection to the organization.[16]

Not all workers were upset about reduced social connections. In the School of Management and Labor Relations, we had several informal discussions (yes, water cooler talk but over Zoom!) about the differences between extroverts who missed the social interaction from being in the workplace and introverts who were happy for quiet, alone time at home. It's also clear that people of color, disabled workers, and some women—especially pregnant ones—were relieved to be excused from toxic or difficult-to-navigate organizational environments. Professor Methot and her colleagues authored recommendations for promoting connection in a remote environment, including encouraging small talk at the start of meetings, creating "virtual lounges," and video-chat roulettes (like virtual speed dating).[17]

The onset of the COVID crisis was rapidly followed by the national and international outrage about George Floyd's murder by a police officer and other killings of Black people by white people. This has led to widespread internal discussions about racism in organizations including at Rutgers. Statements and promises to do better were issued (including by me). Diversity, equity, and inclusion consultants became and remain in high demand.

Much training has taken place. It remains to be seen how much of this reaction in all sectors of our economy remains performative and how much will create lasting change. I cannot do that topic justice in the context of this overview but have tried to honor it by talking about the different impacts of COVID on workers of color.

Aftermath

How many changes around the institutions of work and employment will last? Sadly, the policy changes expanding coverage and enlarging payments for the unemployed came under intense political fire and no longer exist. The retraction in coverage is particularly difficult to justify. On a more positive note, some states, including New Jersey, are investing in technological improvements to their unemployment systems.

During the first year of the pandemic, there were short-term changes at the federal level to employee leave policies. The Families First Coronavirus Response Act required covered employers to provide up to two weeks of paid sick leave for employees quarantined or experiencing COVID symptoms or for caring for a sick relative or a child whose school was closed. These protections expired at the end of 2020. The fight for paid sick leave and for paid parental leave preceded the pandemic and continues. Support for these policies, along with supports for childcare, were part of the "social infrastructure" bill put forward by the Biden administration but not supported by Congress. (Similar laws were subsequently passed by some states.) If the past is a guide, absent statutory requirements, employers will implement these kinds of policies for the workers they are having difficulty retaining or recruiting, but only while those difficulties last.

Many white-collar workers continue to work from home, at least part time, if not full time. This has implications for the life of cities that are beyond the scope of this essay. Meanwhile, employers are grappling with telecommuting policies. Some insist they are "in-person" businesses; others are selling off office space and freeing their employees to live and work elsewhere. In-between options abound. And questions remain. Will employees who consistently work from home be able to progress in their careers at the same pace?

Perhaps the most interesting phenomenon is the number of workers who are unhappy. The reasons are many—safety concerns, family care, work-from-home options, a deeper questioning about the meaning of one's work. We have seen a rise in both exit—in the form of quitting—and voice—in the form of labor organizing and actions—in response.

According to data collected at Cornell's ILR School, a swell of strikes emerged in October and November 2021.[18] Of the 265 strikes involving 140,000 workers identified in the Cornell report for all of 2021, 63 concerned health and safety and 29 "COVID protocols" (these categories are not mutually exclusive, so cannot be added). Sixty-five concerned health insurance, the issue that has roiled collective bargaining relationships for many years. Cornell research identified only eleven strikes concerning racial justice, but other sources identified six hundred strikes—many of them short demonstrations—in support of Black Lives Matter or to honor George Floyd in the aftermath of his death in summer 2020.

Worker militancy tends to come in long waves; some argue that strikes breed other strikes. Many labor observers think we are experiencing a new wave of worker power. There is ample evidence, especially in the gross and worsening income and wealth inequality in the United States and around the globe, for the need for a correction in the relative power between workers and employers.

And then there is the Great Resignation. In 2021, an average of almost four million workers quit their jobs every month, the highest number since the Bureau of Labor Statistics began reporting these data in 2000.[19] Observers do not see this trend stopping anytime soon. Surveys of workers through most of 2022 continued to indicate widespread dissatisfaction with current jobs and high rates of workers planning to quit.[20] Employers are working to figure out what they need to do to retain and attract the workers they want, although the Federal Reserve's attempts to tame inflation are intended to and likely will eventually cool down the labor market and tamp down resignations.

Conclusion

It is not original to observe that the pandemic laid bare significant problems in the United States. Chief among those, for the purposes of this essay, are inequality—racial, gender, and class based—and the many inadequacies of our social safety net and our system of labor protections. There are indications that income and wealth inequality in the United States—and poverty—was reduced by the massive federal aid packages of 2020 and early 2021, but with their end, these problems have returned. The poorest are becoming poorer and the richest are becoming richer. The regulation of workplace safety was and remains largely a failure. The lack of a decent childcare system and confusion over school openings during the pandemic has pulled large numbers of women out of the labor force, not a good outcome for women's equality or macroeconomic success. In ways still not completely understood, the pandemic has provoked the Great Resignation and labor "shortages" in some fields, including in health care. Some of these are not new realities, but they are deeply concerning.

On the more positive side, the pandemic highlighted and celebrated the role of healthcare workers and first responders and brought food supply chain workers under the essential worker umbrella. For at least a period, these workers and others earned the empathy of the general public. The foundational theories of my field argue that none of these problems discussed above will be solved without collective action by workers themselves and their allies both at the workplace level and in the public policy arena. Other pandemics including the plague in the Middle Ages heightened struggles between the haves and have-nots and brought shifts in power. My hope is that the new wave of labor and racial justice organizing and direct actions, including strikes, begins to shift the current balance of power. My fear is that we have failed to learn the lessons of the pandemic and that we will revert to pre-pandemic debates. This fear has been realized in part by the failure of Congress to sustain changes in unemployment protections, to fund the childcare system and otherwise support working families, and to make union organizing easier. Although there is a healthy dose of realism about the near-term future, there is also great excitement in the labor world about the new organizing and especially about the young people leading much of it. I share both the realism and excitement.

The Tolling Bell

KATHERINE C. EPSTEIN

Enough is enough. Across the political spectrum, we Americans are losing the ability to see one another in our full complex humanity. In a national orgy of intellectual incuriosity and uncritical thinking, we're reducing each other to inhuman caricatures. Curiosity about one's adversaries has come to seem sinful. The academic humanities, which more than any other institution might have come to our aid with a full-throated defense of humanism and rigorous civic scholarship, have instead accelerated this descent into anti-humanism. The moral disrepute into which these virtues have fallen is driving Americans further toward the extremes—less because the one extreme attracts than because the other extreme repels.

Rebuilding the center requires a positive commitment to liberal-democratic, humanistic, and scholarly principles in alliance with all who defend them, whatever their politics.

For me, the two texts that best define this vital center are John Donne's "Meditation XVII" and Martin Luther King Jr.'s "Letter from Birmingham Jail." Donne's essay is the most humane work I know for its uncompromising insistence on our interconnectedness: "No man is an island, entire of himself; every man is a piece of the continent, a part of the main." This interconnectedness anchors the most famous line in the essay: when a bell tolls for a dying man, "never send to know for whom the bell tolls; it tolls for thee."

King adapts Donne's humanism to the world of practical politics in a liberal democracy. Throughout his letter, King distinguishes between more and less sinful actions, more and less just actions. He is trying to find a moral center, he explains to the white clergymen who had criticized him as an "extremist." "I stand in the middle of two opposing forces in the Negro community," he tells them. "One is a force of complacency" and "the other force is one of bitterness and hatred." Fortunately, there exists between these two opposing forces a centrist alternative: "the more excellent way of love and nonviolent protest."

Donne's gorgeous humanism and King's loving centrism offer the cure to what ails the United States. The disease is dehumanizing polarization: the severing of often loving, even life-sustaining tribal bonds that cross the political center and aren't based on politics—marriages, friendships, brotherhoods forged in combat—and the formation of new tribes at the political poles, which are based on politics and regard confederation with other tribes as morally polluting. Donne and King light the path away from the political tribes at the poles and toward the tribal confederation of the political center: the exhausted majority.

I'm a lifelong Democrat who has always felt most at home on the political left. From the beginnings of Trump's candidacy, I have viscerally loathed and feared him for many reasons, but two are especially important. One is that Trump shows no sign of a capacity for empathy, for seeing the world through others' eyes. The other is that Trump plays with dark and dangerous forces of dehumanization that are deeply rooted in our nation's history, especially ones related to race. Trumpism isn't only dehumanization, but the dehumanization of an imagined other is its vanishing point, just as every brushstroke on a broad and complex canvas pulls the eyes toward a single focal point.

Democrats have rightly heaped scorn on the Republican Party for failing to stand up to Trump, but they are less eager to consider whether they might be committing the same sins. They should. What might the left find if it listens to the tolling bell and examines its own conscience? It would find, in effect, a Trumpism of the left which feeds the Trumpism of the right: a dehumanization of large swaths of Americans who feel impelled to vote for right-wing candidates not because the right pulls them but because the left pushes them.

Trumpism on the right, to be sure, also feeds the Trumpism of the left. As a friend of mine likes to say, Trump has no character, but he's good at getting others to reveal theirs. Like something out of the book of Job, Trump tests people's faith and commitment to principles. He is so morally repellent that he tempts others to make exceptions to their moral codes to resist him—just this once, we tell ourselves, because this is an emergency. But the emergency lasts, and "just this once" becomes all the time until we've fallen so far that we can no longer recognize ourselves.

Democrats have worked hard to avoid understanding the reasons for this fall. After a brief flirtation with self-scrutiny in 2016, they instead adopted two conscience-cleansing narratives. One was to say that they had been right all along: lots of Americans really are racist, sexist, homophobic, and too stupid to understand their own economic self-interest. The other narrative was that Russian interference delivered the election to Trump. These two narratives were almost perfectly primed to absolve the left of any responsibility for Trump's rise and to eliminate any need for the hard work of self-examination.

In fact, the left's betrayal of its stated values did a great deal to enable Trumpism on the right. Right-wingers are correct to point to the old identity politics and the new wokeness as the principal drivers of this dehumanization, though they typically ignore important shades of historical and moral complexity. Identity politics on the left began as a way to expose and critique the unacknowledged identity politics of the right. That is, the left sought to show that being white, male, and heterosexual was not the default human identity that the right treated it as, and that being nonwhite, non-male, and nonheterosexual were equally valid.

However, the woke left now keeps pace with the right in tokenizing minorities and imposing on them the burden of representation. In effect, it's adopted the same reductionist categories of humanity from which identity politics originally sought emancipation. In so doing, the woke left has swung the pendulum much too far away from the *unum* and toward the *pluribus*, threatening to fragment us into atoms and destroy our molecular bonds. The self-defeating logic of modern wokeness is what gives it its essentially performative quality.

At the same time as they've dehumanized those they seek to help, the woke left has also dehumanized those they seek to oppose. Woke Democrats terribly flatten the complexity of Trump supporters. They grow our food, serve in our armed forces, fight our fires, rescue our animals, and save the lives of our children. Even though the label certainly fits some, to call all these Trump supporters "white supremacists" robs the appellation of any real meaning. Instead of trying to see in three dimensions, or even two, the woke left has collapsed the Trumpist canvas into its vanishing point. Its inability to see the full, complex humanity of its opponents is both cause and effect of its inability to see the full, complex humanity of those it wants most to help.

Another major driver of right-wing Trumpism is the left's inability to offer Americans an empirically accurate and politically emancipatory version of U.S. history. The left is ideologically committed to an all-oppression, all-the-time interpretation of the American past: America was founded as a racist, sexist, homophobic nation, and it has always remained so.

This interpretation isn't just inaccurate; it's also politically self-defeating. If we engage with the world primarily through our race, gender, and sexuality, how can we engage with it as fully human Americans? If our history is all oppression, all the time, why do we want to be American, and why should we hope for a better future? The Democrats' inability to offer compelling answers to these questions—which reflects the Trumpism of the left—represents their signature contribution to the growth of the Trumpism of the right.

If you're on the left, perhaps this list makes you want to say that what the right does is so much worse. But if you react that way, then I have three questions. First, how do you think this list looks to someone on the right rather than on the left? Second, which is more troubling: the fact that you can supply right-wing counter-examples to everything on this list, or the fact that the list is so long and far from exhaustive? Third, and most importantly, *how do you think Republicans justify their behavior to themselves?*

When I began seeking out right-wing media in 2016 to understand why Trump won, it was a revelation that they were just as scared of my side as mine was of theirs. Reading the comments in *The New York Times* and *The Wall Street Journal* is like reading the same Mad Libs script, only with Republicans/Democrats and right/left reversed when filling in the blank: "Typical _____. They have no principles; all they care about is power, so that they can destroy America." It shocked me that people on the right saw the left as a well-oiled machine—because that was how I saw the other side, and precisely the opposite of how I saw mine. I thought Republicans played hardball; I had no idea they thought we did.

I have some sense of how unpersuasive my arguments may seem to those on the left because I used to bristle when people made them to me. It seemed blindingly obvious that criticisms of the left were exercises in false equivalence or whataboutism. I no longer feel that way. I have come to believe that my reaction, multiplied millions of times on left and right alike, is the road to national and moral ruin. What other ending is there to the story of universal unwillingness to examine one's own conscience, coupled with dehumanization of the other side, besides political violence, authoritarianism, and civil war?

While the bell tolls for Democrats as well as Republicans, it tolls especially for academia. Left-wing pathologies exist in their most concentrated form in academia and have emanated from academia.

Healthy societies require healthy universities, devoted to freedom of inquiry for its own sake. They especially require healthy humanistic disciplines. I'm a history professor, and I love what academia is supposed to be: a gift that society gives to itself, a space insulated from market forces and pressures for immediate results, which in return is supposed to generate the knowledge and provide the education that a vital society wants and needs. The particular role of the humanities is to understand and explain what it means to be human. The particular role of the historical discipline is to try to understand and explain the past—our biggest database of human behavior—as much as possible in its own terms, thereby protecting it from being used as a political football or abolished altogether.

When the diseases of dehumanization, intellectual incuriosity, and lazy thinking afflict society, academics are supposed to be experts at treating them. Instead, in our day, the academy has helped to spread the illness. In so doing, we've damaged the country, not least by convincing Americans to rescind the gift they've given to themselves.

All of the condescension, intolerance, hypocrisy, and dehumanization that exist on the left are supercharged in academia, where they ought not to exist at all. Academics proclaim their moral superiority over the people who pay their salaries. Collegiality has been redefined to mean not rocking the boat, rather than as upholding our fiduciary responsibility as trustees for scholarly and pedagogical standards. Even though we tenured faculty enjoy a degree of economic security of which the vast majority of Americans can only dream, we fancy ourselves populists and congratulate ourselves on our solidarity with the masses. From our position of safety, we are amazed by our courage in speaking truth to power. We decry assaults on expertise as antiintellectual while lecturing the hoi polloi on matters beyond our scholarly expertise; then we complain that our credentials aren't respected. Our bad behavior has corrupted the thin ivory line as it has the thin blue line, and it has driven the widespread impulse to defund the academy. That would be a cure worse than the disease, but we've sacrificed too much of the moral high ground to credibly say so.

Wokeness in academia bears a special responsibility for incubating the dehumanizing and self-defeating wokeness of the left more broadly. Woke academics insist on an inalienable right to self-representation, while using jargon that no one else understands and employing labels that many members of oppressed minorities don't use to represent themselves. Woke academics insist that historians can leap continents and centuries in a single bound; yet race, gender, and sexuality pose insuperable barriers. They suggest that members of historically privileged groups should be "allies" to those of historically oppressed groups and also that when we observe someone across the great divide of race, gender, or sexuality being oppressed, we should stand by rather than attempt to speak on their behalf, for fear of misrepresenting them. These messages are incoherent.

The essential anti-humanism of the messages sent by woke academia is also dangerous for the country in at least two respects. First, representation and self-representation are inseparable; together, they build our knowledge of what it means to be human, thereby enlarging our humanity. If scholars in the humanistic disciplines aren't committed to these propositions, America has a problem.

Second, the anti-humanism of woke academics hamstrings their own ability, and that of the left more broadly, to devise effective political tactics. This is a loss for the country, which needs a principled and politically competent left. Strategizing is hard to do when you have no interest in understanding your opponents as human beings.

The anti-humanist currents on the academic left are also anti-scholarly. What makes an intellectual space safe is a shared commitment to the proposition that no idea has a right to avoid scrutiny. Those belonging to historically privileged groups don't get an exemption, nor do those belonging to historically oppressed groups, partly because an exemption infantilizes everyone involved, partly because it precludes opportunities for mutual learning, and partly because no one, however oppressed, is not also an oppressor.

At the same time, treating broad swaths of ideas as so offensive to be unworthy of discussion discourages mutual examination. It would be difficult to overstate the chilling effect on freedom of speech and even freedom of thought caused by the pervasive threat of being labeled racist, sexist, homophobic, or—the special reward of those who belong to an oppressed group but question the tender mercies of wokeness—self-hating.

In the religion of scholarship, universities, especially their classrooms, are sacred spaces. Their intellectual openness is vital to social health. But rather than fighting to keep them open, academics are closing them down to opposing viewpoints. If we in the humanities are so ill that we know not that the bell tolls for us, how can we help others to hear it?

Mutual dehumanization is the path to human desolation on a scale that goes well beyond the unhappiness of our current moment. Democracies cannot survive when neither side is prepared to lose and when the perception of an emergency makes both sides willing to sacrifice their principles but unwilling to compromise.

The only way to get off the path we're on is centrism. This is a dirty word in American politics. Tellingly, both sides speak with contempt for centrists, as though marauding bands of moderates are what threaten the American experiment. It's true that there is a negative form of centrism, defined by relative distance from the poles, that offers no succor. There's also a form of moderation that is really moral cowardice. But I'm talking about a positive centrism, defined by commitment to bedrock principles of liberal democracy, even and especially when they don't immediately produce the outcome we want. The bedrock principles of liberal democracy happen to be the same as the bedrock principles of humanistic scholarship, which are process-oriented rather than outcome-oriented.

I often suspect that I have much in common with many Trump voters. Most people, including me, just want a quiet life, I think. It's a vanishingly small number of human beings who wake up in the morning and go, "How can I be evil today?" (perhaps as few as those who wake up and ask themselves how they can serve the greater good). Most of us are just trying to survive, ideally with at least some ability to think well of ourselves.

When I look at the far right and the far left, I think, I don't want to be governed by *any* of these people. What I want in leaders is moral and intellectual seriousness. They should be able to articulate a vision of America that acknowledges our history of dehumanization but also our history of humanization; that recognizes the shared Americanness of urban and rural residents, conservatives and liberals, or Republicans and Democrats; and that appeals to the better angels of our nature. They should understand that all Americans are caught in an inescapable network of mutuality, tied in a single garment of national destiny. They should treat voters like grown-ups, which means representation when possible but the courtesy of dissent when necessary, rather than pandering.

A hallmark of maturity, in both a person and a nation, is the willingness to live with moral complexity. When we build walls among ourselves for fear of moral contamination, should we be surprised that we elect a president whose signature issue is a wall? Our ability to accept moral complexity in others is tied to our ability to accept it in ourselves. An inability to accept it in ourselves is tied to an inability to accept it in others.

The bell cannot toll for Trumpism a moment too soon. But it will not until we all hear it tolling for ourselves.

Kimberly Camp, *Stagecoach Mary*, 2020. Acrylic on canvas. (Courtesy of the artist.)

Stagecoach Mary

KIMBERLY CAMP

Mary Fields rode a stagecoach through the high deserts of the great Northwest Territory with her Winchester rifle and revolvers close at hand as the first female African American mail carrier. It was said that she never shied away from a fight and thieves were loath to mess with her. Seeing the iconic photograph of her decades ago stayed in my mind. It was how she held her Winchester with her trigger finger ready and the set of her jaw that inspired me to paint her in a bright red dress, in stark contrast to what she no doubt wore. No respectable woman would wear scarlet. It was said that Mary often wore men's pants—far more suitable for hostile territory. Her past self as an enslaved woman appears in the doorway behind her, clothed in the color of ase[1] surrounded by the orbital spirits of her ancestors. For me, she is the embodiment of ase, of power rising from bondage to true liberation. Now was the time to paint her to embrace what her freedom really meant.

Sequestered by COVID-19, I watched men and their guns on television. There were policemen killing Black people with guns. Angry disaffected white men were brandishing weapons of war in public. There were endless fictional characters portrayed as heroic for wantonly murdering "bad guys." Stagecoach Mary reminded me that gun control would take center stage if those same images were of Black men and women armed to the teeth brandishing guns.

On Racism in Museums

KIMBERLY CAMP

Ten years ago, I retired from a twenty-five-year career as a president and CEO for major museums. My work focused on fixing broken museums, launching new initiatives and institution building. When I entered the field, fewer than 1 percent of senior museum professionals were African American. I loved my work and now enjoy museums as a patron instead of an employee. For more than fifty years, I've been a working artist—a painter and doll maker. When I retired from the museum field, I moved back to southern New Jersey and opened Galerie Marie, a small art gallery and studio. The gallery contains art by more than two hundred international artists and my own paintings and dolls. I had just returned from a debut award-winning show with the American Craft Council in Baltimore when the order was given to shelter in place because of COVID-19. COVID exposed the raw underbelly of our worst fears and our greatest regrets.

Fear is often thought to be the cause of outrage and anger, of violence against oppression real or imagined. Regrets come from not speaking your mind when your soul longs for truth. Regrets come from inaction—whether from that room you always wanted to paint but never did, to hugging your parents more once you realized you could only wave at them through a nursing home window.

Kimberly Camp's shamanistic dolls appear to be whimsical, yet they allude to historic struggles for human rights. Camp adorns her dolls with artifacts from her travels, including beads once traded for enslaved persons' lives, transforming the instruments of our ugliest acts into symbols of strength and beauty. *Sentry*, 2020, Kimberly Camp, leather body, stoneware, paper clay, metallic leaf, pheasant feathers, rawhide, bison tooth. (Courtesy of the artist.)

Many artists embraced every solitary second that was uninterrupted space for expression. The everyday distractions that took us from our work just disappeared.

The isolation of the lockdown gave me untethered time to create. Mostly, I sewed cotton three-layer masks for ten hours a day filling orders from people here and all over the country who heard about them through word of mouth. I thought about the last time our country went through a racial reckoning while I worked.

I filled my time with paint, clay, canvas, and audio books. The ones on my list for when I had extra time were the first ones I listened to as background noise while at my easel. These books took the place of the sometimes-incessant jabbering of people who love to talk and never say anything of substance. I didn't have to hear anyone ask if I was making voodoo dolls or asking if what I paint is called Black art. I read Ibram X. Kendi's *How to Be an Antiracist* and *Stamped from the Beginning*, then brutalized my soul by reading *They Were Her Property: White Women as Slave Owners in the American South* by Stephanie E. Jones-Rogers. It was Isabel Wilkerson's *Caste: The Origins of Our Discontent* that gave me the words to piece together my thoughts about the real meaning and impact of racism.

In May 2020, the murder of George Floyd stirred outrage from around the world. We were in lockdown, and everybody saw him die under the knee of former police officer Derrick Chauvin. My anger at the growing anti-Blackness in the social and civic fabric of the country had been growing since the pushback started from white Americans when President Barack Obama was sworn in as our forty-fourth president. White supremacists then in power planted a fertile seed for the emergence of fascism where our democracy once grew. Democracy has always been an ideal for the country to strive for—one that is remembered and recited over and over again by Black Americans when the nation's policies and practices take hard-won civil rights away.

The election of the forty-fifth president in 2016 blew the lid off the safeguards that had sidelined outward expressions of viral racial hatred. I could feel its impact when people visited my gallery in Collingswood, New Jersey. I was told by many that when they were here, they felt safe. White women who came in said they didn't realize that they were surrounded by people who would support the ravings of the newly elected leader of the free world. Wilkerson's book enlightened me about how Nazis studied our country's oppression of Black people and were astonished by how we could be thought of as an idyllic democracy when practicing outward, unfettered discrimination. Some of the women who visited me back then said they were sorry. Some said they didn't have any idea. Some came in and told me they loved me, even though they had never met me before. None of what they said and did was for me—it was to make them feel better about the reprehensible deeds of others. I knew better.

I am still a bit stunned that white people said they had no idea that racism was still a thing. I warned visitors against saying, ". . . in 2016," ". . . 2017," ". . . 2018." With the blunt tongue that I'm known for, I reminded them that they all know haters and ask what they thought these men and women were doing when they weren't at their houses for Sunday dinner. The haters are their brothers, sisters, mothers, cousins, husbands, and friends. Princeton professor Eddie Glaude Jr. says it best when he talks about the "intimacy of our hatred."[1] Unless white people are willing to talk to each other about racism and commit to its eradication, there will be no change.

Black people endure racism every day. Those of us who are still sane steel ourselves to most of it and just move on. We sometimes talk to each other about the egregious actions of perpetrators, but seldom is there an ongoing conversation about what racism does to us physically and mentally. Some practice a form of denial—that the past should be forgotten. But how can it be when there are still hundreds of stone and metal monuments to the Confederacy all over the nation that support the myth of Northern aggression and states' rights? I've always tried to help people be better people by starting the conversation about racism, knowing that without a shared vocabulary we'll never overcome awkwardness. I took to heart a slogan from my Quaker education of speaking truth to power. Steer clear and don't ask my opinion if you don't want to know. Asked if I think racism still exists, I say yes. Asked if it is plausible that in 2022 or whatever year that racists are still around, I say yes. Asked if there is anything that one can do, I say talk to your haters.

One Sunday, a mother introduced me to her son, who supported the forty-fifth president. The transition from talking about photography to politics was swift and obviously purposeful. He said that not all Republicans were racist and that the party was about conservatism. But by their own admission, the Republican Party has built its backbone on white victimization. In a conversation I had with my cousin Clifford Gilchrist, he said that for white people in this country, Black people were optional. No more profound words have ever been uttered. White people can go through their entire lives and never have to deal with us in any significant way. That's what allows the practice of racism to be embraced generation after generation. If it's not directed at you all the time, every day, it's easy to think it isn't a big deal. I often hear people say that this younger generation doesn't even believe in racism and discrimination, but after four hundred years of younger generations, racism and discrimination hasn't stopped.

Artists young and old have created murals that speak to the murder of George Floyd and the multitude of Black men and women killed by police, including Breonna Taylor in her own bed. For Black Americans, these were murders like so many others. Except now, the eyes of the nation were on them. Every thirty years, events turn the nation's attention to the glaring presence of bigotry.

The last time, the pandemic was AIDS. Instead of Senators Ted Cruz and Lindsay Graham, we had Senators Jesse Helms and Strom Thurmond. The atrocity seen around the world was the beating of Rodney King by four white Los Angeles police officers. Anti-Blackness was quelled with calls for cultural equity. The museum world responded to the call by hiring Black managers after being forced to do so by government funding policies that mandated diversification. Outcries from the gay community were met with censorship and worse. The Corcoran Museum in Washington, DC, canceled its Robert Mapplethorpe exhibition[2] when protests about indecency echoed in Congress. Mapplethorpe's photographs of gay Black men in explicit sexual positions were the ones that were used in news reports as indicative of the exhibition's content. Director Christine Orr-Cahill was eviscerated, and funders demanded their money back. Artist Chris Ofili's use of elephant dung on his painting of a Black Madonna at Brooklyn Museum was reason enough for then-mayor Rudy Giuliani to withdraw support for the museum.[3] The Association of American Cultures, a multicultural, multiracial group of nonprofit leaders in the arts was accused by a member of the National Arts Council of co-opting the word *American*. I was reminded of that comment when, in a January 2022 press conference, Senator Mitch McConnell (R-Kentucky) made it clear that when it came to voting, "American" meant white.

People have forgotten we'd witnessed a storm of anti-Blackness before. I documented the stories of senior-level African American museum professionals in a book I wrote in the summer of 2021. I collected stories from these men and women to share anonymously with the newest generation of Black museum professionals hired since 2020. Museums were responding as before to cries for cultural equity. There was a noticeable pattern—senior leaders—facilitators who hired Black staff ran interference protecting them from colleagues resistant to change. Once the facilitator left, microaggressions became so powerful that it whitewashed the Black leadership away. According to Victoria L. Valentine's *Culture Type*[4] online newsletter, there were sixty-nine new, mostly Black curators and senior leaders hired in major museums in the past two years.

People should care about racism in museums because of the role museums play in our broader cultural landscape. Museums are considered to be the epitome of cultural institutionalism. Compared to other arts organizations—dance companies, visual arts centers, theaters, and so forth—museums are seen as far more powerful. They receive enormous grants from philanthropists and government funders to preserve the best of human endeavor. Museum staff make more money and work in grander buildings in picturesque settings. Museum boards are made up of powerful wealthy white men and women, who often pay for the privilege in the tens of thousands of dollars. Museums are trusted more than books and teachers. Museums are the height of our cultural sophistication.

However, museums are not immune to racism. Many were created to promote racism.

Museums are anchored in the wealth created by the transatlantic slave trade. They present white colonialists as the progenitors of natural conservation, literally facilitated on the backs of Black bodies. Dioramas containing animals killed in European colonies are one example of the exploitation of African art, science, and culture, justified by the largess of white care and preservation. Museums promote white supremacy by their exclusion of Blackness in hiring, collecting, programs, exhibitions, research, governance, and audiences. While located in urban centers, their target audiences are suburban and white. Predominantly white museum curators have been elevated above public service, relegating interaction with Black audiences to community outreach coordinators. Museums document the white side of enslavement, emancipation, and Jim Crow. They idealize cherubic-like white children while exhibiting children's literature and toys that depict racial stereotypes. Their commitment to anti-Blackness is watered down and unfulfilled, garbled in euphemisms that reinforce racial hierarchies, like "people of color" and BIPOC (Black, Indigenous, people of color). Yes, there are exceptions. Regrettably, more are the norm.

While researching for my book, a friend told me about Solomon Brown, the first African American employee hired by the Smithsonian Institution—a poet who was hired as a laborer—in 1859. He became a celebrated self-taught scientist, naturalist, educator, mapmaker and illustrator, political leader, and poet. By 1862, Brown became a de facto curator, intimately involved in every branch of work at the Smithsonian. His upward trajectory was abruptly changed when the institution's undersecretary—his facilitator—died in 1887. Secretary Henry demoted him back to a common laborer in the basement of the Smithsonian Castle. Adding insult to injury after almost forty years of service, the next secretary, Samuel Langley, reduced his pay back to his starting wages. Brown had to stay or lose all his income. He worked an additional sixteen years until he left the Smithsonian in 1906. Less than four months later, after forty years at the institution, he died in his Anacostia home. Even as far back as the birth of the Smithsonian, the profession was infected by the cycle of facilitation and elimination. Brown's articulation of the depth to which he understood the vile despicable parts of bigotry and racism would today be called a recognizing of microaggressions and white supremacy. His poem on the subject lays bare the conditions in which he worked, his disenchantment, and his defiance that he, like the people I interviewed for my book aver—"Twist and turn it as you may, the Negro's here, HE'S HERE TO STAY."[5]

People who fear taking an active role in fighting racism have seemingly once again settled on complacency. People who regret missing chances to speak out about racial injustice have reconciled their feelings and moved on to the next thing. The COVID-19 lockdown created a space for inflection. People had time to examine their relationships to work and family and friends and freedom. Floyd's murder gave people a reason to just do something—anything to make racism go away. The enormity of that task often results in inaction. To think we can achieve a racism-free society is fantasy. We can start with the conversation, awkward as it may be. One person can make a difference and start a dialogue. There is no such thing as "reverse racism." Black museum professionals aren't haters. We only want white people to stay out of our way so we can, as my mentor, the legendary curator/thought leader Lowery Sims said, "Find [our] true North."

STYLE Bird

GRACE LYNNE HAYNES

STYLE Bird, by Grace Lynne Haynes for *The New Yorker*, September 7, 2020.
(Courtesy of the artist.)

Meet Me at the Theater at the End of the World

Thirteen Illuminations and an Afterglow

CARIDAD SVICH

Illumination 1: The sound of birds, an eerie calm, the sudden grayness of the skies broken by sunlight. It's the first day of a long week. After all, everything has been rendered seemingly obsolete. Fear and sadness are punctured by the sound of church bells occasionally. Or is it the memory of church bells? Wrap the lunches in tins, stock up on water, shutter the lights of all the marquees, put away the costumes, and wait for what may end up being five hundred days or more of waiting. In this theater, we will live.

Illumination 2: The brisk quiet is remarkable in its efficiency. Three months after the ending of all endings, the fear turns inward, the skies turn outward, rain pelts, and then there is the necessary storm of racial reckoning. Justice cries as just is. The world spins forward. And then snaps back. A high-wire act with people's very lives, as lies are spread like the wildfires that blanket the western coasts. Shouting into the night, global traumas make the news, but in other news, many things are left unseen. It is here where some theaters are born. Just like this. In the spaces of neglect and abandonment. One artist calls another, one worker knocks on someone's door, a play is sent on a postcard, a play is made for the telephone, a fruit basket carries within it the pages of a poem. Here is an everyday theater, humble and low, away from the bright lights of commerce and industry. Through pain shards, a little art to warm the waiting days. In this theater, we make.

Illumination 3: Theater companies from around the world open their vaults and make them available for limited times online, and out come archives of recorded work old and new: Bertolt Brecht's *Mother Courage* from the Berliner Ensemble, Thomas Ostermeier's legendary stagings of *Hamlet* and *Woyzeck*, theater pieces from Hungary, the Czech Republic and Slovakia, Australia, Kenya, England, Ireland, Finland, Norway, Chile, Brazil, and more. Feeding the conversation around the digital campfires, groups spring up on Twitter, WhatsApp, and TikTok. Among them is one called European Theatre Club and another devoted to watching old films. In this theater, we yearn.

Illumination 4: A cough becomes an alert, the weather is a beacon, as theater-makers gravitate to making work on a variety of video platforms. Zoom becomes the most popular for mysterious reasons. Someone says this could have been Skype's big moment, and yet Skype faded into the background and Zoom took over. The new stage space was this video conferencing space. This new black box taught actors and directors new vocabularies, while theater wizards hacked the system and incorporated Isadora software and other online tools to turn this new black box into a fever dream of magic and enterprise. In this theater, we thrive.

Illumination 5: While a coup attempt occurs in the U.S. Capitol, the fires of creativity and renewal stir up older and newer generations of theater-makers, especially those in and of the global majority. We will not be silenced. We will be seen. The voices will ring out, even through our screens. In this theater, we rage.

Illumination 6: Across the universe, a layer of ice cracks, a forest is decimated by greed, a thousand seagulls lose their way and a lone puppet travels from one city to another calling attention to the plight of war and climate refugees. In this theater, we offer peace.

Illumination 7: Walk through the theater districts of cities—old plays and musicals are listed still on marquees, no one is rushing to see a show, the buzz of in-person audience is gone, the buildings called theaters are ghosted by ghost lights, remnants of another time, other priorities, songs sung, words spoken, bodies rendered visible. It was here that we danced once. Nostalgia floods everything with its treacherous sepia tint. In this theater, we mourn.

Illumination 8: A singer stands in the middle of the town square, microphone in hand, boom box at their side. It is a crisp fall day. They sing an old show tune. Their voice is brash and strong and defiant. They are singing for their life, while pop singer Taylor Swift releases two albums that seem to capture some of the tenor of these fragile times—*folklore* and *evermore*—with their bittersweet refrains about heartbreak. I sing a song of letting go, a neighbor says. In this theater, we learn to live.

Illumination 9: The numbered days are not static even if from the outside, they may seem so. Collaborations across nations and states abound, as theater artists take it into their hands to carry on, against insurmountable odds, to keep the fires lit, and the work of collective imaginations speak good trouble to real trouble. Restless is sleep as broken songs for humanity and the planet rise. In this theater, we are.

Illumination 10: Soft petals of a rose against the cheek, the swell ache of morning, cereal in a coffee mug, coffee drips on a pancake, forgotten worlds are called up in the play on the laptop, we wave hello to the actors on the screen, they wave back, emojis in the chat, question and answer for the after-party, we turn our cameras on and see each other's spaces, interiors made public, living rooms become theaters, as once they were long ago, someone's kitchen becomes Lear's palace, someone's attic becomes the lighthouse at the end of the world. In this theater, we touch fire.

Illumination 11: I saw you in the window of another day, the neighbor says, the music came through the speakers and I was dancing in my room; the sirens wailed outside, the sky crisp and blue, how is it that we make anything out of anything when everything is broken? I hold my heart, I press my lips against the horizon, the tendrils of the air caress what's left of the night, to render the invisible, sometimes you need to wear a mask. In this theater, we call on the ancients.

Illumination 12: In the before times before these, before the streets were made of concrete, there was a pulse to the motion of the waves, human and animal, water and mineral. This was the time when the old songs were new, when the theater was but a game played around the campfire, in it we could do anything because we were gods, and we told ourselves the gods would maybe save us. In the before times before these, the world was both heavy and light, much lighter than now; because now, now in these after times, after the wheels of industry have reached the moon and dabbled in Mars and plundered the oceans, there is an unbearable heaviness that not even sitting around a campfire can seem to lessen, and so instead, begins a massive forgetting, and all that had been seen slowly fades because so-called civilized societies cannot bear to face illness. In this theater, we mourn again.

Illumination 13: For some people, theater died in March 2020. To others, that death was a call to imagine a new beginning; sitting with and bearing the face of illness and death, theater is a game of life and death; it is a philosophical endeavor as much as it is an ontological and hauntological and phenomenological one. Around the campfire made of ashes, we inscribe the names of the dead, sing the songs of those passed, dance the lost dances of childhood, and make of our incantations a kind of gospel. Bathed in the light of emergence, theater's rooms are as vast as the sea because the theater rooms do not need buildings; they just need people communicating one to another in whatever manner they are able. Signal fires for and across the ages. In this theater, we breathe.

Afterglow: I want to tell you a story about a theater, a friend says.

It is late. I have been Zooming all day, and I am grateful that a technological platform can forge and sustain connection and foster ingenuity even during the worst of times, making work accessible to so many for whom it had previously been not.

I want to tell you a story so that you won't forget.

I listen.

My friend begins.

Over there you cannot see it, but there was a theater once.

I squint. I try to imagine.

It was made of leaves.

It was stitched together by some insects and squirrels and maybe a raccoon or two. It was a very tender thing. Because when it rained, it flooded over. Through and through. And the insects and squirrels and the raccoons would have to fetch a new set of leaves and build it again. And since it was very rainy then, much more than it is now, they would have to rebuild it over and over. And oftentimes, they were very tired and desperately wanted to give up or hand over the job to some other creature that wouldn't mind the task of rebuilding. But then they remembered that many creatures didn't even know theater existed, and so, they took it upon themselves to remember the patterns of the leaves, the weight of the dirt, and how the sun would come in, just so, and light everything when the birds sang their songs. How else will they know it is a theater if the birds aren't singing?

I want to tell you a story because stories are old fashioned and have been with us for a long time. Some say such stories teach us things, but I think stories merely help us remember everything that has been forgotten.

Look over there. Underneath the theater of leaves, there is a stone. Pick it up. Put it in your pocket. Feel its stoneness course through you.

There have been days and days unlike these, but there have also been days and days like these, and the stone has been witness because it has survived everything.

Inside this stone lives a chorus of stones, and this chorus holds many voices in many languages. The chorus has traveled much farther than you will ever travel, even though it may not have ever left the ground on which stands the theater of leaves.

The stone feels good in your pocket. It is light. It is shaped like an almond. It weighs hardly anything but just enough to remind you of its presence. Sometimes it tells jokes. It is a funny stone, and the chorus is a riot.

Let the stone carry you. Even if it's just to the next neighborhood. For when you get there, you can tell people you have met them at the theater at the end of the world.

What Kind of Pain

LESLIEANN HOBAYAN

does it take
for you to rush up
from behind and propel it
into the belly of an elder,
a Filipina on her way to noon mass,
her regular routine
to spend time with God,
giving thanks, counting blessings?

How much pain
must you carry in your bones
to launch your foot
into her head, her face,
into her prone body,
curled on the concrete sidewalk
washed in spring sun
as she grasped her rosary
asking the Lord for deliverance
from this (wretched) earth?

Over and over:
your foot a catapult of pain
launching yours into hers
kick after kick after kick—

"You don't belong here."
Whose voice do you hear?
What pain must you carry
to explode it all into my lola?

Never mind the soulless
men who watched,
who closed the glass door
on her bleeding body,
still watching.

What pain, what pain—

I never want
to own pain like that.
But it has come closer.

*For Vilma Kari, sixty-five-year-old Filipina who was beaten in New
York City on March 29, 2021*

Be Still

Listen.
Do you hear it?

Above the soft thud
of bullet into tender chest,
above the sharp clank
of shell on concrete,
the clatter of steel blade
on blacktop,
above the wails of sirens
and cries—

There.
In the treetops.

Above "justice is served"
Above knees on necks
Above chokeholds
and hands up—

There.
Threaded in the clouds.

Do you hear it?
Listen.

If you are still,
you can hear
birdsong lifting you,
the breeze holding you,
—be held—
carry you to the light
where you can find peace

There,
breathe
and rest.

*For Ma'Khia Bryant, sixteen-year-old Black young woman who was
shot by police in Columbus, Ohio, on April 21, 2021*

Sorrow

DAVID ORR

Its place is not
in desert heat
or extremities
of frozen seas
but rather on
untroubled lawns
awash with flowers
all the years
the petals falling
short of filling
the yellow, bare
outlines where
some activity
used to be.

The Only Replacement

BEN PURKERT

for a brief minute there
the Earth stopped spinning
it paused like someone about
to cross the street turning

their head to the left then
the right then slowly making
their way through their narrow
slice of time meanwhile the Earth

has so much time on its hands
it's almost obscene almost rude
it does a little victory dance
in our face it spits right

in our eye I know one day
the Earth will be gone though
I struggle to see what will
spin in its place

Acknowledgments

I owe special thanks and deep gratitude to my brilliant friend Chrissy Dunleavy, the spark for this project, and to Barbara Hurd, who offered critical development advice.

This book would not have been possible without the care, dedication, and support from my university colleagues, including Henry S. Turner, Prabhas V. Moghe, Brian Strom, Michelle Stephens, Carolyn Williams, Rebecca L. Walkowitz, Marc Handelman, Donna Piazza, Lara Beise, Michael Meagher, Nicole Ianuzelli, Beth Tracy, and Karen McCarthy. The superb organizational skills of Ava Ginefra and Alice Hernandez proved especially indispensable. Special thanks to the editorial team at Rutgers University Press, including Micah Kleit, Kimberly Guinta, Carah Naseem, and Michelle Scott.

Special thanks also to my personal support team, including my mother, sisters, brother, and especially my nephew Jordan Blair. Also to Billy Ray Church, Pasquale DiFulco, Lori Fleissner, Roberto Guarnieri, Susan Holcomb, Michael Ann Klink, Donna Mancuso, Jean Manhardt, Zoe Marzo, Dr. Lisa Mills, Mary Radich, Kathleen Stewart, Ellen Travers, LuAnn Verbosky, and Kathryne Yoon. And to my family, Pat, Joseph, Anne, and Alex, to whom I owe everything.

Notes

Preface

1. Antonio Machado (1875-1939) ranks among Spain's greatest twentieth-century poets. This poem was published in *Campos de Castilla* (1912).

Looking for a Better End Game

1. N. Racine, B. A. McArthur, J. E. Cooke, R. Eirich, J. Zhu, and S. Madigan, "Global Prevalence of Depressive and Anxiety Symptoms in Children and Adolescents during COVID-19: A Meta-analysis," *JAMA Pediatrics* 175, no. 11 (2021): 1142–1150, doi: 10.1001/jamapediatrics.2021.2482.

2. Nirmita Panchal, Heather Saunders, Robin Rudowitz, and Cynthia Cox, "The Implications of COVID-19 for Mental Health and Substance Use," Kaiser Family Foundation Issue Brief, February 2021, https://www.kff.org/coronavirus-covid-19/issue-brief/the-implications-of-covid-19-for-mental-health-and-substance-use/; Sherry Everett Jones et al., "Mental Health, Suicidality, and Connectedness among High School Students during the COVID-19 Pandemic—Adolescent Behaviors and Experiences Survey, United States, January–June 2021," *Morbidity and Mortality Weekly Report* 71, suppl. 3 (2022): 16–21, http://dx.doi.org/10.15585/mmwr.su7103a3external icon; Ellen Yard et al., "Emergency Department Visits for Suspected Suicide Attempts among Persons Aged 12–25 Years before and during the COVID-19 Pandemic—United States, January 2019–May 2021," *Morbidity and*

Mortality Weekly Report 70 (2021): 888–894, http://dx.doi.org/10.15585 /mmwr.mm7024e1external icon; Mark E Czeisler et al., "Mental Health, Substance Use, and Suicidal Ideation during the COVID-19 Pandemic—United States, June 24–30, 2020," *Morbidity and Mortality Weekly Report* 69, no. 32 (2020): 1049–1057, https://doi.org/10.15585 /mmwr.mm6932a1.

3. Tu-Hsuan Chang et al., "Weight Gain Associated with COVID-19 Lockdown in Children and Adolescents: A Systematic Review and Meta-analysis," *Nutrients* 13, no. 10 (2021): 3668, https://doi.org/10.3390 /nu13103668.

4. J. Tucker and B. Lepage, "Two and a Half Years Later, Women Finally Recover Pandemic-Related Job Losses October 2022 Fact Sheet," National Women's Law Center, https://nwlc.org/wp-content/uploads /2022/10/Sept-Jobs-Day-1.pdf.

5. J. Tucker, "Men Have Now Recouped Their Pandemic-Related Labor Force Losses While Women Lag behind February 2022 Fact Sheet," National Women's Law Center, https://nwlc.org/wp-content/uploads /2022/02/January-Jobs-Day-updated.pdf.

6. "The COVID-19 Pandemic and Women's Unemployment in New Jersey December 2020 Fact Sheet," Center for Women and Work, Rutgers University, accessed November 19, 2022, https://smlr.rutgers .edu/sites/default/files/Documents/Centers/CWW/Publications/fact _sheet_nj_women_and_employment_during_covid-19.pdf.

7. "Family-Friendly Workplaces Policies and Practices to Advance Decent Work in Global Supply Chains," UNICEF, accessed November 19, 2022, https://www.unicef.org/media/85516/file/UNICEF%20 UNGC%20family%20friendly%20workplaces.pdf.

Pandemic Dispatches (East Africa–North America)

1. Freda Kreier, "Ten Billion COVID Vaccinations: World Hits New Milestone," *Nature*, January 31, 2022, https://www.nature.com/articles /d41586-022-00285-2?utm_source=Nature+Briefing&utm_campaign =ad485b9b51-briefing-dy-20220201&utm_medium=email&utm_term =0_c9dfd39373-ad485b9b51-44431689.

2. Larry Madowo, "My Uncle Died of COVID-19 before He Could Get a Vaccine in Kenya, and I Got Mine in a US Drugstore. This Is What Vaccine Inequality Looks Like," CNN World, July 22, 2021, https://www.cnn.com/2021/07/21/africa/larry-madowo-global-vaccine-inequity-intl-cmd/index.html.

3. Benjamin Mueller and Eleanor Lutz, "U.S. Has Far Higher COVID Death Rate than Other Wealthy Countries," *New York Times*, February 1, 2022, https://www.nytimes.com/interactive/2022/02/01/science/Covid-deaths-united-states.html.

4. Henrik Pettersson, Byron Manley, and Sergio Hernandez, "Tracking COVID-19's Global Spread," CNN Health, March 15, 2022, https://edition.cnn.com/interactive/2020/health/coronavirus-maps-and-cases/.

5. Nabil Ahmed, Nafkote Dabi, Max Lawson, Megan Lowthers, Anna Marriott, and Leah Mugehera, "Inequality Kills: The Unparalleled Action Needed to Combat Unprecedented Inequality in the Wake of COVID-19," Oxfam Briefing Paper, January 2022, https://policy-practice.oxfam.org/resources/inequality-kills-the-unparalleled-action-needed-to-combat-unprecedented-inequal-621341/.

6. Oxfam International, "Ten Richest Men Double Their Fortunes in Pandemic while Incomes of 99 Percent of Humanity Fall," Oxfam Press Release, January 17, 2022, https://www.oxfam.org/en/press-releases/ten-richest-men-double-their-fortunes-pandemic-while-incomes-99-percent-humanity.

7. Dawn Allcot, "5 Mind-Blowing Facts about Jeff Bezos' Wealth," Yahoo Finance, July 27, 2021, https://www.yahoo.com/video/5-mind-blowing-facts-jeff-182204262.html.

8. Ahmed et al., "Inequality Kills."

9. Coral Murphy-Marcos, "Keeping New York's Delivery Bicyclists Safe," *New York Times*, October 21, 2021, https://www.nytimes.com/interactive/2021/10/14/business/delivery-workers-watch-groups.html?searchResultPosition=3.

10. Michel Sidibé, "Vaccine Inequity: Ensuring Africa Is Not Left Out," Brookings Institution, January 24, 2022, https://www.brookings.edu/blog/africa-in-focus/2022/01/24/vaccine-inequity-ensuring-africa-is-not-left-out/.

1. H. G. Wells, *The War of the Worlds* (London: William Heinemann, 1898). All quotes in this section come from this edition.

2. United Nations Department of Economic and Social Affairs (UN DESA) and Gapminder, "Life Expectancy (from Birth) in the United Kingdom from 1765 to 2020," [Graph] Statista, June 17, 2019, https://www.statista.com/statistics/1040159/life-expectancy-united-kingdom-all-time/.

3. P. Berche, "The Enigma of the 1889 Russian Flu Pandemic: A Coronavirus?" *Presse Med.* 51, no. 3 (2022): 104111, https://doi.org/10.1016/j.lpm.2022.104111.

4. J. C. Segen, *The Dictionary of Modern Medicine* (Park Ridge, NJ: Parthenon, 1992), 783. Found in J. Frith, "History of Tuberculosis. Part 1—Phthisis, Consumption and the White Plague," *Journal of Military and Veterans Health* 22, no. 2 (2014): 29–35.

5. UN DESA and Gapminder, "Child Mortality Rate (under Five Years Old) in the United Kingdom from 1800 to 2020," [Graph], Statista, June 17, 2019, https://www.statista.com/statistics/1041714/united-kingdom-all-time-child-mortality-rate/.

6. T. H. Tulchinsky, "John Snow, Cholera, the Broad Street Pump: Waterborne Diseases Then and Now," *Case Studies in Public Health* (2018): 77–99, https://doi.org/10.1016/B978-0-12-804571-8.00017-2.

7. J. Snow, *On the Mode of Transmission of Cholera* (London: John Churchill, 1855), 55–98, pt. 3, table 9, reprinted by UCLA Fielding School of Public Health, 2001.

8. Robert S. Holzman, "John Snow: Anesthesiologist, Epidemiologist, Scientist, and Hero," *Anesthesia & Analgesia* 133, no. 6 (2021): 1642–1650, https://doi.org/10.1213/ANE.0000000000005586.

9. G. E. Fox, L. J. Magrum, W. E. Balch, R. S. Wolfe, and C. R. Woese, "Classification of Methanogenic Bacteria by 16S Ribosomal RNA Characterization," *PNAS* 74, no. 10 (1977): 4537–4541, https://doi.org/10.1073/pnas.74.10.4537.

Reflections on Being Human in the Twenty-First Century

1. Historically and contemporarily, highways, railroads, and other man-made infrastructure have long been used to separate Black and white neighborhoods that perpetuate inequality.
2. Audre Lorde, "Poetry Is Not a Luxury," *Sister Outsider: Essays and Speeches* (Berkeley: Crossing Press, 2007).

Risking Delight in the Middle of a Pandemic

1. "A Brief for the Defense" from Jack Gilbert, *Refusing Heaven: Poems* (New York: Knopf, 2005).

We Cannot Escape History

1. Louis P. Mansur, "What Abraham Lincoln Can Teach Us about Resilience in the Face of Crisis," CNN, April 9, 2020, https://www.cnn.com/2020/04/09/opinions/lincoln-inspiration-coronavirus-masur/index.html.
2. "With Malice toward None: The Abraham Lincoln Bicentennial Exhibition," Library of Congress, https://www.loc.gov/exhibits/lincoln/the-presidency.html.
3. Brady Dennis, "Willie Lincoln's Death: A Private Agony for a President Facing a Nation of Pain," *Washington Post*, October 7, 2011, https://www.washingtonpost.com/lifestyle/style/willie-lincolns-death-a-private-agony-for-a-president-facing-a-nation-of-pain/2011/09/29/gIQAv7Z7SL_story.html.
4. "Letter to Fanny McCullough," Abraham Lincoln Online, http://www.abrahamlincolnonline.org/lincoln/speeches/mccull.htm.
5. "Annual Message to Congress—Concluding Remarks," Abraham Lincoln Online, https://www.abrahamlincolnonline.org/lincoln/speeches/congress.htm#:~:text=Fellow%2Dcitizens%2C%20we%20cannot%20escape,dishonor%2C%20to%20the%20latest%20generation.

6. "The Queen's Broadcast to the Commonwealth," April 5, 2020, https://www.royal.uk/queens-broadcast-uk-and-commonwealth.

7. "Lincoln's Second Inaugural Address," National Park Service, https://www.nps.gov/linc/learn/historyculture/lincoln-second -inaugural.htm.

8. "Lincoln on the 1864 Election," National Park Service, last updated April 2015, https://www.nps.gov/liho/learn/historyculture/1864election .htm#:~:text=Human%2Dnature%20will%20not%20change,as%20 wrongs%20to%20be%20revenged.

Paying Attention

1. George Will, "Does Conservatism Mean Anything Anymore?" *Politico*, September 17, 2021; Bette Midler, "By the Book," *New York Times Book Review*, December 5, 2021; Tom Hanks, "You Should Learn the Truth about the Tulsa Race Massacre," *New York Times*, June 6, 2021; Bill Gates, "By the Book," *New York Times Book Review*, February 14, 2021.

Slap Roti and the Story of New York City

1. Thomas Wolfe, *The Web and the Rock*, cited in Kenneth T. Jackson and David S. Dunbar, eds., *Empire City: New York through the Centuries* (New York: Columbia University Press, 2002), 567.

Black and Gray

1. Rebecca T. Leeb et al., "Mental Health-Related Emergency Department Visits among Children Aged <18 Years during the COVID-19 Pandemic—United States, January 1–October 17, 2020," *Morbidity and Mortality Weekly Report* 69, no. 45 (2020): 1675–1680, https://www.cdc .gov/mmwr/volumes/69/wr/mm6945a3.htm?s_cid=mm6945a3_w.

Connectivity, Connection, and Care during the COVID-19 Pandemic

1. We gratefully acknowledge financial support from the Rutgers University Research Council and the School of Communication and Information for this study.

2. National Student Clearinghouse Research Center, "Current Term Enrollment Estimates," January 1, 2022, https://nscresearchcenter.org/current-term-enrollment-estimates/.

3. Chronicle of Higher Education, "On the Verge of Burnout: The Impact of COVID-19 on Faculty Well-Being and Career Plans," 2020, https://connect.chronicle.com/rs/931-EKA-218/images/Covid%26FacultyCareerPaths_Fidelity_ResearchBrief_v3%20%281%29.pdf.

COVID-19 and Spaces of Confinement

1. Jonathan Salant, "N.J. Has More Immigrant Detainees with Coronavirus Than Any Other State," NJ.com, April 10, 2020, https://www.nj.com/coronavirus/2020/04/nj-has-more-immigrant-detainees-with-the-coronavirus-than-any-other-state.html.

2. The Vera Institute has since the beginning of the pandemic archived statistics on COVID-19 in detention from ICE's live database where only the number for the current count is available to the public. See https://www.vera.org/tracking-covid-19-in-immigration-detention.

3. For the Center for COVID-19 Response and Pandemic Preparedness's mission statement, see https://covid19research.rutgers.edu/about-ccrp2.

4. We were fortunate to count on research assistance from Gabrielle Cabrera, a graduate student in anthropology at RU–New Brunswick, and Melani Cruz-Stokes, a criminal justice major at RU-Camden.

5. Our paper in the journal *Ethnography* discusses the benefits and challenges of studying detention centers using remote methods. See U. D. Berg, S. K. León, and S. Tosh, "Carceral Ethnography in a Time of Pandemic: Examining Migrant Detention and Deportation during

COVID-19," *Ethnography* (2022), https://doi.org/10.1177
/14661381211072414.

6. For a full descriptive account of our research findings, see S. R. Tosh,
U. D. Berg, and K. S. León, "Migrant Detention and COVID-19:
Pandemic Responses in Four New Jersey Detention Centers," *Journal
on Migration and Human Security* 9, no. 1 (2021): 44–62.

7. See https://www.vera.org/tracking-covid-19-in-immigration-detention.

8. Senate Budget and Appropriations Committee, Statement to Assem-
bly, No. 5207. State of New Jersey, https://pub.njleg.gov/bills/2020
/A9999/5207_S2.HTM.

9. Jordan Weiner, "ICE Made N.J. Immigrant Detainees Disappear,
Disconnected Them from Their Lawyers," NJ.com, May 3, 2022,
https://www.nj.com/opinion/2022/05/ice-made-nj-immigrant
-detainees-disappear-disconnected-them-from-their-lawyers-l-opinion
.html.

The Climate Crisis and the University

1. Lester R. Brown, *Eco-Economy: Building an Economy for the Earth* (New
York: Routledge, 2013), 276.

2. Pierre Friedlingstein et al., "Global Carbon Budget 2022," *Earth System
Science Data* 14 (2022): 4811–4900, https://doi.org/10.5194/essd-14-4811
-2022; GISTEMP Team, "GISS Surface Temperature Analysis
(GISTEMP), Version 4," NASA Goddard Institute for Space Studies,
April 1, 2022.

3. Friedlingstein et al., "Global Carbon Budget 2022."

4. GISTEMP Team, "GISS Surface Temperature Analysis (GISTEMP),
Version 4."

5. IPCC, "Summary for Policymakers," in *Climate Change 2021: The
Physical Science Basis*, ed. V. Masson-Delmotte et al. (Cambridge:
Cambridge University Press, 2021), 3–32, https://doi.org/10.1017
/9781009157896.001.

6. IPCC, "Summary for Policymakers."

7. IPCC, "Summary for Policymakers."

8. Lester R. Brown, *Plan B 3.0: Mobilizing to Save Civilization* (New York: Norton, 2008), xiii.

9. Liberty Hyde Bailey, *The Holy Earth: The Birth of a New Land Ethic* (New York: Counterpoint, 1915).

10. Kenyon Leech Butterfield, *Chapters in Rural Progress* (Chicago: University of Chicago Press, 1907).

11. Rutgers Task Force on Carbon Neutrality and Climate Resilience, *Climate Action Plan*, 2021, https://climateaction.rutgers.edu/sites /default/files/2021-12/RUClimateActionPlan_Sept2021893.pdf.

2020

1. The U.S. Bureau of Labor Statistics (www.bls.gov) is the source of all the employment data, specifically its Current Employment Statistics (CES) database.

Work in the Pandemic and Beyond

1. https://www.advisory.com/en/daily-briefing/2021/02/10/covid-jobs. Bakers and chefs/head cooks are listed as separate categories. If you add them in to the "cooks" category, we can see that making food was particularly dangerous.

2. Ibid.

3. Devan Hawkins, Letitia Davis, and David Kriebel, "COVID-19 Deaths by Occupation, Massachusetts, March 1–July 31, 2020," *American Journal of Industrial Medicine* 64, no. 4 (2021): 238–244.

4. World Health Organization, Health Workforce Department, *The Impact of COVID-19 on Health and Care Workers: A Closer Look at Deaths*, Working Paper 1 (Geneva: World Health Organization, September 2021).

5. Jane Spencer and Christina Jewett, "12 Months of Trauma: More than 3,600 US Health Workers Died in COVID's First Year," *Kaiser Health News*, April 8, 2021, https://khn.org/news/article/us-health-workers -deaths-covid-lost-on-the-frontline/.

6. Adeel Hassan, "Coronavirus Cases and Deaths Were Vastly Underestimated in U.S. Meatpacking Plants, a House Report Says," *The New York Times,* October 28, 2021, https://www.nytimes.com/2021/10/28/world/meatpacking-workers-covid-cases-deaths.html.

7. Leah Douglas, "Nearly 90% of Big US Meat Plants Had COVID-19 Cases in Pandemic's First Year—Data," Reuters, January 14, 2022, https://www.reuters.com/business/nearly-90-big-us-meat-plants-had-covid-19-cases-pandemics-first-year-data-2022-01-14/#:~:text=Jan%2014%20(Reuters)%20%2D%20Nearly,how%20meatpackers%20handled%20the%20pandemic.

8. https://www.supremecourt.gov/opinions/21pdf/21a244_hgci.pdf.

9. "Unemployment Rates during the COVID-19 Pandemic," Congressional Research Service, updated August 20, 2021, https://crsreports.congress.gov/product/pdf/R/R46554.

10. "Unemployment Rate—New Jersey (April 2020)," *Statesman Journal,* https://data.statesmanjournal.com/unemployment/new-jersey/ST3400000000000/2020-april/.

11. https://www.supremecourt.gov/opinions/21pdf/21a244_hgci.pdf, p. 12.

12. https://sgp.fas.org/crs/misc/R46554.pdf.

13. Make the Road New York and Hester Street, *Excluded in the Epicenter: Impacts of the COVID Crisis on Working-Class Immigrant, Black, and Brown New Yorkers* (New York: Make the Road New York, May 2020), https://maketheroadny.org/wp-content/uploads/2020/05/MRNY_SurveyReport_small.pdf.

14. Kim Parker, Juliana Menasce Horowitz, and Rachel Minkin, "How the Coronavirus Outbreak Has—and Hasn't—Changed the Way Americans Work," Pew Research Center, December 9, 2020, https://www.pewresearch.org/social-trends/2020/12/09/how-the-coronavirus-outbreak-has-and-hasnt-changed-the-way-americans-work/.

15. Parker, Horowitz, and Minkin, "How the Coronavirus Outbreak."

16. J. R. Methot, A. S. Gabriel, P. Downes, and E. Rosado-Solomon, "Remote Workers Need Small Talk, Too," *Harvard Business Review,* March 25, 2021.

17. Methot et al., "Remote Workers."

18. Unfortunately, strike data from the federal government is seriously incomplete, focusing only on those work stoppages that involve one thousand workers or more. Cornell's computation is far more complete but new, so it is not possible to make longer historical comparisons. Johnnie Kallas, Kathryn Ritchie, and Eli Friedman, "Labor Action Tracker Annual Report 2022," ILR, Cornell University, Worker Institute, https://www.ilr.cornell.edu/faculty-and-research/labor-action-tracker-2022.

19. Society of Human Resource Management, "Interactive Chart: How Historic Has the Great Resignation Been?" May 9, 2022, https://www.shrm.org/resourcesandtools/hr-topics/talent-acquisition/pages/interactive-quits-level-by-year.aspx.

20. See for instance, Greg Iacurci, "The Great Resignation Continues, as 44% of Workers Look for a New Job," CNBC, March 22, 2022, https://www.cnbc.com/2022/03/22/great-resignation-continues-as-44percent-of-workers-seek-a-new-job.html; or Tristan Bove, "Great Resignation Shows No Sign of Slowing Down: 40% of U.S. Workers Are Considering Quitting Their Job—Here's Where They're Going," *Fortune*, July 21, 2022, https://fortune.com/2022/07/21/great-resignation-40-percent-want-to-quit-where-are-they-going/.

Stagecoach Mary

1. Ase is a Yoruba word with multiple meanings used to end prayers and to claim power and self-determination.

On Racism in Museums

1. Ivey DeJesus, "A Provocative Conversation on Racism and a Challenge to Commit to Peace and Justice," PennLive, October 20, 2021, https://www.pennlive.com/news/2021/10/a-provocative-conversation-on-racism-and-a-challenge-to-commit-to-peace-and-justice.html.

2. Barbara Gamarekian, "Corcoran, to Foil Dispute, Drops Mapplethorpe Show," *New York Times*, June 14, 1989, https://www.nytimes.com/1989/06/14/arts/corcoran-to-foil-dispute-drops-mapplethorpe-show.html.

3. Dan Barry and Carol Vogel, "Giuliani Vows to Cut Subsidy over Art He Calls Offensive," *New York Times*, September 23, 1999, https://www.nytimes.com/library/arts/092399brooklyn-museum-funds.html?scp=5&sq=sensation%2520saatchi%2520giuliani&st=cse.

4. Victoria L. Valentine, "On the Rise: 69 Museum Curators and Arts Leaders Who Took on Notable New Appointments in 2021," Culture Type, December 29, 2021, https://www.culturetype.com/2021/12/29/on-the-rise-68-museum-curators-and-arts-leaders-who-took-on-notable-new-appointments-in-2021/.

5. Hillary Brady, "'He Is a Negro Still: The Poetry of Solomon Brown," Smithsonian Institute Archives, February 9, 2017, https://siarchives.si.edu/blog/he-negro-still-poetry-solomon-brown.

Notes on Contributors

PATRICIA AKHIMIE is director of the Folger Institute at the Folger Shakespeare Library and associate professor of English at Rutgers University–Newark. She is author of *Shakespeare and the Cultivation of Difference: Race and Conduct in the Early Modern World* and coeditor of *Travel and Travail: Early Modern Women, English Drama, and the Wider World*. She is the mother of two children.

MARC ARONSON earned his doctorate in American history at New York University while working as an editor of books for children and teenagers. An associate professor of public professional practice at Rutgers, he has authored more than twenty books for younger readers and founded the International Youth Literature Collection at the university's Alexander Library.

ULLA D. BERG is associate professor of anthropology and Latino and Caribbean studies at Rutgers University. A sociocultural and visual anthropologist by training, her research and teaching focuses on the racial and affective aspects of transnational migration and (im)mobilities in Latin America and U.S. Latinx communities.

STEPHANIE BONNE is associate professor and trauma and critical care surgeon at Rutgers New Jersey Medical School. She serves as the chief of trauma and critical care at University Hospital in Newark, New Jersey and specializes in gun violence prevention. She is the mother of three children.

STEPHANIE BOYER lives and works in Brooklyn, New York. She holds a BA from the University of California, Riverside (2015), and an MFA from Mason Gross School of the Arts at Rutgers (2022).

KIMBERLY CAMP began her career as a professional artist more than fifty years ago. Her paintings and dolls have been shown throughout the United States in more than one hundred solo and group exhibitions. Her list of exhibitions includes the American Craft Museum, Smithsonian Institution, and the International Sculpture Center, among others. She teaches at Rutgers University–Camden.

JORDAN CASTEEL was an associate professor at Rutgers University-Newark from 2016–2021 and visiting associate professor in 2023. She earned her BA from Agnes Scott College and an MFA in painting and printmaking from Yale School of Art. She is the recipient of a MacArthur Foundation Fellowship (2021).

KELLY-JANE COTTER was a Spanish major at Rutgers and graduated with honors from the Columbia University Graduate School of Journalism. She has been a news reporter and features writer for more than thirty years. She grew up in Middletown and lives in South River with her husband, daughter, and cat.

MARK DOTY, a poet and distinguished professor of English at Rutgers University, has published ten volumes of poetry and three memoirs. Doty's awards include the National Book Award, a Whiting Award, and the National Book Critics Circle Award. He was the first American poet to receive the T. S. Eliot Prize and the first recipient of the Seamus Heaney International Poetry Fellowship in Northern Ireland.

DAVID DREYFUS is an assistant professor in the Supply Chain Management Department of Rutgers Business School where he teaches demand planning and fulfillment, operations analysis, and business statistics courses. His research focus is on healthcare operations, population health, teams, disruptions, and risk. He holds a PhD from Michigan State University. He is the father of two children.

ADRIENNE E. EATON is dean of the School of Management and Labor Relations and distinguished professor of labor studies and employment relations at Rutgers University. She has published extensively in her field on a variety of topics and served as president of the Labor and Employment Relations Association (LERA) in 2020–2021 and was named a LERA fellow in 2017.

KATHERINE C. EPSTEIN is associate professor of history at Rutgers University–Camden. She received the American Council of Learned Societies Burkhardt Fellowship and was a member of the Institute for Advanced Study in Princeton. Her research focuses on government secrecy, defense contracting, intellectual property, and the political economy of power projection.

LEAH FALK is author of the poetry collections *To Look After and Use* and *Other Customs and Practices*. From 2016 to 2022, she directed the Writers House at Rutgers University–Camden and is now director of education and engagement at Penn Live Arts.

PAUL G. FALKOWSKI is the Bennett L. Smith Professor of Business and Natural Resources at Rutgers University. His research interests include evolution, paleoecology, photosynthesis, biophysics, biogeochemical cycles, symbiosis, and sustainable energy.

RIGOBERTO GONZÁLEZ is author of seventeen books of poetry and prose, most recently the poetry collection *The Book of Ruin* (2019). His awards include Lannan, Guggenheim, National Endowment for the Arts, New York Film Academy, and USA Rolón fellowships, the American Book Award, the Lambda Literary Award, and the PEN/Voelcker Award for Poetry. He is director of the MFA program at Rutgers University–Newark.

JAMES GOODMAN, distinguished professor of history and head of nonfiction at the MFA program at Rutgers University–Newark, is author of *Stories of Scottsboro*, *Blackout*, and *But Where Is the Lamb?* He is at work on two books. One, like "Paying Attention," is about what his life has taught him about history and what history has taught him about his life.

DAVID GREENBERG, a 2023 Guggenheim Fellow, is professor of history and of journalism and media studies at Rutgers University. The author of several books of political history, he is now writing a biography of Congressman John Lewis. His work appears in *Politico*, *The New York Times*, *The Washington Post*, and many other national publications.

ANGELIQUE HAUGERUD is professor emerita of anthropology at Rutgers University and former editor in chief of *American Ethnologist* and *Africa Today*. She is the author of *The Culture of Politics in Modern Kenya* and *No Billionaire Left Behind: Satirical Activism in America*.

GRACE LYNNE HAYNES creates lusciously composed paintings containing bright textures and patterns. In her work, black appears aspirational, dignified, and sublime. She is an inaugural member of Kehinde Wiley's Black Rock Senegal residency and is included in the 2020 edition of *Forbes* 30 Under 30 in Art & Style. She earned her MFA in 2023 from Rutgers University's Mason Gross School of the Arts.

LESLIEANN HOBAYAN is a Filipina American poet, essayist, and host of *Spiritual Grit* podcast, who has taught creative writing at Rutgers University since 2006. Nominated for a Pushcart Prize and

2018 Best of the Net, her work has appeared in *The Rumpus*, *Aster(ix) Journal*, the *Lantern Review*, and others. Her chapbook, *Divorce Papers: A Slow Burn* was published in 2023.

JONATHAN HOLLOWAY took office as the twenty-first president of Rutgers University on July 1, 2020. His scholarly work specializes in post-emancipation U.S. history with a focus on social and intellectual history. He is the author, most recently, of *The Cause of Freedom: A Concise History of African Americans*. A paperback version, titled *African American History: A Very Short Introduction*, was published in February 2023.

JAMES W. HUGHES is a university professor and dean emeritus of the Edward J. Bloustein School of Planning and Public Policy at Rutgers University. He is also director of the *Rutgers Regional Report*. His latest book, *Population Trends in New Jersey*, was published by Rutgers University Press in 2022.

NAOMI JACKSON is assistant professor of English at Rutgers University–Newark and author of *The Star Side of Bird Hill*. Jackson studied fiction at the Iowa Writers' Workshop.

AMY JORDAN is professor and chair of the Department of Journalism and Media Studies at Rutgers University–New Brunswick. She is a member of the board of trustees for Sesame Workshop and served as coeditor of the *Journal of Children and Media*.

VIKKI KATZ is professor in the School of Communication at Chapman University in Orange, California. Until 2022, she was associate professor of communication at Rutgers University–New Brunswick (RU-NB). She also serves as editor of the *Journal of Children and Media*.

MACKENZIE KEAN is a Rutgers graduate from Central Jersey. Writing, especially poetry, has always been an important part of

Mackenzie's life. Several of her poems appear in *Philadelphia Stories*, *Writers House Review*, and *Eunoia Review*. Her gratitude goes toward Professors Ben Purkert, Adam Dalva, Yehoshua November, and Susan L. Miller for a great writing experience at Rutgers University.

ROBERT E. KOPP is a climate scientist who serves at Rutgers University as a professor, codirector of the University Office of Climate Action, and director of the Megalopolitan Coastal Transformation Hub. He studies sea-level change, climate risk, and the use of climate risk information to inform decision-making.

CHRISTIAN LIGHTY is the son of hip-hop mogul Chris Lighty. He is an aspiring sports journalist who also produces beats. He was a kid who became an adult at a young age, but that is what made him who he is.

REVATHI V. MACHAN is an Indian American artist studying at Rutgers University, majoring in environmental design and policy. Her works vary in topics and mediums, ranging from polymer clay earrings to realistic scratch art. Recently, she has been exploring abstractions and different systems of philosophy, expressing her discoveries through abstract, three-dimensional models.

STEPHEN MASARYK is a Christian, newly married, and a campus pastor of Rutgers Oasis Church. Born and raised in New Jersey, Masaryk works for the School of Arts and Sciences' Dean's Office in Space and Facilities Management. His hobbies include skateboarding, cooking, and hiking. He has three dogs and a turtle.

LOUIS P. MASUR is Board of Governors Distinguished Professor of American studies and history at Rutgers University. His many books include *The Sum of Our Dreams: A Concise History of America* and *The Civil War: A Concise History*.

YALIDY MATOS is assistant professor of political science at Rutgers University–New Brunswick. Matos's scholarship sits at the intersection of race, ethnicity, and politics (REP), immigration, and identity politics.

BELINDA MCKEON is a novelist and playwright. After seven great years teaching at Writers House at Rutgers University, she recently moved back to her native Ireland to direct a new graduate program in creative writing at Maynooth University.

SUSAN L. MILLER is author of *Communion of Saints: Poems* and has poems in *Collective Brightness: LGBTIQ Poets on Faith, Religion, and Spirituality* and *St. Peter's B-List: Contemporary Poems Inspired by the Saints*. She has twice won Dorothy Sargent Rosenberg prizes for poetry and teaches creative writing at Rutgers University.

YEHOSHUA NOVEMBER is author of the poetry collections *Two Worlds Exist* (a finalist for the National Jewish Book Award) and *God's Optimism* (a finalist for the *Los Angeles Times* Book Prize). His work has been featured in *The New York Times Magazine*, *Harvard Divinity Bulletin*, *The Sun*, and on NPR and Poetry Unbound. He is associate professor of creative writing at Rutgers University.

JOYCE CAROL OATES, a visiting distinguished professor at Rutgers University, is a recipient of the National Book Award, the National Medal in the Humanities, and the Jerusalem Prize. She has been a member of the American Academy of Arts and Letters since 1978.

MARY E. O'DOWD, MPH, a Douglass College alumna, works in population health for Rutgers University and serves on the board of University Hospital, Newark. O'Dowd served as New Jersey's commissioner of health after previously holding positions at New York University Medical Center and New Jersey Hospital Association. She is coeditor of *Junctures in Women's Leadership: Health Care and Public Health*.

KATHERINE OGNYANOVA, associate professor of communication at Rutgers University, studies the effects of social influence on civic and political behavior, confidence in institutions, information exposure/evaluation, and public opinion formation. Ognyanova is one of the founders and a principal investigator for the COVID States Project—a large multiuniversity initiative exploring the social and political implications of the COVID-19 pandemic.

DAVID ORR is professor of poetry and criticism at Rutgers University. His work has been lauded by *The New York Times*, *The Wall Street Journal*, and *The Washington Post*. A longtime critic for *The New York Times Book Review*, Orr's poetry and critical collections include *You, Too Could Write a Poem* and *The Road Not Taken*.

GREGORY PARDLO is author of *Totem*, winner of the *American Poetry Review*/Honickman First Book Prize, and *Digest*, winner of the Pulitzer Prize for Poetry. In 2017, Pardlo was awarded a Guggenheim fellowship. Pardlo is poetry editor for the *Virginia Quarterly Review* and teaches in the MFA program at Rutgers University–Camden.

STEVE PIKIELL is a father of four who has led the resurgence of Rutgers University basketball, both on and off the court, as the head men's basketball coach since 2015. With more than thirty years of coaching experience, the Bristol (Connecticut) native is under contract to remain courtside at the Jersey Mike's Arena through 2030.

TERESA POLITANO is an award-winning writer, editor, and educator. In 2022, she won the International Association of Culinary Professionals Award for Personal Essays/Memoir. She is author of *Single-Handed* and *Celebrity Chefs of New Jersey*. She teaches at Rutgers University and is a member of the university's Academic Initiatives team.

BEN PURKERT'S debut novel, *The Men Can't Be Saved*, was published in August 2023. He is also the author of the poetry collection *For the Love of Endings*. His writing appears in *The New Yorker*, *Poetry*, *The Nation*, and elsewhere. The founding editor of Guernica's Back Draft interview series, he lives in Jersey City.

NICK ROMANENKO is an award-winning visual documentarian and has served as Rutgers University's chief photographer for more than thirty-five years. A 1982 graduate of Columbia College with a degree in economics, he specializes in studio, location lighting, editorial portraiture, and event photojournalism. Romanenko has been a board member since 2004 of the University Photographers Association of America.

EVIE SHOCKLEY, Zora Neale Hurston Distinguished Professor of English at Rutgers University, New Brunswick, is the author most recently of *suddenly we* and *semiautomatic*, which was a finalist for the Pulitzer Prize in 2018. Her criticism and poetry appear widely. She serves as an editor at *Contemporary Literature* and was awarded the Poetry Society of America's 2023 Shelley Memorial Award.

CARIDAD SVICH is a playwright and screenwriter. She is recipient of an Obie Award for Lifetime Achievement and the Ellen Stewart Award for Career Achievement in Professional Theatre from the Association for Theatre in Higher Education. Her plays include *12 Ophelias*, *Red Bike*, and *The House of the Spirits*. She is author of *Toward a Future Theatre*.

DIDIER WILLIAM is assistant professor at Mason Gross School of the Arts at Rutgers University. He earned his BFA from the Maryland Institute College of Art and an MFA from Yale University. His work has been widely exhibited, including at the Museum of Contemporary Art North Miami, Bronx Museum of Art, and the Museum of Latin American Art.

Text Permissions